I DON'T BRUISE EASILY

PREFACE

In twenty-eight years you can make many friends and quite a few enemies, too. You can have labels attached to you and some of them stick. You can be bequeathed reputations you don't want and don't deserve and they can grow. You can do and say things you regret. You can refuse to say things which might put a situation right because, at the time, you feel you don't have to justify yourself. In twenty-eight years so much can happen, and I think it has all happened to me. I have been given a lot of labels and some of them, deserved or not, have stuck. I have been called many things, some of which may have been justified, some which I know were not. But I have never been called a coward. I have never been labelled a whiner.

It is against that background that I hope cricket, cricketers and cricket-lovers will judge my contribution to the game. I will accept my faults and my shortcomings, but I most earnestly hope the public will accept two points from me. Firstly, that whenever I have offended authority and the pundits it has been an occasion when I was doing my damnedest for my team. I don't think anyone has ever accused me of selfishness and I honestly have not played with a consciousness of doing my best for Brian Close. But I have given everything I have got, always, to playing for Brian Close's team. Secondly, I regard myself, honestly and sincerely, as one of the unluckiest people who have ever played the game. I repeat, I emphasise, that I am not a whiner. I don't make excuses for myself where there are none. But sometimes I have sat down and wondered just what – *what* – could go wrong next.

Critics sit on the sidelines; it's their job to do so. The public sit even further on the sidelines and criticise; it's their right to do so because without their money the game would not exist. But I wonder . . . all my life I have wondered . . . if they realise just what effect they can have on a career, and on a life.

A seat in a press box is reasonably comfortable; by and large it gives a pretty good view of what's happening; lunch and tea are available; telephones are available. It's not a bad way to spend a working day. I know one newspaperman who, sitting in the sunshine at Grace Road, Leicester, one day, turned to a colleague and enquired, reflectively, 'Have you thought that we are actually getting paid to sit here watching cricket?' He was, and is, a man who loves cricket . . . who positively basks in his involvement in the game. Unhappily they are not all like that.

Test selectors today are far too close to the press. Newspaper correspondents play far too important a part in influencing selectors' judgement. Selectors will deny it; newspapermen will say I give them too much credit, if credit it is. But it is true. It is difficult for selectors to withstand the concerted battering of daily headlines to stories which say that one player should be in a Test side and another should not. Even ex-Test players turned critics can be cruel, and even though the contemporary player accepts that their views are based on personal experience, he knows at the same time that ex-Test players are required to write the sort of stuff their particular paper wants, and that in some cases a 'ghost' is hovering around at the end of each day.

Of course, the greatest problem of most writers is the lack of sufficient space really to write about the cricket itself. The style of modern 'popular' journalism demands that anything which is not controversial or spectacular should be fairly ruthlessly weeded out of the story. It is difficult not to sympathise with those who know and love their cricket and who would like to expand, sympathetically, on reasons why a player has 'failed', but who are compelled by professional necessity to concentrate on the ones who have succeeded.

So how have I been unlucky?

Well, for twenty-eight years I have been saddled with the title of 'England's youngest Test player'. That has been an albatross round my neck since July, 1949. It is a label which has been trotted out every time I have been recalled to a Test side – and God knows that has happened often enough! – with the implication that I have never lived up to the promise that led to my first selection, or to the future that was said to be indicated when I did the double in my first season. In the meantime I have scored a fair number of runs, taken quite a lot of wickets, held a reasonable number of catches and not done badly as a captain – of England, Yorkshire or Somerset. But always, it seems, more was expected of me.

At the same time, I have not made as many runs as I would have liked to make and I have not made big scores when I very badly wanted to make them. There have been no Test centuries and that is one of the things I regret most of all as I say 'goodbye' to first-class cricket. There has never been a 200. I have been got out when I most desperately wanted to stay in. And this has, over the years, been variously attributed to my being 'a big-head', 'playing irresponsibly', or just plain 'chucking my wicket away'. I say – no, I insist – that it has been none of those things: but I'm hanged if I can put my finger on what it was. Let me give you a few examples of why I believe some kind of bad luck has always dogged me.

In a Test stand of 51 with Colin Cowdrey, I scored 34 of them while Colin was missed three times. Colin went on to get a hundred; I went out to an absolutely brilliant catch off what was not really a chance.

In 1960 I twice went very close to scoring a double century. At The Oval I was 198 when Ron Tindall brought off what must have been one of the most astounding catches of his career – and there would be a lot of them because he was a tremendous fielder. Against Notts at Scarborough I was 184 and going like a bomb when Merv Winfield ran something like twenty-five yards to bring off the sort of catch about which he will never tire of telling his grandchildren.

My career seems to me to be littered with incidents like that – littered with them. If I look back at almost every big innings I have played or every big occasion in which I have been involved, the same jinx seems to have been lurking around. And each time it has happened my critics have had a field day because it has been 'Close, the youngest England player'. For that I suppose many people have instinctively read, 'Close, the most spectacular failure'.

I am not, and never have been, conceited. I am opinionated. I tend to want to be involved in the job of each person on the field. I am intolerant of people who don't give a hundred per cent. I am subjective, rather than objective, when I am playing. I always believe *I* can work something out and I get a bit fed up with people who are not thinking on the same lines. No doubt I have sometimes expected more of players than they were capable of accomplishing because I have never believed any situation was so hopeless that one couldn't do *something* about it. It is probable that I am a bit short on self-criticism because I have always believed in myself and my own ability, all things being equal. Jinxes I obviously cannot cope with – and I seem to have been bedevilled by them.

But never at any time has Brian Close given less than one hundred per cent for the team for which Brian Close was playing. Never has he done anything which he didn't sincerely believe was the best thing to do for his team.

1

THE END...
AND THE BEGINNING

There was, I suppose, a certain savage irony in the way my Test career ended at Old Trafford – the very ground on which it had started twenty-seven years earlier. Even then, after all the many spectacular and controversial phases of a career which had spanned so many years, I didn't mind the sacking so much as the way it was done. From the moment the team was announced for the Third Test of 1976 against the West Indies, I was told in just about every newspaper in the country that I was going to open at Old Trafford . . . not told by the selectors or the captain, mind you. By the press.

Because I believed (despite so much overwhelming evidence to the contrary) that it was the selectors who picked the team and the captain who decided on the batting order, I went to Manchester still expecting – no: I must have come to terms with reality, *hoping* is the right word – to bat at number four. I had done my stuff in the second innings at Trent Bridge and to a much more marked degree at Lord's, and I was convinced I had earned the right to bat in my best position. So it was still a bit of an unpleasant surprise when Tony Greig said 'I want you to open'.

'Look', I said, 'I haven't done that job regularly since 1957. You've got a chap in the side who is opening regularly for Kent.'

'Ah', said the captain. 'We think Bob Woolmer is going to be on the international scene for a long time. We don't want him killed off.'

He said it with the smile that charms the televiewers but the point was still the same. I was now expendable.

From the moment I first joined the Yorkshire side I had been trained, brainwashed even, to think logically and sensibly about my cricket; but no matter how I looked at this it couldn't make any sense. I had been brought back to Test cricket to do a specific job. I had done it and done it damn well enough at Lord's to help put England into a winning position. Now I was being moved to another place in the batting order so I could be dropped.

Thus it turned out. John Edrich and I took another battering and I walked out of the Test match scene with the only battle honours I have ever had – a rash of bruises down my right side and across my chest which required a long session with a pain-killing freezer before I could lie down in bed, let alone sleep. With a rather wry smile to myself, I recalled that on the Wednesday night, before the game started, Alec Bedser and Tony Greig had looked at the pitch and announced that it was going to take spin. These were the brains that were running English cricket and – let me be quite frank about my thoughts at the time – finishing my Test career. Take spin? There were, I think, just two overs from Albert Padmore on the Saturday night and Edrich and I debated whether we ought to buy him a pint or two for the blessed relief they provided!

The game became a nightmare memory as I reflected on the shabby way I was being eased out of the team. Over the years I had been accused of just about everything reprehensible as I had been picked and discarded, picked again and dropped again. But, apart from my age, this time no one could level one single criticism about the way I had played my Test cricket. The answer, of course, was very simple, but no one in any newspaper wrote it. For a long time in Test cricket terms, Greig had not even justified his selection *as a player*. If he had been dropped, as he should have been on form and performance, then the same selectors who had appointed him after getting rid of Mike Denness would then be admitting they had made a mistake. Worse still, the obvious choice for the captaincy then would be me, if I was still in the England side, and I certainly would have insisted on leading players who were going to give a hundred and one per cent for the side. Not every player picked for England during my time in the game has done that, by any means.

So there I was, jettisoned for the eighth (and obviously the last) time. As I left Old Trafford my mind went back twenty-seven years, to my first Test on that ground in July, 1949. It wasn't a distinguished debut – but I did the double in my first season for Yorkshire, and I was awarded my county cap. To a Yorkshire lad in 1949 that represented the ultimate in dreams come true.

Somewhere along the years I have been labelled a 'big-head' who went too far too soon. Nothing, absolutely nothing, could be further from the truth. Far from being conceited, I used to find a quiet corner at intervals throughout that season and pinch myself to make sure I was not dreaming. For most of the time I couldn't believe it was happening to me.

The dream had started seven years earlier. At eleven, I played for Rawdon's first team for the first time. I scored 11 not out and took two wickets for 30. I was on the same cricket field as Norman Grimshaw, who had played for Northants, and Stanley Raper, who had actually walked with the demi-gods of Yorkshire. At the time I don't think I really realised what I was doing. I do remember wondering: 'What do these blokes think about a kid like me being amongst them?'

My father was a very good League cricketer, but I don't remember watching him so much as grubbing about under the pavilion, which seemed a marvellously exciting, secret sort of place, when I was five or six. My cricket, and my football, developed at Aireborough Grammar School and I moved 'up the road' from Rawdon to Guiseley, then to Yeadon who played in the Bradford League. Playing for Yorkshire in the future seemed little more than a dream – for if you had no natural humility, the very fierceness of the competition in those days forced it upon you. Every boy I knew wanted to play for Yorkshire and many of them had plenty of ability. Even so, when you let yourself think that perhaps you *might* be the lucky one called up, you immediately brought yourself back to earth by thinking that that would put you in the company of Len Hutton, Norman Yardley, Willie Watson and others – and you knew at once that you had no right to be thinking anything like that at all.

Just consider the 'opposition' around at the time. Bill Bowes, that great Yorkshire and England bowler-turned-journalist, writing his 1949 preview of the season, described a visit to the nets to look at the Colts:

'Brian Close, the six-foot Rawdon lad, can be singled out for immediate mention. He looks to be a natural successor to Frank Smailes. He could be relied upon to bowl six or seven good overs with the new ball, then revert to off-spinners and with the bat do anything that Frank ever did.'

'Young Ken Smales only needs to prove to himself that he can do it and when he does he will get runs by the fifty.' (Ken was a batsman who bowled off-spinners – at once a rival for me. He ultimately went to Notts and later became Secretary of Nottingham Forest FC.)

'Foord, of Scarborough, a twenty-four-year-old schoolteacher, who has all to gain and nothing to lose by taking up cricket, is bowling well.' (Bill Foord did indeed take up cricket, in harness with teaching, and gave a lot of service to the county over seven years.)

'B. Brooke and G. H. Padgett are promising eighteen-year-old seam bowlers.' (Like Foord, more rivals, and both played for the county – in 1950 and 1952 respectively.)

'Of the faster kind, McHugh (Leeds) has improved considerably and F. S. Trueman (Maltby), a seventeen-year-old with average development seems likely to be a real tearaway Lindwall or Larwood type.' (Frank McHugh played for Gloucestershire and we all know about the 'average development' of F. S. Trueman.)

'Leadbeater and Waddington are bowling that rarity of Yorkshire cricket – right-arm leg-breaks – and from what I have seen of the batsmen, Lowson, Lewis, Illingworth and Horner are lads with possibility.' (Eddie Leadbeater went to Warwickshire, Ray Illingworth's has enjoyed a most distinguished career in Leicestershire and Norman Horner gave long and honourable service to Warwicks.)

'There were two wicket-keepers who impressed me, too, Firth and Booth.' (Jack Firth with Leicestershire and Roy Booth, with both Yorkshire and Worcs, had excellent first-class careers.)

Such was the quality of the opposition around in the early summer of 1949.

'Big-head'? How could any Yorkshire kid brought up on stories of Sutcliffe and Holmes think he could score runs as they had? How could he ever let the thought flicker across his mind that he might run up to bowl in the footsteps of Hedley Verity and Bill Bowes and George Macauley? But that didn't stop him wanting to – and how *I* wanted to. I also wanted to be a centre-forward like Tommy Lawton.

4

In my mid-teens, when I was playing for one of Leeds United's junior sides, I felt that I was a better footballer than cricketer.

Then I was called up to the Yorkshire nets and that provided the thrill of my young lifetime up to that point. I went on tour with the Yorkshire Federation – in effect, the county's third team – in company with a couple of those promising youngsters, called Raymond Illingworth and Freddie Trueman. I made a century against Sussex but I still thought of it as schoolboy cricket, unrelated to the stuff being played by the county team of Norman Yardley. In 1948 I was invited to play for the Colts against Notts at Worksop. Apart from four overs (when we were in the field) it rained throughout both days.

The 1949 season started with me still playing Bradford League cricket for Yeadon after a winter at Elland Road. We had played for, I think, three Saturdays when the call came to join the Yorkshire party going to Cambridge for the traditional start-of-the-season match against the University. My life had begun: I couldn't believe it.

My first cricket was played with my father in the backyard of the terraced house in Rawdon near Leeds which was my first home. In winter it was football on the same pitch. I just loved playing games. Yet I was back in hospital for an operation one month after I was born and I suffered just about every childhood ailment known to the medical profession in 1931, including rheumatic fever.

My elder brother, Peter, followed cricket with great interest once in the Metropolitan Police. Kenneth, three years younger than me, has played local League cricket; Tony, six years younger, concentrated on golf; Alan, ten years younger, dabbled with cricket and was better at rugby; Mary, the baby of the family, had to be content with encouraging us all. But I was lucky enough to inherit from my father – and, indeed, from Grandfather Bill – enough ability to take me beyond the local playing fields. Dad played in the same Bradford League side with *his* father; I played in the same Airedale and Wharfedale League side with mine.

At seventeen, despite that sickly childhood, I was a husky six-footer. We had a marvellous cricket team at Aireborough Grammar School, very conscious that this was Hedley Verity's old school. In fact, I lived in the same Canada Estate where the great bowler had lived. My Higher School Certificate results were good enough to take me to university and in the summer of 1948, despite the wonderful world of sport in which I lived, winter and summer, I had to decide what to do with my life.

While the Australians were making history down the road at Headingley by scoring 404 for three in the fourth innings to beat England, my headmaster, John McDonald, was pointing out the wider horizons which opened up with a university degree. I had achieved some distinction in maths, chemistry, biology and physics and not too far at the back of my mind was a desire to qualify as a doctor. I had been given provisional acceptance at university to continue my studies, but only after my National Service was completed. As I was only seventeen-and-a-half, National Service itself was still six months away; so I suppose that ambition was just a little too remote, just not attainable as quickly as the average seventeen-year-old wants to achieve things: and I signed as a professional for Leeds United. Cricket and football were here, now, all around me and always with me. My decision was not the result of mental laziness; I like to think I have always worked pretty hard at whatever job I have tackled.

Cricket, in particular, was with me personally that summer; and, in a wider sense, the importance of cricket is always accentuated during an Australian tour. The influence was strong; the deep passion I had felt for the game from the first moment I played it was even stronger. So I turned my back on medicine, and chose sport. It has given me immense pleasure: it has given me unbearable heartbreak.

2

A DREAM COMES TRUE

Twenty-eight years afterwards I can recall with absolute clarity the thrill of that moment when I joined the Yorkshire party in City Square, Leeds. Norman Yardley, Len Hutton, Johnny Wardle, Willie Watson, Ron Aspinall, Alec Coxon, Don Brennan . . . they were like gods to me, even the ones who had only played a few games for the county, simply because they had played. I felt I couldn't really look into their faces. I wondered where I should sit on the journey because I was sure I couldn't sit with one of Them. These were the men who were idols to us all at school; they were more important to us than Test players (although some of them were Test players and the others were destined to be), because Yorkshire cricket was more important than Test cricket. I suppose if we thought about it we took it for granted that if one was good enough to play for Yorkshire one would automatically play for England, sooner or later.

At that moment, every ambition had been fulfilled. I was there . . . with Norman Yardley, soft-spoken and gentle in his friendly encouragement; with Alec Coxon, harsh and grating of manner as he was of speech, as hard and uncompromising a competitor in conversation as he was a bowler; with Len Hutton, who kept himself very much to himself until, perhaps, he had had a few beers. Then he would relax and talk superb cricket sense with a touch of magic in his reminiscing, about Wally Hammond and Ray Lindwall and Don Bradman.

Two other new players were there too – Freddie Trueman and Frank Lowson. Frank was about five years older than Freddie and myself and knew a lot more about life than I did. In fact I didn't know anything about it at all – I was a very shy youngster. I had hardly spoken to a girl by the time I was sixteen – and the only thing I knew about the opposite sex was that, so far as I could make out, they didn't play cricket or football. Fred wasn't exactly my cup of tea. I don't suppose, then, that he knew any more than I did, but he was, shall we say, a little less shy.

We beat Cambridge by nine wickets. The university sides in those days were very much stronger than they have been in recent years, and this one included names like John Dewes, Hubert Doggart, Doug Insole and John Warr. I opened the bowling with Freddie (at that time I bowled pretty quick as well as being able to change to off-spinners) and when Cambridge were all out for 283, my figures read 23.3-6-51-2. Freddie returned 20-6-51-2 and he looked rather fast, if a trifle undisciplined in his bowling. Little did I realise then that he was to become one of the great fast bowlers of all time. Equally, little did I realise what was going to happen to me in the future. I didn't think any further ahead than the next ball I bowled or received. I made 28 runs and took two for 52 in the second innings, while Frank Lowson scored two and 78 not out. My first first-class wicket was that of J. H. H. Anton, the Cambridge number three.

In our rather contrasting ways, Frank, Freddie and myself were in seventh heaven at helping Yorkshire to a win, so we had something of a rude awakening when we moved on to Oxford for the next game – and lost. Freddie took four for 31 and two for 41; I had four for 88, four for 71 and scored 22 and 36. Frank scored 66 and seven, so he had had two good knocks in his first two games. Oxford, like Cambridge, were a strong side with Hofmeyr, Boobbyer, Van Ryneveld, Whitcombe, Chesterton and Donald Carr.

Freddie, as a genuine fast bowler, had been 'blooded' and was being brought along gradually, so he went back north after the Oxford game. Frank and I went to Wells for our first taste of county championship cricket against Somerset and found ourselves on a wicket quite unlike anything I had expected in the first-class game. But it gave Frank Lowson the chance to show his real quality as a batsman by scoring 39 out of Yorkshire's first innings total of 83. We won by three wickets, and my first championship wicket went into the bag – Johnny Lawrence, a Yorkshireman who has done so much over many years to develop promising youngsters at his cricket school near Leeds.

Bad wicket or not, that game was really something special because at last I was involved in county championship cricket. The lads back home with whom I had grown up, devouring every word written and every fact included in the newspapers' cricket scoreboards would now be reading about me . . . even if the first one they read said 'Close c Wellard b Hazell'. Arthur Wellard and Horace Hazell . . . two of the names I had been reading throughout the summers. Arthur in particular was a player everyone knew as a big-hearted fast bowler who used to come in at the tail of an innings and smite sixes everywhere. Come to think of it, every county in the old days used to have someone in the tail who caused a rustle of anticipation in the crowd when he walked to the wicket – Jim Smith of Middlesex, Ellis Robinson and Johnny Wardle of Yorkshire, – no frills, no nonsense, everyone knew exactly what to expect and there was a little groan of disappointment even from the opposition supporters if he was out quickly.

In the meantime, my first cricketing feud had developed. While J. H. H. Anton had been my first wicket in the Oxford match, J. J. Warr had been my second and perhaps that was the start of a less-than-cordial relationship. I wasn't really aware of this until we toured Australia together and John wasn't especially friendly. (Perhaps I wasn't sympathetic enough on the day he finished with 0-142 at Sydney!) Anyway, I was due to play against him for the Army in 1951 during my National Service. The night before the game one of our players, second-lieutenant Denis Shaw, said: 'This chap Warr seems to have it in for you. I've just heard him saying he's really going to let you have it tomorrow.' I smiled a bit. John wasn't really one of the great bowlers of his day, though he was renowned as one of the great wits. His first ball to me next day was a bouncer. I let it hit me. The second was a bouncer, too. I let that hit me as well. The next four were beamers. At the end of the over he passed me going to his fielding position and I remarked: 'You've lost your pace a bit, haven't you?' I scored 108 and I think John's renowned sense of humour deserted him – though only temporarily, of course.

After Somerset it was Worcester at Sheffield, and my first encounter with a wrong 'un. Roly Jenkins bowled it, and it was a good one that had me caught at slip. Thus I learned a little bit more about cricket that day. That was the great thing about that season. I was learning everything from scratch in the hardest school in the world – the English County Championship. Every day great players sat talking cricket endlessly. That has always been one of Yorkshire's great strengths – that the players talk about their cricket day in and day out. If they are talking about it, they are thinking about it, and that's half the battle.

I had Dick Howorth lbw in that Worcs game; I can see it now. I was bowling seamers at the time. Then it was Essex at Headingley . . . Ray Smith bowling swingers which went like boomerangs. I scored 88 not out in the second innings and hit Peter Smith on to the roof of the football stand.

It was still like a dream, but a very beautiful dream, and never did I want it to end. But what was real was the batting of Len Hutton. He scored a thousand runs in June and another thousand in August of that year – and they were gorgeous runs. Not the least part of my education was being at the other end whilst he was scoring some of them. He ran me out once, pinching the strike when he was going well, and I didn't even mind. Well, not much. His timing, his balance, the elegance and grace of his cover-driving, the way he instinctively picked the ball to hit and the shot to play made me glad I wasn't bowling, but even more delighted that I was just there to see it. And I was in the same team as that great man.

After seven first-class matches I was picked for the North to play the South in a Test trial at Edgbaston. By mid-season I was on my way to the 'double', with 579 runs and 67 wickets with two months and more of the season to go. One thing looked likely to prevent its completion – National Service, which was due to begin that summer. But an understanding Minister of Labour deferred my call-up until after the end of September, so the road was still open to me. After seventeen first-class games I was selected for the Players to meet the Gentlemen in the traditional game (now just a memory) at Lord's. That was my biggest thrill to date, lining up with Denis Compton as captain, Len Hutton, John Langridge (in his fortieth year, me in my nineteenth), Jack Robertson, Roly Jenkins, Godfrey Evans, Eric

Hollies, Les Jackson and Reg Parks. Completing the eleven was a young batsman, four years my senior, who was said to show great promise – Tom Graveney. I was top scorer in the Players' first innings (my 65 turned out to be the highest in the match) and then the great moment came. I was watching a Sunday afternoon match at Yeadon with my young brother Alan when the news came that I was in the twelve for the Third Test against New Zealand at Old Trafford. By now the whole summer was a dazzling series of miracles. I had not dared let myself believe I would be picked; now I dare not allow myself believe that I would actually be in the side. I would be made twelfth man, I told myself.

My father showed a similar sort of caution when the press arrived to interview everyone in the family. 'Brian and Jim Laker are both Yorkshiremen and they both bowl off-breaks. They won't play them both.' 'They' didn't, but I got my place and, before being capped by Yorkshire, I walked out on to that lovely, lush turf of Old Trafford as an England player on the morning of 23 July, 1949. I was eighteen years and a hundred and forty-nine days old (according to *Wisden*!) and I was in heaven.

That it was an undistinguished debut is a matter of history – one wicket for 39, none for 46, and a duck in my only innings – but that didn't matter so much within the context of the game. Freddie Brown dropped me down the order when we wanted quick runs for a declaration to try to ensure that I didn't have to sacrifice my wicket in my first Test, but I had to go in when wickets fell and the chase was still on. It would have been nice to settle in and play an innings but the pursuit of runs has never been distasteful to me. My instructions from the skipper were: 'Have a look at a couple and then give it a go.' So in I went, played two back to the bowler, Burt, and then I went for a six and would have got it – if the tallest New Zealander in the team, Geoff Rathbone, hadn't been posted at long on! It was as near as that. I had hit the ball well, and this was in the days when we used the full arena at Old Trafford, not just a reduced field as they do now. It wasn't a team disaster that I had been dismissed, and except in arithmetical terms I was not disappointed. Jim Laker replaced me for the Fourth (and last) Test, also got a duck in his only innings, took none for 11 and then four for 78 in the second innings. Both games were drawn, as the first two had been. I had been 'blooded', had my first taste of the top flight of cricket and was eager for more. I was sure my chance would come again.

I went to Scarborough for Yorkshire's Festival Match against MCC with 100 wickets already in the bag; I needed 63 more runs for the double. Scores of 44 in the first innings and 46 not out in the second took me past that milestone, and it was at Scarborough that Norman Yardley awarded caps to Frank Lowson and myself, to complete for me a hat-trick of 'youngest-evers' – England and Yorkshire caps and the double – in my first season.

On 6 October, 1949, I became No. 22185787 Signalman Close, D. B., Royal Signals, Catterick. The Army was to be my life for the next two years. Or was it?

3

LEEDS UNITED TO AUSTRALIA ~ VIA THE GUARD-ROOM

When I first played cricket for Yorkshire I was, by profession, a footballer. Three months earlier, when I had registered for National Service, under 'occupation' I had put 'professional footballer'. So when I joined up the following October, that was my trade as far as the Army was concerned even though, in the meantime, I had played cricket for Yorkshire and England. My call-up was delayed in the first place because I had a football injury; and it is rather interesting to speculate on whether my sporting life might have taken a completely different course but for that. In February, 1949, I reported for my medical with the injury, and I was told: 'We'll delay your call-up for a month or two to give it a chance to get right.' In fact I was fine in a couple of days, but no call-up had come by the time Yorkshire summoned me to play at Cambridge. After that I stayed in the side and by mid-July a member of the Yorkshire Committee had enlisted the aid of Maurice Webb, then MP for Bradford Central, to get my call-up deferred until after the cricket season.

But I am getting ahead of myself. Football had been one of my great loves since my earliest days and at sixteen and seventeen I think I was better known as a promising football talent than a cricketer with a future. I had been on Leeds United's books since I was fourteen, playing first with their 'nursery' side, The Stormcocks. It was a great side and they were happy days. At fifteen I toured Holland with the West Riding FA Youth side and then became the first Leeds product to play for the England Youth XI. That was against Scotland on Aberdeen's famous ground at Pittodrie and I got rather a good press (perhaps I should have stuck to football!) although we lost 3-1 –

13

mainly because Ronnie Simpson, the Scottish goalkeeper (later with Newcastle and Celtic), was in brilliant form, I remember.

At seventeen, after leaving school, I signed professional forms for Leeds United, then managed by Billy Hampson. The club captain was Tom Holley, a disciplinarian but a great character with a wonderful sense of humour – a characteristic I am glad to say he retains to this day. I was an inside forward, and as such I expected to work hard throughout the game, attacking up front when required, then fetching and carrying the ball up from mid-field and distributing it. There wasn't anything like the degree of specialisation in football that we see today. Neither were Leeds the soccer power they became under Don Revie in the sixties, but they were a good crowd of lads and I was getting paid for playing a game I loved. I was a happy young man. Then a new manager arrived – the legendary Major Buckley, never without his plus-fours and his little terrier called Bryn (after Bryn Jones, the great Welsh inside forward). The major was extremely publicity-conscious, a great hogger of the headlines, and he loved to be lauded for the discoveries he had made – 'the Buckley boys'. Well he hadn't discovered me, but once the cricket season started and one of his players was called up first by Yorkshire, then by England, that was fine for the major. He could bask in reflected glory. But that wasn't enough; he had to make me into a Buckley boy. So he decided that I should be a winger. If it came off, he had 'discovered' me: if it didn't, well, I was still an England cricketer playing football for his club.

He said I was a good crosser of the ball and would be better out on the left wing. My ambidexterity has always extended to my feet and while I was a two-footed player, with the reputation of being an outstanding header of the ball, I instinctively liked it just a little better if I could get the ball on to my left foot. So out to the left wing I went – and I didn't like it. In those days of orthodox wing play, when you had to stay in position, you could spend ages in a game without ever seeing the ball. No, I liked to be involved and to be working.

All this happened shortly after I had joined up and was allowed weekend leave to play for Leeds United's Central League side. Before that, the major had done me an earlier mischief. Coming back from cricket I was as fit as a flea, and I had three marvellous games at

14

inside forward, one of which was against Derby County. They had just bought an expensive new player, and were giving him an outing in the reserves. I ran rings round him – it was one of those games you dream about. So the following week Major Buckley took me on one side and said, 'I see you had another good game. I am going to play you in the first team next week but you are not fit enough.' Not fit enough! Can you believe it? Back from a full season of first-class cricket, six days a week, six hours a day, and I wasn't fit enough! Oh yes, he was a man of strange notions, the major. So he had me out on the pitch on my own doing special training, twisting and turning. I came a cropper near the corner flag and so joined the Army ten days later with a sprained ankle.

In a situation rather like the old TV series *The Army Game* I was excused duties from the start of my military career. A month passed before the injury cleared up and then I started getting forty-eight hour weekend passes to play for Leeds. The major now had me on the left wing. But Tom Holley, in the later stages of his football career, had dropped out of the first team and was skippering the Central League side. He used to exercise his authority by calling me into the middle for the last fifteen or twenty minutes. The first time he did this we were 1-0 down but won 2-1; the second time we were 3-1 down and won 4-3. The third time it happened was against Newcastle United at St James's Park where they got enormous crowds even for reserve team football. Well they might, because the side read like an international XI and the game was like an FA Cup Final. Ted Robledo had smashed into me earlier in the game and my leg had gone completely dead. As the game went on it gradually got worse, swelling and stiffening up. So when Tom called me into the middle (we were losing 1-0) I wasn't exactly feeling full of the joys of life. But at least I was back in the thick of it and I smashed in three shots. Jack Fairbrother made two marvellous saves to keep out two of them and the other whistled just past the post and hit a little boy full in the face. I can see it now. It bowled him right over and I felt sick.

By next day my leg was a mess. It was more swollen and desperately painful, needing immediate attention – but the dear old Army doesn't work like that. I was told to report sick next morning, went on the sick parade and was given 'Excused Duties': but no treatment. I couldn't get any either, no matter how hard I tried, and there was no question of my having a weekend pass to play football.

So I sat around for something like six weeks doing neither the Army nor my leg any good at all. At last I managed to get home for the weekend and by this time the leg had stiffened up so much I couldn't bend it. I went to see Bob Roxburgh, the Leeds United trainer, who started heat treatment. But it was too late. I went sick whilst on leave and stayed at home getting what treatment I could, but then I received a call to report to an Army medical centre in Leeds for a check-up. The MO examined me, decided I was fit enough to travel back to my regiment at Catterick, and off I went. Still no treatment. I was unfit for duties, no use to anyone, and my leg was not improving. With Christmas approaching, I persuaded the CO to let me go home on leave for the holiday but this had to be subject to medical clearance. I reported sick once more and this time there was a different MO from the one who had been (not) treating me. I gave him my case history of the last couple of months and he said 'if this is what I think it is you had better have an X-ray'. So I was sent to Catterick Hospital where the X-ray showed an ossification. I spent the next two months in hospital, just lying still, which is not exactly the way I like to pass my time. Thank you Ted Robledo and the Royal Army Medical Corps! From hospital I was sent to a convalescent depot at Hereford and in March I went home on leave.

I used that fortnight to practise cricket, but during it I ran into Ken Willingham, the great Huddersfield Town and England wing-half, now on the Leeds United staff. He said, 'You are going to get nowhere in football at Elland Road. You are not a Buckley boy and the major just doesn't want to know anyone who isn't. I can fix you up with any club you want.' A number of clubs had shown interest in me as a lad, amongst them Arsenal, but I had signed for Leeds because they had given me my first chance as a junior and I have never liked being disloyal. Because I hadn't played since November, the major gave me a free transfer, so when one of Arsenal's scouts came to talk to me during the early part of that summer, I signed for them and regarded myself as privileged to do so. Arsenal were the greatest club in the land, a club of proud traditions and enormous success. It was marvellous to think that next season I would be part of it. However in

August I found myself selected by England for the tour of Australia.

It's a fairly safe bet that I am the only man ever to be picked for an MCC tour whilst serving a period of jankers. And even though the Army hushed it up at the time, the story leaked out a week or two afterwards as these things have a habit of doing. Cricketers were not the only people doing National Service in 1950; a newspaper reporter was in uniform at the time and he flogged the story to the *Daily Express* with great glee.

What happened was this. In the season immediately following my 'double' and first England cap, my cricket was limited largely to service games during the week, League cricket with Leeds on Saturdays and charity matches in Roundhay Park, Leeds, on Sundays. In fact I had played only one first-class game for Yorkshire in 1950 when my selection was announced. In one way I was anxious to continue my career in county championship cricket, but National Service had to be done and I couldn't complain that my military duties were particularly taxing. In fact the Army hadn't bothered to give me a job, because the official view was that I was away so often playing either football or cricket that it wasn't worthwhile. I wasn't complaining. Yorkshire League cricket was good stuff and in the Sunday matches, which brought enormous crowds to Roundhay Park – Jack Appleyard raised thousands and thousands of pounds for charity with those games – I was playing in such distinguished company. Arthur Wood, Eddie Paynter, Ticker Mitchell, Bill Alley, George Tribe . . . there was always a glittering parade of international stars. Mid-week, when I wasn't playing for Combined Services or the Army, there were unit games and I was a bit surprised when I was instructed to play in a practice match at Catterick one weekend. After all, I had played a season for Yorkshire and a Test match for England; I had played for the Army and Combined Services; and it seemed just a bit pointless to play in a practice match for a unit team when I could be in Roundhay Park helping to raise money for charity. So I had a word with Captain Pocock, who was captain of the Royal Signals team, and he agreed. 'Yes, we can let you off', he said. 'Go home and play.' So I went, and it rained all weekend in the West Riding, but not in Catterick. At that time I was opening bat for the Signals, and in my absence the Brigade Major, normally number three in the order, moved up to open and some silly sod bowled him for a duck. 'Where the hell is Signalman Close?' he demanded. 'He's gone home', he was told. 'Then he's absent without leave', snarled the major. It's remarkable how getting a duck can affect some people. When I got back on Sunday night I found myself on a fizzer!

So next morning it was cap off and march in. 'Number 787 Signalman Close, SIR.' The CO gave me seven days 'CB'. Now I wasn't really very familiar with the more esoteric aspects of Army life. I hadn't really had a lot of military experience. So someone explained to me that 'confined to barracks' wasn't exactly like being kept in after school. It involved parading rather a lot in something called Field Service Marching Order and that meant I had to have the said FSMO to parade in. I had been issued with a great deal of equipment when I first joined but I had left it with a friend down in the Camp Centre because kit had a habit of disappearing if one left it untended. As I was away a lot, mine would obviously be most vulnerable.

So off I went on the bus, down to Camp Centre for my FSMO, blissfully unaware of the fact that by doing so I was committing another offence straight away – leaving the confines of the barracks to which I was confined. At the precise moment I was boarding the bus the news came through to the company office that I had been picked to tour Australia and suddenly everybody was looking for me. 'Where's Close?' 'I've just seen him getting on the bus.' *WHAT?* 'On the bus.' 'Good God, find him.'

Well, I had been to see my friend, picked up my equipment, had a pleasant bit of lunch and was just getting back to the unit when I ran into a guard. I was marched back, not quite sure what I had done wrong but with the distinct feeling that it was something serious. Then the Army's press officer arrived and everybody seemed to be tickled pink by the news that was now passed on to me. The press of the country, it seemed were heading for Catterick *en masse* and the PRO felt it wouldn't be a good thing if every paper in Fleet Street announced that the young lion was in fact a naughty soldier who was serving a period of jankers. The War Office would not like it and might not let me go on tour. That bit frightened me. I wanted to tour with England more than anything in the world – more even than to

18

play football with Arsenal. Certainly more than to be stuck in Catterick as a minor jailbird. So the CO, bless him, cancelled that one night of my seven days CB and arrangements were made for a press conference. It was decided to hold it in the NAAFI Club at Camp Centre and everybody arrived there except one reporter from the *News Chronicle*. Later that evening he turned up at No. 7 Selection Regiment guard room and asked if there was any chance of seeing Signalman Close. He was told, 'There should be. He won't be off on one of his sporting jaunts at the moment – he's doing seven days CB.' CLANG. The reporter was redirected down to Camp Centre and arrived just as the press conference was ending. When the PRO learned that he knew all, the reporter was taken on one side and asked to keep quiet about the CB bit because the War Office might not like it etc, etc . . . He played ball and for a week all was well. And then a little clerk working on the camp newspaper, who was a reporter in civvy street, heard about it, telephoned the *Daily Express* and sold the story.

A certain amount of hell was let loose and my CO had to issue a statement with suitable Army dignity: 'The fact that Close has been given CB is purely a domestic affair. We treat him as we treat any National Serviceman. If he contravenes military regulations he must be treated in the same manner as any other signalman.'

4

A TOUR OF MISERY

I was a very young nineteen when I sailed for Australia in October, 1950. True, I had played for England, I had achieved the first-class double, I had my Yorkshire cap and I had played representative football in Holland and Scotland. And I had had a decent education which had equipped me for an academic or professional career had I not opted for full-time sport. But I was an inexperienced youth who didn't drink and didn't smoke; girlfriends took second place to sport, and I had had very little opportunity to develop any sort of worldliness. The MCC party included giants who were more or less names on cigarette cards to me . . . Denis Compton, Cyril Washbrook, Doug Wright, Freddie Brown and, of course, Len Hutton, had all been master cricketers before the war. Now, more than ten years afterwards, I was with them setting off on tour. I badly needed someone to advise me. I was desperately anxious for one of those great players to take me under his wing, to talk cricket to me, to tell me what a tour involved, to discuss the opposition and what it was like to play against the greatest of all Test opposition. From the beginning to the end of that tour none of the senior players offered me one single word of advice about anything.

I needed to know how to build a long innings, how to study the special significance of certain field-placing, the risks that certain shots involved. Looking back at all the things I needed to know, I knew virtually nothing. I played my games in only one way – for the sheer joy and pleasure of playing them. I loved my life because sport was my life, and I played it according to my natural instincts.

When I boarded the *Stratheden* I had never even seen an ocean-going liner, let alone sailed in one and, in the words of one writer, 'I spent the first day exploring her from top to bottom'. It's true; I did. It was all part of a great adventure; everything was a marvellous novelty. I was the only one of the party not exhausted by a hard season, so I didn't waste any time resting in bed or on a deck chair. By eight o'clock each morning I was running round the decks for half-an-hour. After breakfast – and I ate well in those days – I would swim or play one of the deck-games, quoits or tennis. If one of the team was available I would play with him; if not, with other passengers.

To this day I am completely unable to sit down and do nothing. Ask my wife. When we go on holiday Viv just wants to lie down and sunbathe; I want to be up and doing things . . . swimming, or playing a ball game of some kind. So at nineteen I was all the more restless. In the evening I could find no pleasure in sitting having a drink so I danced for a while, then went to bed early. I did find one rôle which involved me with my own party. In the usual shipboard 'race-meetings' Godfrey Evans and Denis Compton would run a 'book' and I did the calculations for them. But apart from that I was not really involved with my fellow tourists to any great extent. It never occurred to me that I was doing anything out of the ordinary. It seemed perfectly normal to me to be busy, to be active, to be involved – and I was loving every minute of it.

I was lacking in discipline in that I didn't know how to conform. No one told me what was expected of me so I just did my own thing, as they say. I was not inconsiderate; I had no desire to be a loner and I most certainly was not conceited as a youngster who had come a long way in a very short time. On the contrary, the senior members of the party were my heroes. I would dearly have loved them to take me on one side and talk to me . . . about anything. I didn't know how to approach *them* simply because they were such demigods in my eyes. Perhaps it didn't occur to them that I could be lonely, that I needed their company and their help and their guidance. As things were I had to make the best of things in the only way I knew – by taking part in everything I could. I had no inkling of the utter misery that was to come, of the treatment that was to leave its mark on me for the rest of my life.

I did not play in the first game against a Western Australian Country XI and against the WA Colts I was bowled for five and had bowling figures of 7-1-21-1. Not the most spectacular of starts – but in the first first-class game of the tour I made 108 not out, took four for 104 and I was in my own personal heaven.

After that I played in successive games against South Australia, Victoria, New South Wales, and the NSW Country XI, missed the Northern Districts game and returned to play against Queensland, so I had been in six of the first eight matches and played against all the Sheffield Shield sides. I was not in the team for the First Test, nor had I expected to be. My form was inconsistent. Then I had an upcountry game against a Queensland Country XI in which I bagged a pair and did not bowl! Against NSW Southern Districts in Canberra I made 105 not out, but during the innings I stretched and strained a tendon in my groin – so I missed the Sydney match against an Australian XI. We all came back to Melbourne for the Second Test. In the earlier match there, against Victoria, I had made 30 and played pretty well against their unique unorthodox spinner, Jack Iverson. I had not had a lot of trouble with him, having worked out his variations, but against England, in the second innings of the First Test, he had taken four for 43 and we had lost the match.

Before the Second Test, I went through a series of movements to test my fitness. I thought that I was fit, but as I dashed back, twisting to take a catch during fielding practice, I felt the groin again. Freddie Brown called me over and asked me how it felt. I told him that I was fine until that last twisting motion. 'How bad is it?' he asked. 'It's still there, but I think it is only slight', I replied. 'That's a pity – as an all-rounder you could be invaluable in balancing the whole side up if you were fit', he said. Not wishing to let the side down, I answered 'It should be all right if I have it strapped.' So I had it strapped. And I played. And that was one of the greatest mistakes of my life. In retrospect, I think that as a captain I would have killed anybody who told me he was fit enough to play when he wasn't. But I was nineteen. I very, very badly wanted to play in a Test match against Australia, and I thought I could overcome the effects of the injury. If I was ever big-headed in my life it was at that moment when I thought that my enthusiasm and the natural ability in which I had boundless confidence could take me through a Test in Australia with a groin injury, however slight. I paid for it later . . . oh, how I paid for it.

In the Test itself you might say I bowled better than I batted. I took the wicket of Sam Loxton in the first innings, but the ball I remember was one I bowled to Lindsay Hassett. It dipped in, then nipped away and just went over the off stump. After twenty-seven years I remember bowling that one. But my batting . . . I went in with four balls to go before lunch when we were 54 for four. I was tense; I was strung up.

At that age – or, more to the point, with such a limited degree of experience – one doesn't appreciate the significance of certain field-placings and how they can affect what seems to be a bad ball. Iverson was bowling and despite my tension I was conscious that I had played him well in our previous meeting; I was confident he wasn't going to fool me. He bowled me what I thought was a bad ball down the leg side. I did not think about letting it go. I didn't think about just pushing and surviving till lunch. If I had done, I could have established myself steadily afterwards, getting used to the pace of the pitch and the bounce and fixing all the field-placings on a radar screen in my mind. My thinking in those days was, you might say, imperfect, and no one had sought to improve it. It was, in my judgement, a bad ball and I decided to hit it. I didn't bargain for the extra bit of bounce Iverson got; attempting to sweep the ball, I got a top edge and I was caught by Loxton, just behind square leg, for a duck.

Jack would not claim it was the best ball he ever bowled and I certainly thought it was a loose one. But I was out and England were 54 for five. When I got back into the dressing-room, there was a deathly silence. I sat in the dressing-room through lunch nearly in tears. I was sick with misery. Years later (during the Centenary Test celebrations of 1977 as a matter of fact) Ian Johnson told me he saw me in the dressing-room and said to Freddie Brown: 'Young Close is a bit down. Go and have a word with him. He needs a little help.' Evidently, my captain replied, 'Let the ——— stew. He deserves it.'

The groin strain began to get worse as the game went on. I caught Ian Johnson on the boundary in the second innings and by that time I could hardly run. In our second innings Bill Johnston got one to nip back and had me lbw. I had got off the mark, but only just. And I was only beginning to pay for the groin injury, for playing when I ought not to have done. I missed the next two games which were against New South Wales and then the Third Test at Sydney. Because of my leg I couldn't even do my share of twelfth man duties. Others had to take my place, instead of having time off, and that started murmurings of 'swinging the lead' – the anti-Close lobby had begun to develop.

My room-mate on the tour, Gilbert Parkhouse, was as good as gold all through. I became pally with Bob Berry and Eric Hollies was always pleasant. But from the senior players I faced a wall of first, indifference, and later, hostility. The only man who took the trouble to talk cricket or to try to give me a bit of advice was Bill Bowes, who was following the tour as a newspaperman. By the time we went across to Tasmania in January I was beginning to feel like a leper.

Freddie Brown and some of the others were staying on the mainland while Denis Compton skippered the party of thirteen in Tasmania – a lovely island with great, friendly people. I would have loved the trip in any other circumstances. Before we set off the captain had told me: 'I have arranged for you to see a specialist in Hobart. We'll get to the bottom of it and find out what it's all about.' So the appointment was made for lunchtime on the first day of the match. Before play started Compton, who had lost the toss, came into the dressing-room and said: 'Get changed. You are doing twelfth man's job today.' I explained about my appointment with the specialist and he said, 'You can go when you've finished here.' 'What if I am required to come out and field?' I asked. 'You do it', replied Compton.

The team went out, and I was in a right state. Gil Parkhouse, the thirteenth man, said quietly, 'Change back into civvies and go and see your specialist. If it's necessary I'll go out and field.' So I went and after examination was told I had ruptured the roots of a tendon in the pubic bone. 'It's going to be quite some time before you are right', said the specialist. 'It could take three or four weeks – providing you don't do any further damage.' He put this in a letter which I took back to the ground and handed to Brigadier Green, one of the two joint managers of the tour. He read it, looked a bit shattered and said: 'You'd better show this to Denis. He is planning to play you in the next game.' The team came in from the field. I gave the letter to

Compton. (He wasn't in the best of moods, as we weren't doing particularly well.) He read it, tore it in half, threw the pieces on the floor and said: 'I couldn't care less what the —— doctor says. You are playing in the next match.' The next match was in Launceston three days after the Hobart game ended and Compton put me down to bat at number three. I went out for a net and in a grim attempt at a joke I said to Gilbert (who was number four), 'Get your pads on. I haven't had a bat in my hand for a month.' In the event I played over a half-volley from Graeme Hole and was bowled for four. When we went into the field Compton posted me at slip and I asked him: 'What if one goes through? Do I chase it? I have been told not to damage this injury any more.' Compton looked at me. 'Of course you do. You do your job like the rest of us.' So I did. But still it was not all over. When we returned to the mainland, in Renmark I was told I was wanted in the skipper's room. Freddie Brown was in bed, the curtains were drawn, and in that rather strange location I was cross-examined about the remark I had made to Parkhouse before the Launceston game. Only by now it was said that the remark had been 'I am going to get out deliberately'. That was the sly way in which things were now happening.

Somebody had overheard the light-hearted exchange between my room-mate and myself, and twisted it. I protested to the skipper that he had been given a distorted version of a perfectly harmless and insignificant remark. I pointed out that I had been played in a game after the specialist (to whom *he* had sent me) had warned against causing further damage and that Compton had torn up the specialist's written opinion. 'I couldn't care less about any of that', said Freddie Brown. 'You're a professional. If the captain tells you to play with a broken leg, you play.' So I had to carry on playing with the injury getting worse and worse. In the return match with South Australia I opened the bowling with Brian Statham. I missed the Fourth Test, of course, then went to Melbourne where I bowled 33 overs against Victoria. By now my leg was dragging as I ran. Finally, at Geelong (playing my fifth game out of the six to take place since I had been told my injury would take time to heal) I had bowled four overs when I felt something snap completely. I collapsed, couldn't get up and had to be carried off the field. I lay on a table for the rest of the day, sick and feverish with ice-packs being applied to my head. And at the end of it the senior players gave me a solid cursing.

I went out to Australia in 1950 a naïve and unworldly boy. Many times I retired dejectedly to my room at the end of the day, in sheer misery at the wall of hostility built by men I had hero-worshipped for years. Not one of them offered me one syllable of advice when I needed it. Not one of them offered a kind word when I was depressed. Not one of them sought to point out the error of my ways except by abuse. Gilbert Parkhouse was a good friend. Bob Berry and Eric Hollies became pals as the tour deteriorated. Without Bill Bowes I do not know what I would have done because there were one or two occasions when I felt so completely out of my depth that I even contemplated killing myself. But Freddie Brown, Len Hutton, Cyril Washbrook, Reg Simpson, Denis Compton – you made my life hell. And I had so admired and respected you all when I set out.

I grew up on that tour. If I became any sort of captain at all in my cricketing lifetime it was because of what I experienced on that tour. I learned that there are times when a player needs a bollocking and times when he needs encouragement, times when he needs guidance and times when he needs to be left alone. I learned them by default of my first tour captain. A very different young man came back from Australia.

Because of my injury, I was sent straight home at the end of the Australian tour, with Eric Hollies and Bob Berry, not required for the New Zealand part of the trip. The return journey by ship gave me ample time to relax, and rest my leg. On arriving back in England, I reported once again at Catterick to continue what was left of my National Service.

Whatever sad experiences I had had on the tour, time is a great healer. With my leg mending, I threw myself back into the coming summer, to pick up the loose ends and re-establish myself. I had learnt a great deal on the tour in terms of life in general and cricket in particular. Now I had to restore my damaged confidence. It didn't take me long to do that. That summer of 1951, I found myself playing a lot of cricket – for Army teams, Combined Services, and others. A much wiser young man than I had been, I scored a great many runs, including quite a number of hundreds. One of these was against the

South African touring side, which gave me great satisfaction. In that match I managed to score 66 and 135 not out. That was some consolation for what I had suffered in Australia.

5

THE PALATIAL PORTALS
OF HIGHBURY

By the time I passed under the portals of Highbury, having completed National Service, I had lost almost two seasons of football, first with the injury and then the MCC tour of Australia. I had probably slowed down a bit and put on some weight. But I didn't think about that in the excitement of joining the staff of the most famous football club in the world, a club whose name had been synonomous with great achievements for more than twenty years, a club whose dignity and prestige were just as important to everyone connected with it as its playing record. Once again I was in a world populated by men who were names on cigarette cards to me, and that, to a youngster growing up in my world, was immortality. From the great Arsenal team of the 1930s, Alex James and George Male remained as members of the coaching staff to provide a link with the days of invincibility. I was installed in club digs in Muswell Hill and started to rub shoulders, literally, with players like Alex Forbes, Arthur Milton (for so long a cricket opponent, too), Dave Bowen, Lionel Smith, Laurie Scott, Jack Kelsey, Peter Goring and Jimmy Logie. I really worked to get back to match-fitness; I trained hard. After two or three games in the A team I graduated to the reserves, and without blowing my own trumpet I knew that Alex James had a regard for my potential as a forward.

Football is entirely different from cricket because it is a matter of split-seconds, of spontaneous action rather than sustained and considered thought. There is no time to weigh up possibilities and alternatives. You have to decide what needs to be done almost as you are doing it. I hadn't yet learned to think long and deeply about my cricketing

29

methods; I was more at home in a game where you did everything by instinct.

Yet my luck did not seem to improve. I was due for a game in the first team because Jimmy Logie was injured, but in training immediately before the big chance I damaged a knee myself and was out for the next three weeks. I was back in the game again soon, but so was Jimmy, and my chance had gone – but only temporarily, I felt. I had been playing well; above all I had loved every moment of every game. Football (and cricket) were not badly paid in those days – at least in relation to what one could earn outside sport – and how many people are lucky enough to have a job which they enjoy one hundred per cent? So I wasn't unduly concerned about money. I had enough to live comfortably and to put a bit by as well. I thought quite simply that I was very, very fortunate to be doing something I loved, winter and summer – and getting paid for it!

There was an easy, gentleman's agreement between Arsenal and Yorkshire that I would be released as required for both games. Arsenal allowed me time off midweek to go up north to practise for the coming cricket season, but called me back at weekends. If there was any clash of interest, it would be worked out in an amicable manner. As it happened, the opening day of the cricket season – the traditional (in those days) match, Yorkshire v. MCC at Lord's – clashed with a reserve team cup final for Arsenal. They required me to play, and gave me enough time to make arrangements with York-shire. They didn't mind me playing cricket during the day, as long as I was available for the evening match. I discussed the situation with Norman Yardley, the Yorkshire captain, and he was most consi-derate, remarking: 'That's all right, Brian, we'll let you go early from Lord's.' So everything seemed fine.

When we came to Lord's, Norman stayed up north because his wife was expecting a baby. Don Brennan took over as skipper and, unfortunately, it was not until the Wednesday the cricket started that I learned Norman was not playing. At the same time I couldn't see any reason why my arrangement with the captain should not hold good, so I got a shock when I approached Don Brennan and John Nash, the Yorkshire secretary, who was acting as match manager. 'No', they said. 'Your job's cricket now. You cannot be released early.'

30

I arrived at the Cup Final as half-time was approaching and Arsenal were not exactly amused. I was asked to ring Highbury next morning and I spoke to George Male. He said, 'I'm very sorry, Brian, but we've decided to give you a free transfer.' Thus another branch of a promising career was summarily lopped off. I loved everything about Arsenal. The place was like a palace. You were immediately conscious of belonging to something really big, really important. Everyone at Highbury lived, breathed, talked, ate and drank Arsenal. Everyone believed in the club; everyone was proud to be a part of it. It was just like playing cricket for Yorkshire.

A number of football clubs approached me informally . . . Chelsea, Aston Villa . . . and several others, all in the south, but I was now into the cricket season. After two years in the Army, the most important thing for me was to re-establish myself in the Yorkshire side, and I preferred not to make a decision about football until the summer's end. As it turned out, that was easier than I anticipated. Things went well for me, and by the end of the second week in August I had completed my second 'double' – the first player to do so that season.

At the end of it, the time had come to think about football again. I decided that if I was going to play, it was going to be up north. I didn't want to be involved in a lot of travelling; I preferred living at home to being in digs. The Bradford City manager, Ivor Powell, approached me and we agreed that I would have a month's trial at Valley Parade. It was handy, about ten minutes' drive from my home, and I liked Ivor immediately. After two Midland League games City said 'OK, we've seen enough', and signed me as a full-time professional. Ivor was a tremendous enthusiast and motivator. He had the knack of making you think you could run through brick walls without sustaining any damage. He made you believe you could beat any team. And because he got such obvious enjoyment out of everything he did, the players enjoyed it all as well. Ivor also had an endearing habit of lapsing into malapropisms when he got carried away by his enthusiasm. He used to tell the press that our success was due to 'the great harmonium' we had in the dressing-room. Once he denounced a gang of friends of directors trying to scrounge a lift in the players' coach: 'What do you think this is – a public convenience?' And he always enjoyed a good meal, especially 'steak with all the tarnishings'. But he was a lovely feller and I was happy to be with Bradford City.

I scored nine goals in about seven games and everything was going well, until I played against Port Vale. I caught a ball on my chest, brought it down and hit it out to the left wing. As I turned, the centre-half, coming in late, locked my right leg. I went on, the leg stayed behind and my career was halted once again. At first it was thought to be ligament damage. Within a few weeks I was back in training, running, turning, everything except hitting the ball flat out. Because of this I had another examination and it was decided to operate. The internal cartilage was found to be torn; the external was all right except that the membrane round the joint had been frayed. After the operation I put in a lot of effort to get fit again. Five and a half weeks later I played my first game for the Reserves in the Midland League. The knee, regretfully, wasn't strong enough to cope with the twisting and turning of a match, and after the game I suffered quite a lot of discomfort and swelling. For me that was the end of football, and cricket, for the next eighteen months.

Yorkshire tried playing me in one game during 1953 to see if the injury would stand up to it, but I was simply a passenger. I made regular visits to an orthopaedic specialist; I had regular treatment. But the knee never improved. I couldn't, of course, restart football for the 1953-54 season and I was living on my savings. I got a bit of a job as a rep but there was plenty of time to brood. Was I ever going to be able to play cricket or football again? Had I chucked away a decent education and the chance of a career in medicine, or accountancy? Life was grim. There were times when I was close to despair.

The 1954 cricket season arrived, and still my knee was not right. I practised and trained during April, and every night I went to bed with hot compresses on to bring down the swelling which occurred with each bit of exercise. The skin became red-raw with the constant application of those compresses. So I started the season playing solely as a batsman. After each day's play I had a quick meal and went to bed. That knee *had* to get better. But each morning there I was, carrying out an anxious inspection to see if the swelling had returned. And gradually it started to get stronger. I'll never know how or why.

32

No medic was able to tell me but explanations were not really what I was looking for. I was managing to do my stuff as a batsman and the leg was getting stronger – that's what mattered. Halfway through the season, with my knee on the mend, Bob Appleyard, who had been plagued by illness, had a setback and I had the opportunity to bowl again. I ended the season with 66 wickets. The following season I just missed my 100 wickets by a hair's-breadth and the world was a beautiful place once again. Then I started to have troubles of a different kind.

The wickets were coming, but I got into a bad trot with the bat. The lads were marvellous. Every member of the team helped, telling me to relax, not to worry about it and that it would work itself out. But I was getting severe headaches and my vision became so blurred at times that I thought my sight was going altogether. I worried myself sick, to such an extent that I became afraid to play for fear of failing. At Lord's, against Middlesex, I was twelfth man and went out to field as substitute. I made a complete and utter mess of two straightforward stops and I go hot and cold every time I think about them even now. At the interval Norman Yardley took me on one side and asked: 'What's the matter?' Sadly I replied, 'I wish I knew. I am on edge the whole time. I can't concentrate. At times I don't seem to be able to see properly.'

The captain sent me down to St George's Hospital where I had a thorough examination and the specialist told me, 'You have been having attacks of migraine. That's the reason for the headaches and, in consequence, the blurred vision.' And twenty-five years later there is still not a great deal medical science can do about migraine, as its sufferers know only too well.

So I went back to Lord's with something else to worry about. Could I beat this new enemy? Was I exaggerating its effects? Was I a coward, unable to face a loss of form and to fight to overcome it? Would I ever get back to those carefree days when I had no problems and played every day for the sheer joy of being involved in top-class sport? Should I go home and rest and try to overcome my problems that way?

The next game was in Somerset. Yardley, sensing something of all that was going through my mind, gave me a choice: 'Do you want to come on to Taunton or would you rather go home and rest?' I replied, 'May I let you know at lunchtime, skipper?' And I sat and wrestled with it all again. I have always liked to examine a problem from all angles, to think and deliberate for as long as I can, then, having made up my mind, to get stuck in and get on with it on the course I have chosen. At lunch, I said: 'I'll give it one more go, skipper, and then, if I still can't get going, I'll have to go away and sort it out.'

Off we went to Taunton where Somerset scored 288 and we had lost four wickets by close of play. Next day we were all out for 157 and so in a bit of trouble but things had, for no reason that I could think of, come right for me. I had scored 30 when I was given out stumped, off Johnny Lawrence, the leg-spinner. I knew I wasn't out and that annoyed me a bit but, miraculously, I had got back into form. I felt good and knew I was batting well. I wasn't idiot enough to think that everything in the garden was going to be lovely from then on but at least I was getting out of my mood of despair. For a moment I considered that stumping decision and allowed myself the thought that nothing ever went right for me for long – but Norman Yardley soon sorted that out, with an inspired bit of thinking. Somerset scored 152 in the second innings and so we had to get 284 to win on an early finish day. It wasn't going to be easy. I was standing in the dressing-room in my civvies when the skipper said, 'What are you doing like that? Get changed, you're going in first.' I had about five minutes to get into my whites and put the pads on.

I had no time to think about batting in a strange position, no time to wonder whether my eyes would give me trouble, no time to ponder on my run of low scores, no time to brood about my first-innings dismissal. In a flurry of clothes and tackle I was out in the middle opening the Yorkshire second innings. We scored 285 for two, won by eight wickets and I got 143. It was the most marvellous feeling I had ever experienced – to be back out of the wilderness. After this game I continued to open the batting for Yorkshire, and five weeks later I was selected to open for England against South Africa in the final, deciding, Test at The Oval. I made top score in the first innings against Heine and Adcock in full cry. We won the match, and hence the series – it was very satisfying. The migraine did not desert me. It wasn't a miracle of that dimension. I still experience the trouble today, but not so frequently. What had happened was that my belief in myself had been restored, and that was due in no small measure to Norman Yardley's intuition.

6

SURREY'S SEVEN YEARS OF PLENTY

Throughout almost the whole of the 1950s Yorkshire had a side of tremendous ability which never won a single honour. This was due to a variety of reasons, not the least significant of which was the domination of the county championship by Surrey, a splendid team who played all their home games at The Oval. We'll come back to that in a minute, but first let's look at Yorkshire.

We had some great players – Hutton, Watson, Wilson, Lester, Appleyard, Wardle; we had developing all the time the potential of Trueman, Lowson, Illingworth and myself; we won matches but we couldn't win a title. Why? Well, to win titles you have to be prepared to bowl the other side out twice. Surrey could do it regularly at The Oval. We had much more difficulty doing it at Headingley, Bramall Lane, Scarborough, Hull and Harrogate, all of which had good wickets and some of which were beauties. Even Bradford was good for a big total if the weather was dry. Bob Appleyard had two or three fantastic seasons but was plagued by illness; Freddie Trueman never really had a settled opening partner through something like ten years. For one brief moment, in 1957, we thought we had cracked this one when a lad called David Pickles came on the scene. He was terrifyingly fast, and when he came in late that season he rolled over one side after another. They had never seen anything like him. But that winter the coaches got hold of him and afterwards he had difficulty in bowling within reach of the batsmen, let alone hitting the stumps. That is one of the great tragedies of Yorkshire's cricketing history – what a pair: Pickles, with a bit more experience, and Trueman! No side would have been able to cope with that opening attack. Yorkshire wickets didn't help the spinners much and we were always struggling to force a win on home grounds. Remember that none of those grounds *belonged* to the county club and we had no say in the preparation of the pitches.

Now let's look at Surrey. They had four great bowlers in Alec Bedser, Loader, Laker and Lock. To back them up they had the skipper, Stuart Surridge, who was not only a useful performer with the ball and an excellent slip fieldsman but a dynamic, driving captain. Their batting had one truly great player in Peter May and the rest were adequate players – Eric Bedser, Fletcher, Clark, Constable. The up-and-coming men were Edrich, Barrington, Stewart. Now don't let anyone try to kid you that The Oval pitches were not specially prepared to suit Surrey's attack. It is the bowlers who win matches in the last analysis and, if you have the chance, you give your bowlers the sort of pitch they like. I remember one match there where we lost the toss and Trueman's very first ball of the game to Eric Bedser took a piece out and, to a man, every one of our batsmen (out in the field, of course) let out a groan: 'Oh, God. Here we go again.' It was going to be turning square by the second day and in the fourth innings Laker and Lock were going to be unplayable. Still not convinced? Then try this.

My brother Peter was in the Metropolitan Police and spent his spare time watching cricket at both Lord's and The Oval. He knew a lot of people, and talked to them. Amongst the people he was able to talk to was Bert Lock, the Surrey groundsman. Towards the end of the fifties there was a little fluttering in the Surrey dovecote which left Bert furious. 'Right', he said. 'They think they are good enough to win matches on their own. Let them try.' So ask yourself how many times Surrey have won the championship since that point. And reflect, if you will, that for nearly twenty years The Oval square has been getting slower and slower until it is now one of the worst featherbeds in the world.

This is not to say for one second that in the fifties Surrey were not a fine side, but contrast the help they got from their pitches with what we found on ours. Towards the end of the fifties we started to play one match a season at Middlesbrough and we arrived there for a game to find the pitch completely indistinguishable from the rest of the square. 'For God's sake get some grass off the pitch', the players said to the groundsman. He complained to the Middlesbrough committee, they complained to the Yorkshire committee and after their next meeting Brian Sellers, the chairman, told us in the dressing-room in no uncertain manner: 'It's your job to play cricket on whatever wicket is provided. Don't try to interfere in things which don't concern you.'

Oh yes. It was a struggle. Then again everyone played just that little bit harder against Yorkshire. Forgetting The Oval, we used to get the 'royal' wicket on other counties' home grounds – the one right in the middle which was used just once, when Yorkshire visited. We were a drawing power and the counties wanted the game to last three days. Every match was a needle match. Not when the day's play was over, of course; we were all pals together then. But during every minute of every game it was WAR. It was at once Yorkshire's pride and Yorkshire's burden that everyone played that way against us. And let me say that no Yorkshireman ever wanted it any other way.

It was interesting watching the development of Tony Lock as a left-arm bowler. I won't, just for the moment, say *slow* left-armer. When he started, Tony was a gentle little cafeteria bowler. 'Cafeteria'? You just helped yourself. Then, suddenly, the next season, stories were flying around the county scene. 'Have you seen Lockie?' people were asking. He had changed his action through the winter, quickened up, and was knocking wickets over like ninepins. At times he bowled as fast as Bedser, and when the ball was turning and lifting as well on a worn wicket, he wasn't the most pleasant bowler to face. It was some time before 'chucking' purges had started and for quite a time Lockie was an exceedingly difficult performer to handle. It got him a lot of Test places which Johnny Wardle ought really to have had – and while no one talked about bowlers who threw it, there was a lot of muttering going on around the circuit. Then a film was made of Lockie's action and almost as suddenly his action changed again. But by this time he had gained in experience, learned a lot and was a good slow left-armer against whom there was no complaint – except when he 'bowled' his quicker ball!

In post-war terms, it was a vintage time for slow left-armers. At Northampton was the inimitable George Tribe, the great Australian bowler, who had so many unorthodox variations of attack that he sometimes fooled himself. He bothered almost everyone and on a helpful wicket he could almost make the ball talk. I had one great advantage in playing George. Before he qualified to play in county cricket he used to take part in Jack Appleyard's charity matches in Roundhay Park, Leeds, on Sundays in 1950 and 1951. I always fielded first slip to him and I watched and watched until I felt reasonably sure I knew something about his variations. In later years it was funny to hear the greatest batsmen comparing notes and complaining bitterly about misreading his spin. I took 91 and 58 off him in a match at Bradford and that amused me more than ever, especially as George took 14 wickets in the game and ended on the losing side!

Bradford seemed to be a good ground for me in the fifties, even if we did have a lot of rain. There was one game against Notts (with Bruce Dooland, another great Australian wrist-spinner) in which the second two days were washed out, but not before Len (Hutton) had scored 149 not out. While everyone else was struggling Len was really enjoying himself, counting the balls in an over (which, like many great batsmen before him and since, he did so expertly) and pinching the strike off the fifth or, more usually, the sixth ball. No one could get 'in', but Len carried on stroking it superbly. We were 211 for five when I went in and it was, for no accountable reason, one of those joyous days when every ball you hit seems to go for four. We put on 91 in thirty-two minutes, of which my share was 62 – quite laughable considering Len was trying like hell to farm the bowling the other end! I would have had a great chance of the fastest 100 that season if rain had not intervened and washed the rest of the game out.

Those were such golden days with a team of great players, all seasoned campaigners, all strong personalities, tough men, hard men, knowledgeable men, uncompromising men . . . Hutton, Watson, Lester, Wilson, Wardle, Appleyard . . . but we couldn't win the championship. That was still Surrey's personal property in the 1950s.

7

JOHNNY WARDLE, NOTHING SHORT OF A GENIUS

Norman Yardley retired as Yorkshire's captain at the end of 1955 after eight seasons. He was a fine, knowledgeable skipper, a good player in his own right and a thoroughly decent man. If he had a fault it was that he didn't seem able to play hell with senior players when they needed it. But he helped me a lot in my formative years and I had a great regard for him. Whoever followed was going to find it difficult. Len Hutton had skippered England, but Yorkshire's committee still shunned the idea of any captain who was not brought up in the amateur tradition. Their choice was William Herbert Hobbs Sutcliffe, son of the great Herbert.

Billy was a super lad. He was at once 'one of the boys'. He was not a bad player though he did not have a great deal of natural ability. He made himself into a county cricketer because it was expected of him, and because he believed in Yorkshire cricket and its divine right to pre-eminence. He was happier having a pint and a natter when a day's work was over than he was cracking the whip on the field. His problem as a captain was that he had fixed, preconceived ideas about the way a day's play would go. You cannot be as rigid in ideas as Billy was and lead successfully, because circumstances can change completely with one ball in a long cricketing day. The side was still full of strong, positive personalities, of whom F. S. Trueman had now become one. Every man in the side knew a great deal about cricket. Most of us had something to say about the way things were going in the course of a day. Billy did not have as much knowledge as his players but he had a good, pleasant personality. His trouble was really in handling the bowling and the field-placing. Because he wasn't a bowler he couldn't think with a bowler's mind – and what made it worse for him was that we had some outstanding bowlers in the side with minds of their own. He could not stand up to them in the practical arguments which develop in the normal course of events during a long hard season. We had two bad seasons and he retired. In 1958 Ronnie Burnet took over.

Ronnie had been captain of our young second team – who had been fairly successful in the minor counties scene – and also captain of a Bradford League club. He was a good, likeable man, friendly, a good mixer, and he tried hard to fit the bill. In first-class cricket terms, however, Ronnie just wasn't good enough. In terms of running a side of tough, experienced and somewhat frustrated players – it was as different as chalk from cheese to his previous experience. It wasn't too long into the season before irritations and frictions arose.

We all had our own ideas about who *should* have been captain, of course. Several names had been bandied around, some of them the names of senior players in the side. But the committee were still obsessed with the philosophy of an amateur captain and Ronnie Burnet was appointed. Before his first season was over Johnny Wardle, a bowling genius, had been sacked, and in Ronnie's second season Yorkshire were back as county champions. This has led some people to believe – and, over the years, the belief has strengthened in those same circles – that his appointment was an inspired one, that the committee in one sublime moment found a man strong enough to stand up to the hard characters established in the team and then to lead a side composed partly of experienced men, partly of youngsters of great potential, back to greatness. Well, he did it, and you can't take that away – but they were two very complex years.

My own choice for the captaincy, being a professional myself, would have been Wardle. He probably wouldn't have been everyone else's choice in the team but he was respected as being the most knowledgeable cricketer in the side and he had a strong character too. It is sometimes felt, for obvious reasons, that a bowler does not make the ideal captain, but there are other reasons, equally obvious to me, why a bowler does. Johnny was interested in winning matches. He hated losing and most of all he hated losing games which could be won. He was a vastly experienced player and certainly would not have hogged the bowling if it wasn't his type of wicket or if he thought someone else was capable of doing better. He knew his cricket inside out; he knew the opposition; he knew about field-placing; and, by God! he knew about bowling. He had come up the hard way. When Wardle first got his chance with Yorkshire, Arthur Booth, who had been understudy to the great Hedley Verity in the thirties, was resident left-arm bowler, and his ability had been proved over the years. But Johnny competed for the place and won it. During his reign, he had just one sticky patch. That was in 1949, when after a lean spell he changed his approach to the wicket and his bowling action slightly, on the advice of a Yorkshire coach; for a time he was replaced in the team by Alan Mason, a young Colt. It wasn't long before Johnny discarded the change, went back to his normal action, and working hard soon regained his place in the side.

Johnny was a good close fieldsman and a very handy customer with the bat. Above all he had a shrewd, calculating cricket brain. He knew the bowling changes – who was the best bowler in a particular situation. As a bowler himself he was, in my view, nothing short of a genius. Not only was he a superb left-armer of the orthodox kind. On wickets where the orthodox would not turn, he could switch to the back-of-the-hand 'chinaman' and drop it straight on a length. He was a master of variations of flight and pace. And he thought, soundly and responsibly, about what he was doing.

On good wickets, often he would drop a man three-quarters back, behind square leg, for one specific ball. In the middle of a spell of orthodox stuff he would suddenly slip in the chinaman's googly about the line of the leg stump. The batsman would go to sweep, hitting against the spin, and more often than not the ball would go straight up in the air to the fielder. I remember Nigel Howard coming in as skipper of Lancashire in a Roses match at Old Trafford, just after Johnny had claimed a wicket in that very way. Nigel walked across for a word with the other batsman, Ken Grieves. We learned afterwards that what he said was: 'Watch Wardle with this funny stuff and cut out that leg-side shot. He's fooled too many people with it'. And first ball Nigel did exactly what he had told Ken not to do and holed out!

Yes, Wardle was the greatest slow left-arm bowler of my time but the appointment as captain of a man who was hardly a first-class cricketer brought about his downfall. As I said earlier there had been speculation in the newspapers as to who would be captain for the 1958 season. Both Ronnie Burnet and Johnny Wardle attended a cricket dinner in the preceding winter, as speakers. During the evening, Ronnie asked Johnny over for a quiet drink and told him that the committee had asked him to be captain the next season. 'Should I take it?' he asked. Johnny was speechless. Ronnie continued, 'Well, if I don't take it, Derek Blackburn' (another amateur from the League) 'will get it'. Johnny's cricket brain began to examine the situation. He mused 'They're both decent fellows in their own way, but in the hard, professional, first-class cricket sphere that Yorkshire competes in – well!!'. Disappointed by the shattering news, he said aloud, 'Only you can decide that'.

The news broke publicly, and Johnny consoled himself with the fact that since Willie Watson had left to join Leicestershire at the end of 1957, he was officially senior professional. Now he would be able to contribute much more than just playing ability to Yorkshire's fortunes. I must admit that in my experience up to that time, I (and others) had learned more about cricket from Johnny than all the senior players put together. In my judgement of the contribution needed from the senior professional, Yorkshire had been sadly lacking.

Before the 1958 season began Johnny, as senior professional, had been asked by the committee to give all the help he could to the new captain, not just by his play but with advice too. (Perhaps they had got around to realising that a complex mechanism like a cricket team just doesn't run itself on the field and there is more for the captain to do than toss up!) Johnny offered advice, a lot of which was not taken up. I suppose Ronnie, as is human, felt he had to justify being appointed captain by doing as *he* felt fit. Good honest emotions perhaps, but we were getting nowhere and were becoming a little frustrated. By mid-season we were having a mixed series of results . . . beaten by Middlesex, then by Surrey (by an innings, too – that smarted), then Sussex, but wins over Kent and Somerset. Things were not going well on the field.

Johnny had had several brushes with the skipper, attempting as it were through the normal channels to get the right bowlers on, and more important, to get them on at their most effective ends. For instance, there was the match we lost to Sussex at Worthing. It was Test match time, and England had deprived us of Freddie and Ray leaving Johnny as our only experienced regular bowler in the side. Other bowlers we had were the young and inexperienced Mike Cowan, Mel Ryan, Jack Birkenshaw (a promising all-rounder making his first-class debut), and myself. By this time I was only regarded as an occasional bowler and had just started to have trouble with the remaining cartilage in my right knee.

Heavy rain the night before the match had got under the covers, leaving one end of the wicket wet and helpful. Obviously during our time in the field Johnny, being first a left-arm bowler, and secondly, the most regular and experienced one, should have been bowling to this end – and said so. Ronnie on the other hand thought, and said, that being the most experienced he ought to bowl to the other end, and leave the wet end to the 'lesser mortals' – the youngsters. As a result, Jackie Birkenshaw and I, bowling off-spinners, gave away too many runs for our wickets and we lost a low-scoring match by more than 100 runs. Another awkward situation in that match arose in the second innings, when Ken Suttle was batting. Johnny Wardle had always been trouble to Kenny when bowling his chinaman and googly. Not getting much response to his orthodox spin at the dry end, he tossed a few 'funnies' in. A couple were hit away for runs, and the skipper went to tell Johnny to cut them out. But Johnny tried another, and had Ken caught by Vic Wilson.

We reached Sheffield for the return game against Somerset and the wicket completely immobilised our opening pair, Freddie Trueman and Mel Ryan. The spinners took over – Johnny and Ray Illingworth, and Wardle really looked the only bowler we had capable of troubling the batsmen. He was going steadily, making them play, keeping them on the alert, when Ronnie took him off and put me on. I didn't get a ball past the bat, couldn't do a thing and I remember saying, 'For God's sake get Johnny back on'. Wardle returned and, in fact, took two or three wickets. We came in to lunch and on the way to our dressing-room a row started. The skipper inferred that Johnny was 'not trying'. He could not have made a more false accusation. Johnny

Wardle *not trying*! He could as soon stop breathing as stop trying like hell to win every match he played in.

The row developed and Johnny told the captain: 'The committee asked me to help you. Most of the things I suggest you won't do, and because you won't listen you are making us professionals look like fools to the public.'

The committee were meeting that afternoon to pick the side for the next game at Old Trafford. The captain left the field to sit in on the meeting, as was usual, and Johnny, as senior pro, handled the side. He bowled 33 overs and took six for 46. If that's what you get when you are not trying, what sort of figures might you expect if you do try? We were back in the pavilion when Ronnie returned from the meeting. He said to Johnny, 'You are wanted in the committee room.' Johnny put on his blazer, went out and came back some time later looking shattered. He had been told he was sacked from the end of that season.

Of course it was a sensation. Wardle was at the height of his powers. There was a scramble by the newspapers for his story and the *Daily Mail* bought him up. A series of articles was to start the following week and when Johnny arrived at Old Trafford for the Roses match he said, 'In view of some articles which will appear under my name next week I think it would be better if I didn't play.' He never played for Yorkshire again – it was a tragedy. Instead of bowling for England on the tour of Australia the following winter he reported it for the *Mail*. And that was a tragedy for England. We lost four Tests, drew the other and Tony Lock, our slow left-arm bowler in the series, took five wickets for 380!

8

CHAMPIONS AGAIN

Vic Wilson was appointed senior professional for 1959 with the same brief as Wardle – to help and advise the captain in every way he could. There could scarcely have been a greater contrast in personalities. Johnny was tough, hard, uncompromising and had that fierce determination to win. He was a real Yorkshireman. Vic was quiet, unassuming – a nice man. He wasn't a great thinker about cricket. He was a fine close fieldsman and played some good innings without ever altering his style to suit the circumstances. He played just the same on all wickets and against all types of bowling. If the ball was turning and a class spinner was in action he was lost. If he was facing really quick bowling with movement in the air or off the pitch he was in trouble again. Yet his imperturbability sometimes became an asset. I remember one incredible innings against Derbyshire where Les Jackson and Co were booming it all over the place. Everyone was in trouble, Vic as much as anybody, but somehow he would be beaten two or three times an over then crash the others to the boundary. He scored 230 of the most amazing runs I have ever seen and at no time was he playing well!

Well, *he* certainly wasn't going to give unpalatable advice to the captain. We were going to be struggling again. We won the first game of the season, against Notts at Middlesbrough, and Vic got 76 and one, but after that he got into a bad seam. He had scores of three and zero against Lancs (we lost that one), seven not out against Warwicks (drawn), 27 against Glamorgan (won), 25 against Somerset (drawn), five and 14 not out against Northants (drawn), 35 against Derbyshire (drawn), a pair against Hampshire (won), seven and two against

Surrey (lost), and two not out against Notts (drawn). Then he was dropped. Yorkshire had a lot of talented young players developing – Brian Stott, Ken Taylor, Philip Sharpe, Jackie Birkenshaw, Don Wilson (Taylor played in the first two Tests that season) – and Vic didn't get his place back for just over a month. So from 20 June I became senior professional. Ronnie told me before the start of the match with Sussex at Bradford and I said, 'Fair enough, skipper, but I don't want the same thing to happen to me as Johnny. If I offer you advice it will be something which has been reasoned out as the best thing for the side. If you disregard my advice I shall stop offering it.' And Ronnie began to listen and to take notice.

Nothing was done ostentatiously. We exchanged views as we crossed between overs. I talked to the close fieldsmen and the wicket-keeper because Ronnie, who was not exactly a gazelle in the field, was usually posted at mid-on or mid-off. In this way the whole accumulated experience and knowledge of several senior players was made available to the captain. And he listened – and acted. We beat Warwicks at Sheffield by six wickets in the last few minutes of extra time. (I remember that one in particular because F. S. was involved in a car crash on his way to the ground. He tried to force his way into a pub called, of all things, The Cricketers Arms! He arrived late and I had to deputise for him with the new ball – 10–3–12–5!) Then we defeated Essex at Colchester by seven wickets and suddenly we were up near the top of the table. If Surrey had been having one of those seasons that we had come to regard as normal they would have had the championship sewn up by this time.

Then, for some reason only he can tell you about, Ronnie stopped listening to the advice of his pros. Perhaps he thought he had learned enough in the two previous games to work it all out for himself. Maybe he felt it was beneath his dignity to be told what bowling switches were necessary or where fieldsmen ought to be. I just don't know what caused the change, but we lost to Hampshire at Bournemouth, beat Derbyshire at Chesterfield and Essex at Scarborough, drew with Gloucestershire at Leeds after being 116 behind on the first innings, lost to Surrey at Bradford, lost (heaven help us!) by an innings and 144 to Northants. About this time I was recalled fleetingly by England, but I was dropped again after just one Test at

48

Headingley. I scored 27 runs in my only innings when we were heading for a declaration, took five wickets for 53 in the match and four catches.

Meanwhile, after getting only 34 runs in five innings, Vic Wilson had been dropped by Yorkshire again. No county was having a particularly good season and we could still win the championship if we got stuck in. So I started to *natter* Ronnie. It was going back on my resolution not to offer advice if the captain wouldn't listen, but winning the title was more important than any personal feelings of pique. I tried a different tack. I got the bowlers to ask for field-changes. Ronnie could scarcely ignore the specific requests for placings from bowlers like Freddie and Ray. One way and another, we pestered him into taking advice. After the defeat by Northants we beat Leicestershire at Grace Road, drew the return Roses match, beat Middlesex at Scarborough, Kent at Leeds and Middlesex at Lord's.

That Kent match is worth recalling because it was one of the few in which Colin Cowdrey ever made many runs against Yorkshire, in my experience. It was the usual peach of a wicket. David Pickles, as I have mentioned before, had lost all his control as a quick bowler. (He was back in the side because Fred was away.) He couldn't get the ball anywhere near the stumps. Only six wides were recorded but there must have been a lot of near-misses and his 12 overs cost 59 runs as Kent piled up 365 (Cowdrey 108). We declared 134 behind their score to get at them at the end of the second day – they had batted on into the second day – and we had to score pretty quickly to get into any sort of position where we might possibly win. Pickles bowled three second-innings overs and once again couldn't get the ball anywhere near the stumps. That was one of the few occasions in my life when I have asked the captain to let me bowl. The next morning, the sky was overcast. It was one of those heavy days when the ball swings around at Headingley, and I took eight for 41 in 19 overs. Kent were out for 109 and we scored 247 for eight to win by two wickets with two minutes to spare. Ray Illingworth hit 74 (what a marvellous all-rounder he was) and Don Wilson had one of his hurricane knocks for 34.

We ran into trouble against Somerset at Bath with both Freddie and Ray called up for the last Test at The Oval. They scored 342 for five declared and the wicket (as usual at Bath) was starting to go a bit when we replied with 275. Doug Padgett and I put on 205 for the third wicket but everyone else struggled somewhat. So it wasn't really a surprise when we had Somerset out for 187 in their second innings. (Don Wilson, who had taken the only five wickets to fall in the first innings, got three more for 64, and doing the off-spinning in Ray's absence, I got six for 87.) A draw was no good to us: we had to go for a win on a pitch which was breaking up, and with the time left setting us a helluva striking rate. Brian Langford, who was a damn good bowler, and loved operating at Bath, was in his element. Everybody else got a few runs and we were still in with a chance of winning when Ronnie Burnet went in at number ten. I said, 'For God's sake get your left foot down the pitch and hit Langford anywhere between mid-on and fine leg. He's hardly likely to get you lbw and you can pull him anywhere in that arc with reasonable safety'. Well, Ronnie got his leg down the pitch all right but somewhere outside the line of the leg stump! The whole lot went over – and he blamed me. '*You* told me to do that', he complained. Oh Lord! We lost but we had a laugh!

We soon motored the sixteen miles to Bristol for the next game against Gloucestershire. Arriving early, we booked into our hotel, and still smarting over our near miss at Bath, went out to the local Rummer Bar to let off steam and relax – with schooners of draught sherry.

Next day, Ronnie lost the toss. It was a scorching hot day, and with Freddie and Ray still away in the Test match, I had to open the bowling with Bob Platt. The wicket was good, with little bounce. After bowling seamers for three overs and seeing no movement, I remarked to the skipper that we'd get nowhere fast with these and changed to off-spinners. I bowled almost through to lunchtime. After lunch conditions were the same but by bowling tidily we restricted Gloucestershire to 160 for 6 by late afternoon. (Tom Graveney had been at the wicket for all but the first half hour, and we'd just got him out for 67.) I seemed to have been bowling most of the day up to then, and we'd got through our overs pretty quickly because by four o'clock the new ball was due. Ronnie said,

'I'm thinking of taking it; then we can have two bites of the new cherry.' (A 'bite' both before and after tea.) I couldn't believe my ears. 'Hold on a moment', I said, 'who's going to bowl with it?' 'Why, you and Plattie of course.' I replied: 'You must be joking, skipper.'

I managed to dissuade him from taking the new ball before tea, but not afterwards. Its arrival (coming on quicker to the bat), plus tired bowlers, enabled John Mortimer and Company to cut loose and murder us. We took two more wickets and one was run out at that as Gloucestershire piled their score up to 294. I bowled nearly 50 overs that day, and that's a lot for a 'part time' bowler. Come Monday morning, the climatic conditions completely changed – no sun, but just cold, dampish, overcast clouds. Tony Brown (7 for 11) and David Smith (3 for 16) wobbled the ball all over the place and despatched us for 35. When we followed on, they did it again, but to a lesser degree, and we lost by an innings. Only Brian Bolus, I think, came out of the game with any credit as a batsman – 12 not out and 91, exactly half our total.

With that win, Gloucestershire themselves were in contention for the title. No one had run away with the lead and we were still very much in the hunt when we won the next game, at Worcester, by six wickets, with Brian Stott carrying his bat through the first innings for 144 not out. So we went to Hove for the last game of the season needing to beat Sussex to win our first championship since 1949 (and even that had been shared). They were not a bad side at all in those days – Alan Oakman, Les Lenham, Kenny Suttle and Jim Parks as experienced pros, Ted Dexter, Hubert Doggart, Robin Marlar and the Nawab of Pataudi as the products of Oxbridge at a time when the Universities produced a vintage crop each year. For three days we had one of those off-shore gales at Hove with the wind blowing straight down that not inconsiderable slope. This meant there was only one end to bowl at – if you had a choice. Fred had a choice. And he bowled like a drain. For 19 overs of the first innings and 24 of the second he performed as though it was a game of no importance. Maybe he was tired after a season in which he had bowled more than 800 overs for Yorkshire and another 177 for England. He had a right to be. But this was an occasion which demanded everything from everybody and conditions were right for him – slope in his favour, wind behind him and the big occasion which Fred loved.

But somehow, he didn't respond. Sussex scored 210. We had to fiddle around a bit with the bowling and Ken Taylor came out with the best figures of four for 40. We lost two wickets (Brian Bolus and Doug Padgett) for six and it was largely because of a super 122 by Ray Illingworth that we got a first innings lead of 97 – what a season he had had! Fred again bowled indifferently in the second innings and now time was our biggest enemy. In those days, before motorways took you from one end of the country to the other in a few hours, playing periods were arranged to give you as much travelling time as possible each Tuesday and Friday if you had a long trip to the next match. We were due at Scarborough for the first day of the Festival next morning and that was a mammoth drive in 1959 – so it was a four or four-thirty finish on the Tuesday. A few overs before lunch, Sussex were 270 for seven. I was bowling to the Nawab of Pataudi and he hit me high in the air towards mid-on. Mid-on was the captain. As the ball came down we could all see that Ronnie was not underneath it and, sure enough, it dropped about a yard in front of him. He never laid a hand on it. Sussex were 173 on, three wickets left and there was a maximum of two hours ten minutes play left after lunch. There could be no declaration. Sussex couldn't make one, with the championship at stake and we didn't expect one. We had to bowl them out. I suggested to Ronnie: 'Give Fred these last overs before lunch and tell him to really let it go.' Ronnie gave Fred the ball and he didn't put a bit of effort into it. During lunch I played hell with Fred – the first time I had ever done so. As we walked out after lunch I asked Ronnie, 'What are you going to do now?' He said, 'What can I do? I'll have to give Fred another go.' I said, 'Wash your hands of Fred. Let Ray bowl downwind and Don Wilson into the wind. If they can't do it, then we've had it.' Illy took the last three wickets in about a quarter of an hour and we had to score 215 to win in 112 minutes!

That was an afternoon of Yorkshire cricket I shall never forget. Brian Stott and Doug Padgett put on 141 for the third wicket with a staggering mixture of beautiful shots of purest finesse and old fashioned slogs of the crude-but-effective type. And their running between the wickets had to be seen to be believed. Marlar helped considerably when we got going, by putting his fieldsmen back on the boundary – the two youngsters were taking twos where one should have been barely possible. I wish the people who exult over present-day Sunday afternoon knockabouts could have seen that stand. It was marvellous. We won with seven minutes to spare. Yorkshire were back on top again.

It was a lively convoy which drove northwards that evening of 1 September, 1959, stopping here and there for a break and a little more celebration. We were too delighted to be tired by the time we arrived at the Balmoral Hotel in Scarborough – alas it is now no more, but it was for so long the focal centre of Festival social life. And there were the members of the MCC team we were to play the following day (well, it was *that* day by this time) including that master of the sardonic sally, Peter Richardson. As ever, he pitched straight in with a prime bit of stirring . . . 'You have been lucky all season . . . you are not a good enough team to be champions.' And he very nearly got filled in. Fred was all for it . . . 'Come on, Closey. Just listen to this cheeky bastard . . .' Fortunately we got away to bed without any blows being struck but Richardson was at it again when MCC scored 329. (And Vic Wilson, Yorkshire's senior professional at the start of the season, played for the opposition!) But with 83 from Brian Stott and 53 from Dickie Bird (perhaps the best-known Test umpire in the world, now) in a first-wicket partnership of 146, plus another century from Ray, his fourth of the season, we topped them with only four wickets down. They declared at 261-5 in the second innings and set us to score 260 at, I think, 112 an hour! It was ridiculous. Doug Insole, later chairman of the Test selectors, said, 'Come on. Let's see if you really *can* score quickly.' As I say, it was ridiculous. But we did it for the loss of only five wickets and with time to spare. Even Peter Richardson kept quiet after that.

So that left us with one more game – Champion County v The Rest of England. The selectors paid us the compliment of picking a side in which one man (Mike Smith) had scored 3,000 runs that season, four more had scored 2,000 and there were four international bowlers – plus Godfrey Evans behind the stumps. This match came one week after the Scarborough game and it had been a week of celebrations. Everyone in Yorkshire, it seemed, wanted to give us a party and we

53

had had a great time. It was back to earth with a vengeance when The Rest declared at 384 for eight and bowled us out for 160. Now let me go back a day and a half to a discussion I had with the captain before play started.

We had taken twelve players to The Oval and for the last place in the side it was a choice between Vic Wilson and Jackie Birkenshaw. Vic had had 23 innings for Yorkshire during the season and totalled 359 runs. Birkie was an all-rounder of considerable promise but was very inexperienced. Also, he was an off-spinner and we already had Ray Illingworth in the side and me as well, if necessary, to take care of that department. Ronnie was always keen to bring on the youngsters. I was as keen as the next man to do that if it was the best thing for the side. But I reasoned – and this was a game we badly wanted to win, to establish that our championship was no fluke and that we were worthy of the title – that Vic had got to come good some time and that with his experience he had a better chance of making runs against that standard of bowling than Jack, who was, after all, a bowler who batted a bit. I talked Ronnie into playing Vic Wilson and by doing so probably changed the course of his career. He was top scorer with 41 in the first innings, batting at number six.

So we followed on and by this time the euphoria of the past week had gone. We had been brought back to reality with a bump and it was now a matter of getting down to it and playing like Yorkshiremen and champions. We got 425 in the second innings – and who was top scorer? Vic Wilson, with 105. I got 86 to add to my first innings 34 and we rolled over The Rest for 135 to win a game in which we had followed on. (Ray took four for 40, and I finished with five for 47.) During the winter, Yorkshire announced that Vic had been appointed the county's first professional captain.

Now I don't know what was in Vic's mind as that season drew to a close. It might well be that having had a good innings – he first played for Yorkshire in 1946 – and then that dismal 1959 season when he was dropped to make way for the developing youngsters, he would have decided to call it a day and concentrate on his farming. Equally, I don't know what the committee's thinking was. But the team had heard a few rumours that the committee thought that Vic had reached the end of the road, and that they had sent him down to the Champions *v* Rest match as a matter of courtesy. If either of those conjectures is true, by talking Ronnie Burnet into playing Vic against The Rest, for the good of the side, I had talked myself out of the Yorkshire captaincy, at least for three years.

It is ironic that years later, in fact only recently, I heard this version of what happened that winter. Apparently Ronnie Burnet was asked to dine with the chairman, Brian Sellers, at the Raggalds Inn just on the outskirts of Bradford. He was told that having done a good job in putting Yorkshire cricket back on top, he was fully entitled to lead the team for another year. But if he did that, Vic Wilson would be away and out of the team by the end of that year and the committee would have no alternative but to give the captaincy to Brian Close . . . and 'that won't do – we can't have that' or words to that effect. However, if Ronnie retired immediately, first of all he would finish on top and secondly they would be able to appoint Vic as captain for the following year, which was, it seemed, more acceptable. Ronnie, always wanting to do what was good for Yorkshire cricket, retired. Talk about intrigue and manipulation!

9

VIC WILSON

Vic Wilson was a sound, solid citizen in county cricketing terms. He made a lot of runs for Yorkshire – 27 centuries, two double centuries, well over 20,000 runs in all – and was an excellent close-to-the-wicket fielder, especially at leg-slip. He was a quiet man with his own interests and at the end of a day's play he was the first to pack his gear and slip unobtrusively away. Not for him a pint or two in the club or our hotel bar, and an evening's chat ranging over the past day's play and the battle still to come. A quiet man in every way, Vic. We never knew what became of him when the day's toil was over. Certainly he wasn't talking cricket with his men and it was a fair bet that he wasn't thinking cricket, either. In fact in almost every way Vic was too introverted. Maybe he wasn't sure of himself, or of others.

This proved rather irksome to the magnificent team he took over at the start of the 1960 season. There was a lot of experience in the side, by this time represented by players who were far from being at the veteran stage . . . Ray Illingworth, Freddie Trueman, Jimmy Binks and myself. At the next level came Doug Padgett, Brian Stott, Ken Taylor and Mick Cowan who had all been playing for the county with varying degrees of regularity for six or seven years, while a fine band of younger players was developing – Philip Sharpe, Don Wilson, Brian Bolus, Bob Platt, Mel Ryan and Jack Birkenshaw. The only weapon we still really lacked was a regular opening partner for Freddie, someone who could break through and who could also take over as senior bowler when he was away – as he was with great regularity in those days of his Test heyday. As it was, once we had had to accept that David Pickles was never going to get back any sort of rhythm or accuracy, it was a matter of perming a combination from Cowan, Ryan and Platt with all sorts of other names being tried from time to time but no one ever making the job exclusively his own. I did a filling-in job and took 64 wickets in the season, some with seamers, some with spinners, although for quite a time now I had regarded myself primarily as a batsman. Perhaps no one knew exactly what I was going to bowl – sometimes I didn't myself! If ever we were stuck with two batsmen for long, the lads would natter the skipper: 'Give Closey a go – he'll get us going again.' More often than not I would, too – not always with a good ball, but that didn't really matter. The lads would really pull my leg if I bowled someone in an unorthodox way (my tactical full-toss was something of a dressing-room joke) but at least we would be on the move again. Then I could be replaced by the regular bowlers; I had done my job.

No-one could ever say throughout my career that I was a 'negative' bowler. I always believed in giving the ball to the batsman in such a way as to make him act positively, hoping that something would happen. The cricket was certainly never dull when I was bowling! Either the opposition got runs or we got wickets – sometimes both. Considering that I was never regarded as a regular bowler after the 1955 season, I don't think I did too badly at all. I bowled my share of good 'uns in amongst a few bad ones. I did what was possible, given the circumstances, and didn't let my team down. Funny thing, the two best bowling performances of my career occurred when I was filling in for regular bowlers.

Fred was really in his pomp around this time and such was his power that we missed him all the more when he was called up for Test after Test. When you look round at some of our fast bowlers today, and consider the amount of work they do and the frequency with which they break down, the Trueman story becomes little short of fantastic. In 1960 he took 150 wickets for Yorkshire at 12.72 and bowled 873 overs. Yet he also played in all five Tests against South Africa that summer – another 180 overs and 25 more Test wickets at 20.32. Ray Illingworth played in four of the Tests, too, and Doug Padgett in two, so the ability of our Colts was seriously tested.

The first flaw to show itself in Vic's captaincy was the way he handled Freddie. Vic seemed obsessed with the idea that F. S. was the only bowler who could win matches for us, irrespective of the state of the wicket and the game and regardless of the strengths and weaknesses of any particular opposition against speed or spin. Vic almost literally bowled Fred into the ground and it was during that time that my resolve formed to use him, if I ever became captain, as I felt strongly he should be used – in short, sharp spells.

Don Wilson had the fearsome task of succeeding to the title of Yorkshire's slow left-armer, the latest in a great dynasty going back through Wardle, Verity and Rhodes, into the mists of time. Yorkshire's slow left-armer had always been a truly great bowler. Don was a great lad, bubbling with enthusiasm, devoted to Yorkshire cricket with the fanaticism which made it great and which brought out that little bit extra from all our opposition. He was a super chap to have in a side because he was always cheerful and never grumbled no matter what he was asked to do. He loved playing cricket and most of all he loved playing cricket for Yorkshire. Don was not a great spinner of the ball, and batsmen knew this, but just occasionally he would produce something entirely unexpected and startle the best of batsmen. Less frequently he would try a little experiment, such as when he decided to see if he could bowl a chinaman. He had been talking about it to one of his friends in the press corps and when he finally slipped one in he turned round to look at the press box and bellowed right across Bramall Lane 'did you see it'? That was absolutely typical of a lovable cricketer. He was involved and he wanted everybody else to be involved as well.

A word about that Yorkshire press corps. Not only had we to contend with the fiercest opposition of their season from every team we played, not only did we play half our games under the critical scrutiny of the biggests crowds in cricket – crowds reared on the greatness of Rhodes and Hirst, Robinson and Waddington, Holmes and Sutcliffe, Bowes and Verity, of Hutton, of Leyland, of Mitchell (and as we all know, no contemporary cricketer is ever as good as those of yesteryear as far as spectators are concerned!) – but we played all the games under the eagle eye of a regular gallery of cricket writers from the major Yorkshire papers and the northern editions of the nationals. The *Yorkshire Post* and the *Yorkshire Evening Post*, the *Yorkshire Evening News*, *The Sheffield Telegraph* and the *Sheffield*

Star, and the *Bradford Telegraph and Argus* all had their own writers following us to every match. They were joined by reporters from the northern offices of the *Daily Mail, Daily Express, Daily Herald* (later *The Sun*) and *The Daily Telegraph*. Occasionally they were joined by someone from the now-defunct *Daily Sketch*, the only one of the 'nationals' to print its northern editions in London. Consequently, that reporter's copy had to be 'phoned through much earlier than the others whose editions were printed in Manchester. One day a young reporter arrived at Bramall Lane for his first county match and suffered a marathon rearguard action by Derbyshire's skipper, Derek Morgan. During the tea interval he borrowed one of the press box telephones and, in some embarrassment (surrounded by men who were totally steeped in cricket) began to dictate his story of the day's play in characteristic *Sketch* phraseology: 'Derbyshire skipper Derek Morgan yesterday plundered the Yorkshire bowling as his namesake once plundered galleons on the Spanish Main. Full point, paragraph . . .' When he had completed his story he put the 'phone down and for a moment there was utter silence. Dog doesn't usually eat dog. Then, with the quiet dignity for which he was renowned, T. H. Evans-Baillie, of *The Daily Telegraph* (a fine writer in the Robertson-Glasgow, A. A. Thomson mould), said to him: 'Young man. I think you were a trifle uncomplimentary to Morgan there, if I may say so.' 'Why?' demanded the blushing and defensive new boy. 'I thought I gave him a pretty good mark for such a diabolical innings.' 'Not *Derek* Morgan, Captain Morgan', came the gently reproving reply. 'Th' feller was not a pirate, y'know. A privateer, and never sailed without letters of marque.' Collapse of entire press box which rather hurt 'Bill' Baillie.

*   *   *

The seven lean years (of Surrey dominance) had grieved our public and our press as much as they had disappointed and frustrated us, so having pulled off the title in 1959 we had to hold on to it. Second place has never been any good to Yorkshiremen, players *or* public. So it was fortunate that we had settled into a good side, with top-class Colts waiting in the wings. But we could not have made a worse start because we lost the first game of the 1960 championship season to Sussex at Hove – where we had won the title nine months earlier. And, incredibly, it was a match in which we didn't lose a wicket until after tea on the third day! It wasn't because of the weather either: it happened like this. Sussex batted first and scored 280 with Ted Dexter hitting 96 (and 76 in the second innings). We declared one run on without losing a wicket, Bryan Stott making 138 and Ken Taylor 130. Sussex then declared at 250 for two and we started another frantic chase to get 250 before six o'clock. The match actually finished at three or four minutes past six but no one argued about that – and though we lost by 32 runs it was a fine game of cricket. I can still remember it with a smile (and I can't do that about many defeats!) because I was stumped off a wide. I had pulled a muscle in my chest, and thus handicapped, I dropped down the order. We were still in the race when I went in to bat at number ten. I went down the pitch to Kenny Suttle. He saw me coming and lobbed the ball well wide of me, far out of reach. I could neither get across nor back and I was stumped by a mile. Every time I see Kenny, or any of the Sussex lads in that game, that stumping is always brought up.

It was a bad start but we hadn't played badly and no one was particularly concerned about one defeat. We knew we would play worse and win matches. So we went off to Bradford and beat Gloucestershire in two days, hammered Somerset by 10 wickets at Hull and had an innings victory over Hampshire at Portsmouth. There was another innings win over Kent at Gravesend which again was completed in two days, and included a whirlwind 69 by Fred Trueman. We beat Northants at Sheffield, Sussex by 10 wickets at Middlesbrough and then, disaster – defeat by 10 wickets at the hands of Lancashire at Headingley. Not only were they the ancient enemy, they were our main rivals for the championship throughout that season. Geoff Pullar had a tremendous record against us, with an average of 70-odd in Roses matches, and he scored 121 out of a total of 210 after we had been bowled out for 96 in the first innings by their leg-spinners, Bob Barber and Tommy Greenhough.

We beat Derbyshire at Hull after that, drew a rain-ruined match at Lord's and then, at Worksop, I cost Don Mosey a quid for which he has never forgiven me. At that time Don was northern cricket correspondent of the *Daily Mail* and just before lunch he was sitting with Len Shackleton, that marvellous entertainer of the football field who at that time was writing on cricket in the summer for the *Daily Express*. I was 96 not out and the non-striker, with the pavilion clock showing 1.28 p.m. Shack said to Don, 'It's a pity Closey is going to miss a century before lunch, isn't it?' 'Oh, I don't know', was the reply, 'I still think he'll do it'.

Shack leapt in. He would bet on two flies walking up a window. 'D'you want to back that up with a quid?' 'Certainly', replied Mosey, who was never known to wager more than half-a-crown and only then on a certainty.

A puzzled, mildly incredulous Shackleton watched Vic Wilson play out the rest of the over and turned with a demand for his pound. Mosey refused to hand it over, saying, 'Just wait a minute'. And to his astonishment Shack found the field changing over and Bomber Wells preparing to start another over. 'What the devil is going on?' asked Shack. 'Did you know the clock was wrong?' 'No', replied Don, 'but surely you know that lunch in Notts home games is at two o'clock?' Shack called him every kind of name under the sun and was still haranguing the cackling Mosey when I holed out at deep square leg – still 96. The laughter subsided immediately, and Don has never had another bet with Shack in his life.

'Bomber' got me out more times than I care to remember. He was a great character, with his aldermanic figure and Cotswold drawl, who looked and sounded more like a Chipping Sodbury postman than a county cricketer. But he had a marvellous wit and loved to exercise it on the field. I got 198 in the next match when we beat Surrey late on the third day, the nearest I have ever been to a double century. I chucked it away by trying to hit for four a very wide delivery from Peter Loader, which pitched in the bowler's follow-through. I should have taken my time and looked for two singles instead. On a good Oval wicket, I had been belting every bowler about. Three sixes off Lockie – two on top of the Ladies' Stand and one through an open window in the pavilion – gave me particular satisfaction. They made up a bit for the times he had got me out. Just two runs short of my 200, Ron Tindall took an absolutely marvellous catch, diving to his right – and I was walking back. Later that season, I had reached 184 against Notts when Mervyn Winfield took the catch of his life at deep square leg off (you've got it) Bomber Wells. Stamping back to the pavilion, cursing myself at every step, I had to pass the hugely grinning Bomber. 'Ar, Closey', he said. 'Tricked you again. Caught in my leg-trap!'

On 25 June, 1960, I captained Yorkshire for the first time when Vic Wilson missed the game against Derbyshire at Chesterfield. It was a tremendous thrill and the only thing I didn't enjoy about it was something I discovered in that game and which remained with me through the rest of my career – I absolutely hated walking out on to the field first. I don't know what it was, but I felt embarrassed, uneasy, exposed if you like, and in all my years of captaincy I have always felt the same. In fact I used always to slow down as soon as I stepped out on to the turf to allow the next player to catch up with me.

I was bowled for a duck by Les Jackson in my first innings as captain. It was a typical Jackson delivery, pitching about middle, whipping away and just taking the off bail. It was a bit of a struggle with no big scoring but we managed to beat them by 58 runs, without Freddie, Ray and Vic. I wasn't nervous about being in charge. I felt, I suppose, I had been building up to this moment all through my career. I was confident I knew my cricket and I knew the opposition and it was good to be able to put my own ideas to the test. Vic was not proving a good listener to the views of his senior players but at that time we were still steam-rolling most opposition so no great disaster had resulted from the skipper going his own way. He came back for the next game, against Northants, and we lost after declaring at 377 for seven, getting a first innings lead of 146, and declaring again at 139 for seven. Now it takes some doing to lose a game like that but we did it by setting Northants something like 50 an hour for five hours. It was a typical Northampton shirt-front of those days – even Frank Tyson, banging it down, could manage only two for 70 and one for 59. We threw that one away. Vic's trouble was, basically, a lack of imagination. He worked to certain set, straightforward formulae of which his favourite was: 'Bowl Fred until he can hardly stand and if that doesn't work, well, we've tried.' He didn't seem capable of doing anything other than the obvious and this led to trouble between us.

On Saturday, 9 July, we scored 253 at Gloucester on a wicket with a bit of grass on it which was useful to the seamers. Mel Ryan and Mick Cowan bowled Gloucestershire out on the Monday morning for 77, sending down 15 overs each. It was a morning of good attacking cricket in which Sharpie, Binks and myself picked up catch after catch around the wicket.

We enforced the follow-on, but it was pretty obvious that Ryan and Cowan were jiggered after bowling all morning and were not going to be as effective in the second innings, no matter how hard they tried. The spinners were going to have to play a part even though they were going to get no help from the relatively well-grassed pitch. But in the morning I had noticed that Cowan (left arm over the wicket) had been given a remarkable amount of latitude by the umpire, Harry Baldwin. In Cowan's follow-through, the umpire had allowed him to run very close to the line of the right-handed batsman's off-stump, making a bit of rough that could help an off-spinner. However, the wind direction (from right to left), blowing against the bowler's chest during his action and against the spin on the pitch made that end wrong for an off-spinner. With Ray in the Test match at that time, I was filling in in that department. Both Ray and I, when bowling on a wicket that might turn, preferred the wind to help the spin (left to right) particularly if the wind was strong – which it was. I wanted a patch of Mick's rough at the other end. With the start of the second innings, the umpires crossed over to opposite ends, but Mick and Mel continued to bowl at the same ends as in the morning. Perhaps the wind had taken out what little moisture there was in the wicket, and most certainly the bowlers were tired and had lost most of their 'bite'; whatever the reason, they were having no success. After a while I went to Vic and suggested that he gave Mick a go from the other end before he was too tired, explaining my reasons. He wouldn't listen. I could see his reasoning, Ryan had taken six first-innings wickets from the end he was now using again; Cowan had picked up three from *his* end. Why change them? Well, I told him why. I did not say that attacking the opposition is much more than putting your bowlers on and then hoping. It's a matter of looking ahead, of thinking about what might work if the first ploy fails, of trying to be one jump ahead of the batsmen. So I kept on asking and Vic kept on refusing until finally he told me: 'If you open your mouth just once more I'll send you home on the train.' So I shut up. At tea, Stott, Taylor, Padgett, all of them got on to me . . . 'Can't you make Vic do something?' I replied: 'I've been told to keep my mouth shut. I'm saying no more.' We bowled 125 overs in that second innings without getting more than four wickets; then rain came in the late afternoon of the third day, by which time we should have won the match.

Rain interfered with the next two matches but it didn't prevent Don Wilson hitting 83 off Surrey at Bramall Lane – he had the time of his life belting Alec Bedser with the new ball – and promptly acquired a new car registration plate: DON 83. That was getting in on the act a bit. Mine at that time was BC 100. We lost to Essex at Headingley in a game in which I took eight for 43 so I had some idea how George Tribe had felt a few years before, but Trevor Bailey had seven for 40 and five for 61 – splendid bowling. I was one of his victims in each innings. In the second a ball lifted, faintly brushed the little finger of my glove, hit me on the shoulder and rebounded to slip. I walked. The close fielders looked a bit surprised and Doug Insole asked, 'Where are you going, Closey?' I have remembered that incident, and other similar ones, over the years when opposing batsmen have damn nearly knocked the cover off the ball but stood their ground.

The return Roses match at Old Trafford was a fantastically exciting game of cricket, and by this time I was offering suggestions to the captain again. I fact I asked to be given the ball, but was turned down. Lancashire needed to score only 78 to win on the last afternoon and had all the time in the world to do it. (Two and a quarter hours.) 'What are you going to do?' I asked as we went out on to the field. Vic said, 'Well, we can't do any more than try our best', which meant that we were going to go through the normal motions and hope that something might happen.

'Look', I said. 'It's too good a wicket to *expect* that we can bowl them out for less than they need. But they are not a good batting side. So let Freddie and Mel bowl short of a length at the off-stump, set the field to save ones, and put a man on the boundary where they might get a four. Then if that works, they might panic.' So that's what we did – and in the first hour they scored only a dozen runs. Fred, downwind from the Stretford end, and Mel Ryan, into the wind, kept them quiet; the fielding was tremendous, and the atmosphere gradually became highly charged as the clock ticked away.

Lancashire tried hard to get out of the stranglehold and lost wickets. They were 43 for five with time getting really short. Mel had taken four of those five wickets and had bowled magnificently into a brisk wind but he could only do so much. He'd already bowled for almost two hours, and he began to tire, to bowl the odd loose delivery. The score began to creep up. With fifteen minutes to go, Lancashire still needed 28 to win. I asked the captain to let me take over from Mel. I said, 'I'll bowl tight enough, I'll keep them under pressure and that's still our best chance of getting them out.' Lancashire just had to keep going for the runs now, having been required to score only 78 to win. But the tiring Ryan was kept on and, inevitably, gave runs away. What made it all the worse was that his performance had been absolutely superb; he deserved something better than to concede the runs which ultimately cost us the match. Even so, the contest lasted to the very last ball of the match when Fred opted for glory rather than the requirements of the situation. Remember, Lancashire were challenging us closely for the championship. With one ball to go and two wickets left, the chance of a win had gone so we needed to draw. And with seven men festooning the off side, Fred bowled at the leg stump and gave Jack Dyson a glance to deep fine leg and a two-wickets victory.

However, we won five of the next seven games to take the championship with an average of 7.68 points per match against 6.68 by the runners-up, Lancashire. We won 17 of our 32 championship matches, Lancashire 13, and so went into 1961 with two consecutive titles under our belt. But we were only runners-up that year, which was little short of a disaster. That comment will no doubt raise a smile south of the Humber, but that was the way Yorkshire people had always thought. The team were supposed to win the championship as of right – and if they didn't there was an inquest at all levels, from the county committee right down to the smallest cricket society. We won 17 matches, lost five and drew 10. Hampshire, who finished above us for their first title, won 19, lost seven and drew six. Who could begrudge them their first championship, led by that likeable 'clown prince' of cricketers, Colin Ingleby-Mackenzie? Other good cricketers in the Hampshire side at that time were Roy Marshall, Butch White, Derek Shackleton and Peter Sainsbury. Theirs was a great victory – but we could still hold our heads high when we looked back over the season's play. After all, the opposition had declared in ten or eleven of the matches won by Hampshire, while that had happened only two or three times to us.

When Colin Ingleby-Mackenzie was interviewed about his team's win, he was asked the usual sort of question – 'What was the secret of your success?' With the champagne corks still popping about his ears, he replied: 'Wine, women and song. As long as my players were in the hotel before breakfast, that was OK by me.' What a character!

We had started the 1961 season with a win in the traditional fixture with MCC. I made 100 at Cambridge where a young man called J. M. Brearley kept wicket for the University and scored 33 not out in their first-innings total of 78. At Oxford, the Nawab of Pataudi scored 106 and 103 not out against us. What a good player he was! And what sort of player might he have become if he had not so tragically lost an eye in an accident. Even after that he came back to score lots of first-class runs in and for India. We started the championship season at Swansea and beat Glamorgan by five wickets and then trekked from South Wales to Hull without the benefit of a motorway. Does anyone wonder why I have gained a reputation for fast driving! For once Bomber Wells didn't have me caught in his leg-trap; he bowled me. I can't have been looking that time. And dear old Norman Hill, that genial heavyweight who was once disciplined by his committee when it was reported that he had eaten twenty-three pieces of toast at breakfast, tried his usual caper of talking Fred out of his bowling stride. He must have succeeded that time, because Fred took only one wicket in the match – most unusual for him against Notts!

Norman never stopped talking apart from one occasion in an early-season game at Old Trafford. The wicket was pitched close to the pavilion, giving a very long boundary on the railway side and Brian Bolus, who had recently joined Notts, ran him for *five*. The windows rattled as Norm's sixteen or seventeen stones pounded up and down the pitch five times, then there was a long delay while he got his breath back. Finally, he walked down the pitch and told Bolus: 'If you ever do that again you will field permanently at short leg. And with *our* attack you won't live for long.'

But the most successful man at talking to Fred was undoubtedly Bill Alley. He could keep his face straight while trotting out the most outrageous nonsense and impressionable newcomers to the game had to be very, very careful if they were listening to him. Fred himself was not exactly impressionable, but he had a great personal regard for Bill and found himself listening, from time to time, when all his instincts told him to ignore the big Australian. 'Why are you bowling your guts out on a pitch like this, Fred?' he earnestly inquired one morning at Taunton when F. S. was in full cry. 'I've been bowling on this bloody track for years, mate, and I tell you it's not worth the effort. Now look at Plattie down there. He's got the right idea – just gentle swingers and letting the shine do the work. I tell you, Fred mate, he'll live longer than you.'

And before Fiery Fred knew what was happening he was bowling medium-paced and Alley was belting him. He once walked in at Hull with the scoreboard reading 13 for three and Fred, pawing the ground like a charger before Agincourt, couldn't wait to improve on his figures of 5-3-5-3. Bill glanced up at him with what approximated to an engaging smile on those ruggedly handsome features and inquired, 'Feeling good, Fred?' 'Look at t'bloody scoreboard', snarled Fred, clearly having no nonsense on this occasion. Bill sighed, 'Well, mate' he said reflectively, 'you know you can't bowl at left-handers. It's only going to be twos, fours and sixes down this end for the rest of the morning so make the most of it.' And an outraged F. S., who had been bowling magnificently, was sufficiently disturbed to bowl a full pitch down the leg side. Those two would go at it hammer and tongs every time we met and each, in his own particular style, meant it all. Then at close of play, off they would go together to the nearest pub and try to out-talk each other all night.

We went to Old Trafford without Fred, lost the toss and were clearly going to struggle on a beautiful pitch. Close and Cowan formed the opening partnership but it was Ken Taylor who took the wickets – 44 overs, six for 75, with his little 'darts', as we called them.

What a useful man he was to have in a side . . . good batsman, brilliant cover point, a bowler who could break a stand or bottle one end up. He was a natural games player – he played football for Huddersfield Town, when they were a more distinguished side than they are today, and was an excellent golfer too.

The course of the game might have been changed completely by one brief spell on the Monday morning. We had lost five for 101 (replying to 216) when Ray Illingworth joined me on the Monday morning with both leg-spinners in action – Barber and Greenhough. With the ball bouncing a lot and leaving him, Illy was in all kinds of trouble and twice was nearly caught in the covers. So I got down to that end, hit Barber for three fours in an over, and as captain he took himself off, never to return in the innings. He'd just taken two cheap wickets, too. If I'd been him, I would have stayed on, put a few men back on the boundary for the left-handers and bowled at the right-handers, who were all in trouble. Illy got over his shaky start and added 117 for the fifth wicket with me (Illingworth 61, Close 111). Thus we led Lancashire by 85 valuable runs. Later the wicket became useful for the orthodox finger-spin bowler, and Ray demoralised the Lancashire batsmen with eight for 50 in the second innings. In the end Yorkshire won by 10 wickets with plenty of time in hand. A spinner has got to believe in himself and when the batsman is attacking him he should realise that he is always in with a chance. But to take himself off at that point . . . we won by 10 wickets not long after lunch. We drew with Hampshire, beat Leicestershire and Warwickshire, then went to Worcester. There the game had an incredible finish and we won it purely because of a remark made by one Worcestershire player.

We gained a first-innings lead of 38 and needed to make 190 to win on the last afternoon. Don Wilson had broken a bone in his hand fielding and was not to bat except in an emergency – but the old firm of Flavell and Coldwell got to work and there *was* an emergency. They were a great pair, especially at Worcester, where Jack Flavell used to bang the ball down hard with the help of a fine pair of shoulders, getting life which few other bowlers could extract, while Len Coldwell was always swinging and seaming it about all over the place. And so we found ourselves 154-9 with quite a while to go.

Wilson, enthusiastic as ever, insisted he could do something by helping Bob Platt to bat out time, even though it meant batting with one hand. Plattie was a stylist among tail-enders, playing immaculate-looking strokes straight from the text-book but entirely without any power. If he managed to survive a few deliveries, he took some shifting at times. Anyway, he went in, and, offering a dead bat to everything, looked as steady as a rock. But what of Wils – naturally a belligerent striker of the ball, revelling in the six over long-on and mid-wicket, but now hamstrung by a broken hand? Well, like the great trouper he always was he got his head down and grafted and, not unnaturally, the bowlers became frustrated as time inched by. Wilson got an edge to a ball from Flavell which flew over the slips for four and in a momentary fury Jack called Don 'a spawny bastard'. 'You what?' exploded Wils. 'You WHAT? Bowl me another like that and I'll belt it back over your bloody head.' And Flavell did. And Wilson did.

Bob Platt immediately walked down the pitch and in hushed concern chided his partner. 'Hey, Wils. Take it easy. We're supposed to be saving this game, not trying to win it.' 'Sod 'em', fumed Wilson, who felt his role as a wounded hero had received less generosity from Flavell than it merited. 'Sod 'em. I'll show 'em whether I'm spawny.' And he carved 29 runs, not out. The Yorkshire handbook, with fine disregard for drama, soberly records: 'Yorkshire won by one wicket at 5.28 p.m. on the third day.'

Wilson, the hero of a Yorkshire win which should never have been, did not play for the county again that season. It was one of those savage ironies which I thought only affected me, but while he was recovering from the broken hand we introduced a slow left-arm bowler from Huddersfield called Keith Gillhouley. In his first game – against Essex at Harrogate – he took four for 35 and one for 47; he was joined in that game by an off-spinner from Middlesbrough called Brian Bainbridge, who took six for 58 and six for 53. He was our fourth-choice off-spinner! Such was the depth of talent in the Yorkshire Leagues. Gillhouley had three for 34 in the next game against Glamorgan, and then, with Don Wilson nearly ready to return, two for 44 and seven for 82 against Middlesex at Bradford. He continued to bowl so well, right to the end of the season, that Don could not

70

find a way back into the side. Keith was a pleasantly genial character, a steady bowler who unerringly kept on line and length and he took 73 championship wickets for 21.49 – a remarkable performance for a totally inexperienced spin bowler. Later he went to Notts but never had the same success, partly because he had to bowl most of his overs at Trent Bridge and partly, no doubt, because he didn't find there the same attitude to orthodox left-arm spinners. Perhaps he missed the support of the high quality close catching that Yorkshire had given him.

The Essex game in which Gillhouley made his Yorkshire debut gave me my second experience of skippering Yorkshire because the captain was a guest at the wedding of Miss Katherine Worsley to the Duke of Kent – the bride's father, Sir William Worsley, was the Yorkshire president. We won the match by 52 runs and, as on the first occasion when I led Yorkshire, we were without Trueman, Illingworth and Vic Wilson (and, of course, Don Wilson this time) so I felt reasonably pleased with my record. I remember the game, too, for a catch I took. We wanted a breakthrough when Essex started their second innings late on the second day. I didn't waste time with the new ball. After two overs from Mel Ryan I brought Gillhouley on at the town end. As he bowled his first over to Gordon Barker, the batsman played a perfectly correct defensive shot with the bat angled down. He couldn't have played it any more correctly. But as he did so, I anticipated the outcome and dived in from silly point. As the ball fell from the face of his bat to the ground, it lodged in my fingers – and it took Gordon a couple of minutes to realise he was out.

We drew with Glamorgan (I made another 100), lost to Middlesex, then went to The Oval where Ron Tindall again came into my life! After bowling us out for 84, Surrey scored 319 and so we were in a position where we were going to have to bat for a long time even to save the game. There was no way we could get into a winning position; it was a grafting job. And we lost Philip Sharpe for none and Duggie Padgett for five.

Our next wicket fell at 220 and we should never have lost that. It was a beautiful track, I was rememembering my 198 here the previous season and I was quite sure I was going to better that. I felt that good.

Musing over the time aspect, I thought I could reach about 300 by close of play if I wasn't out, because we just had to keep on batting. As there was no hope of winning, circumstances were ideal for the batsman – for once he could play for himself. By staying there as long as possible he would be doing the perfect job for his side. Thus I was enjoying myself. I had run well ahead of Brian Bolus and was 130 as the clock came up towards lunchtime. Lock bowled me one wide on the off side and I played a square slash out towards cover. That meant a long chase for deep third man so as I cantered past Bolus I said, 'Don't rush it. Just a nice, easy two.' I completed the two and trotted some yards past the wicket. Suddenly, behind me, I heard a cry of 'run, run, run' and turned around to find that Bolus had run a third and was staring me in the face. I belted off as hard as I could as the throw came back from way, way out on the gas-holder boundary. And what did it do, but hit the stumps direct? And who was the fielder? Ron Tindall, of course. I stamped up the steps of the pavilion, banging my bat on every step and fuming, 'I'll kill the bugger. I'll kill him. I'll kill him', referring, of course, to my friend Bolus, not Tindall. Run out 132. And I had been so happily contemplating not my first 200, but my first 300. When Bolus came in for lunch he stayed outside the dressing-room asking each of the team as they trooped off for their meal, 'Is it safe to go in?' And with great delight each of them assured him that it wasn't. I don't know what he did about lunch. But we saved the game and Boley got 132 not out, so he saved his face.

I was recalled by England for the Third Test at Headingley but I didn't play. Nevertheless, on the eve of the game I was asked what I thought of the pitch as someone with a fair amount of experience at the ground. The wicket had a whitish look, unlike anything I had ever seen there before. I felt it, had a good look at it, and remarked: 'It'll be a slow turner. There won't be many runs in it, if the spinners push it through quicker.'

Of the top brass who went out into the middle with me, no less an authority on wickets than Gubby Allen said it would *not* turn out like that. Australia scored 237 and 120, England replied with 299 and 62 for two and Freddie Trueman took six for 30 in the second innings (five for 58 in the first) bowling off-cutters. Fred never tires of talking about the game, and the Australians never stop complaining about that wicket . . . Headingley, 1961.

I was back with Yorkshire on the Saturday (the Test, in fact, only lasted three days) for the Derbyshire match at Chesterfield. There was interference by rain but we still won by an innings and 18 after totalling only 268 for eight. Then we drew at Taunton, beat Sussex at Bradford and Gloucestershire at Scarborough. My benefit match against Surrey at Headingley was drawn; so was that against Sussex at Hove and then we had a bad run of results until the very last match when we beat Hampshire at Bournemouth – after they had already made sure of the championship. The players were not happy. They felt that we had failed to win games which could have been won. Second-best was never any good to any Yorkshireman, even though the championship that year was a two-horse race – Middlesex, in third place, were 36 points behind us.

We started 1962 at Hull on one of the coldest days I can ever remember. For my part, I went out to field wearing two pairs of socks, two pairs of flannels, two shirts and three sweaters. Everyone wanted to bowl as the best way of keeping warm, and it was not long before the consumption of a modest cup of coffee before the start was driving one umpire, Paul Gibb, from the field in search of relief. By the time he had been gone for five minutes we were damn near frozen to our spots in the field; when the delay stretched to ten minutes we thought we had better go in search of him. And three of us found Paul in the lavatory, so cold that he was totally incapable of unfastening the necessary buttons! It was a game against Somerset in which I was caught at slip by Geoff Lomax, diving to his left. By one of those accidents which cause 'literals' to appear in newspapers, his 'diving catch' appeared in the *Daily Mail* as '*divine* catch'. Geoff came down to breakfast next morning, minced up to the table where the writer was sitting, brandished his copy of the *Mail* and said, 'Why, thank you, darling', to the consternation of non-cricketing residents at the next table. Sharpe held three catches in the Somerset first innings and how he held on to them with numbed fingers, I'll never know.

I have played in the annual Boxing Day matches in Leeds run by the Northern Cricket Society but I have never been as cold as I was in that searing east wind. And just for good measure it wafted over the ground a fragrant reminder of the presence of the fish-docks only a few miles away.

Our first innings total of 246 was good enough to give us an innings win and when we had crushed Gloucestershire at Bradford by 196 runs and beaten Warwicks at Edgbaston by an innings, we had got off to a flier. Then came a draw with Middlesex at Middlesbrough in which Peter Parfitt scored 132. We couldn't stop him talking, either on or off the field. I play a lot of golf with him these days and we have just the same trouble! Then came a defeat on the first innings in a drawn game at Worcester where Tom Graveney hit a beautiful 89. He had moved up (geographically) from Gloucestershire where he had never been involved in a chance of playing for a championship side and one could see the difference in him. He had always looked a fine player but being in the more competitive atmosphere (Worcestershire finished runners-up that season) provided a fine edge which had been missing. What a player he looked now! If he had been involved in fierce competition when he was younger who can guess at how great he might have become. As it was, the boost he gave to Worcestershire's batting, allied to their bowling strength, made them a side to be respected. Tom was now in a situation where it really mattered if he got out before making a big score, a situation where he really had to do his stuff not only for his side but for his personal reputation.

The game at Worcester was a personal disaster for me because Flavell moved one back into me off the seam which cracked me inside the pad and on the inside of the knee. God, it hurt. I struggled on for a bit and then was caught behind. After the match a bruise developed and a week later I detected a slight stiffening. I thought it was just taking a long time to heal and carried on, expecting it to sort itself out. That sort of injury was fairly commonplace, after all, and nothing to worry about usually. I got 140 not out against Warwickshire at Sheffield in an innings in which Ray Illingworth had 107 – and we lost. Then I got 80 in the next match at Lord's which we also lost. By the time we reached the Roses match nearly three weeks later, the knee was extremely uncomfortable. In spite of that it did not appear to be seriously damaged, and as the match was an important one I decided to play, after consultations with the captain and our physio. By the Monday evening, my knee was visibly swollen and throbbing. I struggled to the ground on the Tuesday morning, and using two bats as walking sticks I limped into the dressing-room. The lads thought it was a huge joke. The physio looked at the knee again, which by now was a horrible sight, and took my temperature, which was above normal. He telephoned for the county's consultant orthopaedic specialist, Reg Broomhead, who whipped me into Leeds Infirmary straight after the game ended. We won by seven wickets thanks to Freddie taking 5-29 in the second innings and Jimmy Binks' six victims.

That evening Mr Broomhead operated on what turned out to be an abscess. Next morning he told me, 'If you had gone another day with that you would have lost your leg.' That was on 13 June; I didn't play again until 14 July and in the meantime I had missed the debut of a young Colt with an impressive run of good scores in the Second XI, one Geoffrey Boycott. Also whilst I was away, Fred had turned in one of his more spectacular performances against Notts at Worksop. He had none for 49 overnight after the first day's play, went out and had a particularly thick night in one of the pubs of his youth (just over the north Notts border) and next morning, with a severe hangover, he reduced Notts to ruins by taking eight for 35. Then at the end of July, he was in disgrace – but, as ever, it was the sort of disgrace which made him a page one story in every paper in the country.

Fred, and Philip Sharpe, had been in the Gents *v* Players game at Lord's while we were playing the return with Notts at Headingley. We made the long trip to the West Country and when we went to bed our two men at Lord's had still not arrived. The next morning it was getting perilously close to time to report at the ground, but there was still no sign of Fred. So Sharpie, used to Fred leaving everything to the last minute, decided to beg a lift from one of the others. Ten-thirty came, but still no Fred. Sharpie was in a fix, because his kit was locked up in the boot of Fred's car. But there was no real anxiety for F. S.; we knew he would turn up sometime. Eleven o'clock, still no Fred. Vic Wilson was in a spot, because he had to toss and to declare his team. He confided to me, 'I am thinking of leaving Fred out of the side.' Now F. S., in terms of parade times and similar team matters, had got away with murder throughout Vic's captaincy and I had to say to him, 'Well, it's your decision, but if you are thinking of disciplining him you should have done that three seasons ago, in your first season as captain, not your last. If you had, all would be well now.'

Fred was left out, and told to go home and report to headquarters. He didn't go, of course, until he was ready, which was a day and a half later. He spent most of the intervening time having a field day with an extremely receptive audience of pressmen. There was quite a storm.

Vic had announced, just before the Trueman incident, that he was to retire at the end of that season. We had been through a lean time by Yorkshire standards, winning only two of our last eight games, and we were slipping in the championship. There had been various criticisms of Vic's leadership in the field for some time, which had been unsettling; we had not had success to bind us together. But the recent events, and our natural pride and traditions, finally jolted us out of our apathy. After the Taunton game we talked things over amongst ourselves; we knew we weren't a patch on the team we should be. We were doing nobody any good – not Yorkshire, the captain, or ourselves. We resolved to try to put things right, and see if we could send Vic off to his retirement with another championship win.

I wonder if Vic ever reflected later on the sudden change in his team: the lethargy of the previous few weeks was replaced, almost overnight, by all the old urgency and resolution to win. He led us at Bristol against Gloucestershire, whom we beat easily, and then we steam-rollered Essex to an innings defeat. Freddie had missed those two games, but rejoined us at Middlesbrough to play Kent. There was a certain coolness between the captain and the man whom he had regarded as indispensable; but Fred soon caught the spirit of the team at its best, and we were all united once more. Of the last twelve games that season, we won seven outright, led on first innings in four, and thus lost on first innings in only one. But it took us until the very last day of the season, at Harrogate, to make sure of the championship – and even then we won by only four points from Worcestershire (0.13 in average points).

It was tense in the extreme at Harrogate because of a constant fear that the rain, which caused many delays, might wash the game out completely. A hat-trick by Jeff Jones (Don Wilson and Mel Ryan with the last two balls of the first innings, Ken Taylor with his first ball in the second) passed almost unnoticed. But at four minutes past four on the afternoon of Friday, 7 September, 1962, we saw Vic Wilson off to retirement with a second championship in three years. Complaints and niggling were forgotten as the champagne flowed and although no decision about his successor had been announced I had started looking forward to the job which would fulfil my fondest ambitions and hopes – the captaincy of Yorkshire.

10

CAPTAIN OF YORKSHIRE

My first season as captain of Yorkshire was a marvellous summer. We won the county championship in spite of heavy Test calls and we had some absolutely magnificent games. Remember, no one gave us anything. We had to dig our own victories out of nothing, to fashion and contrive them entirely by our own efforts with bat, ball and brain. This brought some dramatic finishes which kept everyone on his toes for the full span of each match. We had some brilliant players who played brilliantly; we had some promising youngsters who developed in spectacular style. Boycott, who was still an up-and-coming Colt at the start of the season, finished top of the averages, scoring 1,628 runs; Hampshire, who had just established himself as a first-team player, consolidated with 1,236.

Philip Sharpe, in his third season as a capped player, got into the England side and topped the Test averages, while F. S. topped the England bowling taking another 34 Test wickets. Captaincy came to me as a joyous relief, rather than a strain. I had spent something like six or seven seasons watching successive captains dabbling with a job which I regarded as highly specialised and vitally important. For five of those seasons I had been in a position where I urged, coaxed, pleaded with first the senior professional, then the captain himself, to take action which seemed to me at the time to be necessary, even essential. Sometimes my advice had been taken, sometimes it had been ignored. It had been a highly frustrating time and now, at last, I was free of all those frustrations. I could follow my own instincts, put my own ideas in operation. To back me up I had a team of superb professionals who were not only great, or very good, players, but who all thought about their cricket day and night. The advice born of their cumulative experience was available to me when I needed a second opinion as everyone does at some time or another. There was a pure, unalloyed joy in playing cricket in 1963. In addition, I got back in the Test team, played in all five matches against the West Indies, and finished third in the batting averages. It was the first time I had ever had more than two consecutive Tests and I felt that at last I, too, had consolidated my position.

We started the 1963 season with a win at Northampton which was accomplished right on the last stroke of the clock. It was a remarkable game in some ways. At 106 for five in our first innings we were in a bit of trouble against David Larter and that lovable character, Ollie Milburn. I was in the forties when I was joined by F. S. Trueman, batting number seven, no less. When I was out we were 272 for six and Fred went on to complete his maiden first-class hundred. It was a bit of a seamer's wicket and at 56 for four we were in real trouble. Then Boycott and I put on 50, of which Geoff got eight, and I had a good long look at his defensive technique. Now when Fred came in it was none of your block-one-and-belt-the-next-over-long-on of which we saw a great deal over the years. He played really well, got behind it and treated us to some magnificent shots. He knew no one was going to drop it short at him. Whenever that happened to Fred – and it was usually an accident if it did – he would fix a long, meaning gaze on the bowler which clearly said, 'I've got to bowl at *you* yet'. Fred, remember, was the most respected and the most feared bowler in the country.

So no one bounced it at him, and when the bowlers overpitched he played some superb cover drives. It was a real treat to be batting with him because, as ever when he was on top, the chat flowed freely. He offered all kinds of advice to the bowlers, directed fielders into position, invited approval of his batting . . . it was an afternoon of immense fun. We scored 339, bowled them out for 137, but in following on Ollie scored a brilliant 123, full of shots of tremendous power from those heavily-muscled forearms, and they totalled 303. It was one of those fascinating situations – with the wicket now playing much more easily – where we had to winkle them out by constantly changing our strategy while keeping one eye on the clock. In the end we had to score 102 in very quick time, and I had the satisfaction of adding

53 not out to my first innings 161 as Yorkshire pulled off a win, bang on five o'clock, in my first championship match as captain. I had an intensely satisfying sense of achievement, allied to an equally important feeling of enjoyment. It had been fun; every minute of it. The strain of having to think about a thousand and one things at once was all in the future.

We drew with Kent in a rain-affected game at Hull where a very young Derek Underwood had four for 40 off 21 overs – the shape of things to come – and then we crushed Warwicks at Edgbaston by an innings and 171. Freddie took four for 18 in the first innings, six for 18 in the second; Mel Ryan had four for 13 and three for 29 and between them our opening bowlers took every wicket to fall to bowlers (that is other than run-outs) in the game and that is something that can't have happened *very* often. We were now a really good side and we were a confident side. We had all grown in experience together and were still growing and improving every day. Freddie took 8-45 in bowling out Gloucs for 80 at Park Avenue and he was in incredible form. For my part I was relishing the novelty of being able to put my ideas into operation whenever they occurred to me instead of suffering the frustration of seeing things which ought to be done and not being able to get them going. At the same time it was now brought home to me that with so many things to think about, you can't always spot straightaway things which seem more obvious when they are not your immediate responsibility. So I consulted. There was a lot of experience in that side, a lot of cricket know-how and I would have been a fool to ignore it. Illy and I talked things over whenever a stand looked like developing; I talked a great deal to Jimmy Binks who, as wicket-keeper, was constantly in the picture about pace of the pitch, movement off it, problems the batsman was encountering, errors on the bowler's part. Round that wicket there was a sort of round-the-clock surveillance with one completely single-minded purpose – to get the batsman out. So we came down to earth with a bit of a bump when we lost to Hants at Headingley by 130 runs. We had to chase a fourth-innings target of 275 at a virtually impossible rate. If anyone declared against us you could bet that the target was going to be unattainable – and in trying to reach this one we reached the point of no return in our batting and lost just five minutes from the end.

Faced with a pre-Bank Holiday Friday evening return journey from Kent to Yorkshire, roads packed with holidaymakers, we flew from Headingley to Rochester. Our next match was at Gravesend, and Rochester was the nearest airfield. Our flight was a little (and short-lived) private enterprise on the part of Peter Richardson and a friend of his. Peter had told one of Yorkshire's personal press corps about the flight just over a fortnight previously, during the game at Hull, and it would have been a nice, 'exclusive' story for the *Daily Mail*. But Richardson at that time was renowned as the greatest practical joker in cricket. His favourite target for leg-pulls was the press in general and Jim Swanton in particular. He used to concoct the most ludicrous stories of unusual feats of batting, bowling and fielding (usually in public school cricket, a bait which Swanton could never resist) and send them to *The Daily Telegraph* with a suitably unctuous covering letter asking if the great man was interested in the enclosed. The great man was, and week after week catalogues of fictitious nonsense appeared in his Monday morning 'Commentary'. It developed to such an extent that Jim's secretary, the lovely 'Daffers' (now Mrs Richie Benaud) used to comb through the letters, see which unlikely story arrived in an envelope postmarked in the town where Kent had last been playing, and make sure that her boss never saw it. Richardson retaliated by giving his latest composition to someone in the opposition team to post at *their* next port of call. Everyone in cricket knew about all this – except E.W.S. So when Peter offered the *Mail* man an exclusive about Yorkshire's flight to Rochester it was politely acknowledged and quickly forgotten. So it came as a bit of a shock when Crawford White, in the *Daily Express*, produced the exclusive story a couple of days later and it proved to be true. A classic case of crying wolf, I suppose.

So we went to Gravesend, gained a first innings lead of 64, declared at 187 for nine and left Kent needing 252 to win. They really went after the runs and the result was an absorbing afternoon's cricket which finished with a win for us by 22 runs with just eight minutes remaining. And yet we might never have done it if a certain message had been delivered. Kent had made a tremendous effort to get the runs. They hadn't a lot of time, and we hadn't a lot, either, to bowl them out because there had been interventions by the weather. In the event, they were all out 229 in the 54th over! Who needs one-day cricket with a third afternoon's play like that? They had to chance their arm; we had to buy wickets – e.g. Don Wilson 8.4-0-72-4. Kent 205 for six, then 212 for seven. I caught Alan Dixon, and Freddie came back to knock over Underwood. We were watching the signals from the pavilion – and watching them a little more closely, it turned out, than the in-strike batsman, Alan Brown. The last man, John Dye, came out with instructions (we learned later) for Brown: 'Put the shutters up. We've had a go. It hasn't come off. Now it's our job to save the game.' For some reason we never discovered, Dye came and never said anything to Brown who was left to believe the chase was still on.

I stationed myself at silly mid-off for the start of Wilson's next over. We didn't know about the undelivered message but we had seen the signals from the pavilion and I expected Brownie to block. To the third ball he had an almighty swipe and drove the ball straight into the middle of my forehead. It ricocheted high into the air and before I had time to think about being hit I instinctively whirled round to see where it had gone, shouting 'catch it'. Instead I found myself gazing into the horror-struck eyes of deep mid-off who just kept looking at me as the ball sailed over his head and bounced over the boundary. I was livid, delivered a hell of a rocket to the fielder, and crouched for the next ball. Brown decided to repeat the stroke, missed the ball and was stumped. We had won – and only then was I ready to think about the bump which was beginning to swell in the middle of my forehead.

We flew back north for the sweetest of all victories – by an innings and 110 in the Roses match at Bramall Lane. There we saw Geoff Boycott show what a great batsman he was going to be. Lancashire's batting was a bit thin but there was nothing wrong with the attack which faced us after bowling them out for 151 . . . Statham, Higgs and Lever, Marner to back them up with medium-paced seamers, Tommy Greenhough and Ken Grieves with leg-spinners and Jack Dyson's off-breaks. Ray Illingworth was out of our side at this time with a recurrence of Achilles tendon trouble which had developed in Australia the previous winter, and with my swollen forehead throbbing a bit I dropped down to number six in the order and moved Boycott up to number five.

We were 56 for three when he went in and in those days the

atmosphere of a Roses match was something special. In personal relationships we had developed a bit from the days when, as Emmott Robinson used to say, 'We say "ah do?" on't first morning and then we say nowt but "how's that", for t'next three days,' but out in the middle it was as intense as it had ever been for a hundred years. It was war with an audience, and the audience were as much a part of it, in spirit, as the combatants. So it wasn't exactly an ideal situation for a young Colt having his first taste of a Roses match. It was 56 for three when Boycott joined Bryan Stott, 305 for four when they were separated, the following afternoon. Boycott reached his maiden first-class hundred in his first-ever Roses match with as fine a back-foot cover drive as anyone will ever see – and off Brian Statham with the new ball. Boycott went on to get 145 (Stott 143) and he has never looked back since the afternoon of 3 June, 1963. This was the player who (I had learned at my first committee meeting as Yorkshire captain) had been recommended by my predecessor for non-retention 'because he was unlikely to make a first-class cricketer'.

Now the real depth of Yorkshire's talent began to appear. Freddie and I were called up by England, Ray Illingworth was still injured so Jimmy Binks became fourth-choice captain and led the side to victory by an innings in each of his first two games as leader – against Somerset at Harrogate and Derbyshire at Chesterfield. Jimmy had joined the county in 1955 and took over the captaincy with a record behind him of 200 consecutive county championship matches. And he kept that up, too. Only after he had retired – prematurely, alas, but he was thinking of his future outside cricket – did he reveal that more than once he had played with broken fingers. He was a highly intelligent cricketer, and invaluable to me with reports of what was happening and suggestions of action we might take. He could be opinionated and stroppy and we had our share of arguments. But the great thing about all these arguments on the field was that every aspect of every one of them was designed to bring about a Yorkshire win. I had often disagreed with captains' policy; now I found that players from time to time disagreed with mine. It was healthy; it was positive; we all had the same objective in view – winning. When he retired, Jimmy sent me a letter which I shall always treasure. It did not omit a reference to our arguments, either!

Fred and I were back for the return game with Somerset, where we scored no points in a rain-spoiled game. But twenty-one of us got one of our great laughs of the season, and I had one of my major arguments. In our second innings Freddie stuck around for a bit and Fred Rumsey let him have a couple of bouncers. F. S. was outraged. Bowlers just didn't do that sort of thing to him. But Rumsey was a great character with a sense of humour of his own. His captain, Harold Stevenson, watched the second of his bouncers with some interest and most of the crowd listened to the Trueman reaction with immense delight. Stevo warned Rumsey, 'Watch it. This isn't the last time you are going to play against Yorkshire, you know.' But Rumsey, having provoked F. S. to seething fury, couldn't let it alone and he even had the satisfaction of catching Freddie off the slow left-armer, David Doughty, for 42. Then Stevo allowed his own sense of humour a bit of free rein. There were just a few minutes of play remaining and no result possible when we were all out, so he sent in Rumsey to open the innings.

F. S. couldn't wait to get hold of the ball. He marked out his run, hitched his trousers and stood pawing the ground as Rumsey walked to the wicket with Brian Langford for a token five minutes batting. 'Take it easy, Fred', said I, and threw the ball to Jackie Hampshire. F.S. went mad. He cursed me all over the field. He called me every name he could think of. And when, at the end of an over which gave Langford nine runs, I put Duggie Padgett on at the other end, the Ball of Fire started all over again. No one could play for laughing. In the Somerset dressing-room, I gather, there was a little disappointment at being deprived of the spectacle of big, bulky Rumsey ducking and weaving to avoid Freddie's counter-attack, but it wasn't worth risking having someone killed. Padgett conceded a single to Langford, was struck for a four by Rumsey and then bowled him, to his own ecstatic delight. He spent the rest of the season telling his room-mate, travelling companion and friend of his youth (Illy) that he should have been there to see it. Bowlers always love to bat and batsmen invariably love to bowl and when, in either context, something comes off for them, it's their main talking-point for the year.

I went off to the Second Test with Freddie as the team went on to Bristol for the next game with Gloucs. It was rain-ruined from the start and on the second evening there was a bit of a party led by two of the more bucolic members of our press corps. This led to a certain amount of disturbance in the hotel, a complaint from its management to the Yorkshire committee, and an official rollocking for Fred! Oh, committees . . . it is quite unbelievable how utterly out of touch they can become. They knew I was in the Lord's Test (presumably because my second innings there received quite a bit of publicity) but – don't ask me how or why – they never noticed that Fred was playing, too. So in my absence, a corporate body two hundred miles away in the north assumed that F.S. was the captain and therefore responsible. He never tires of telling of the official reprimand he received. Mind you, in that same season, a Yorkshire committee man sat in the pavilion at Chesterfield, watched Duggie Padgett score 142 and remarked, 'Taylor is playing well today, don't you think?' Ken Taylor was not even in the side. As I said, committees . . .

We returned from the Test – Fred to his rocket, me nursing my Griffith and Hall bruises – to bowl out Glamorgan on a greenish wicket with a swinging atmosphere. The conditions seemed to suit me and I took six for 55, feeling every bruise with every step. In the second innings I had 16-9-19-4 (not my sort of figures at all; I wish I could remember more about that day!) and we won by 10 wickets before lunch on the third day. In the next game at Trent Bridge, Notts opened with two Yorkshire exiles – Brian Bolus, who scored 2,000 runs in his first season there after talking himself out of a place with Yorkshire, and got two England caps in the Fourth and Fifth Tests, and Barry Whittingham. Bolus, as he invariably did *against* us, got runs – 77 out of the first 90 – as well as indulging in a non-stop dialogue with Fred. We lost to Middlesex at Headingley without Fred, Illy and myself so we missed another talkative innings from Peter Parfitt, drew with Surrey at The Oval and against Sussex at Bradford we needed a new opening partner for Jackie Hampshire. The regular pair that season were Hampers and Doug Padgett, but with Doug temporarily out of the side I had to decide who should take over. I decided on Boycott.

Up until then he had been batting at number five or number six and he wasn't too happy about that. Even though there was no restriction on the length of a first innings in those days he was not

Above: Aged sixteen, with West Riding FA Youth XI. (*H. Hoggarth*)
Right: Training, 1948–49. The shorts were longer then – and the ball bigger? (*Central Press*)

Above: Old Trafford 1949, with another Test debutant – John Reid of New Zealand. (*Sport & General*)
Left: It's a different ball-game . . .
Right: With my young brother Alan at Yeadon – just after I had been told of my delayed call-up. (*Topical Press Agency*)
Following pages: Victory over West Indies at The Oval, in 1966. (*Central Press*)

Above: With Derrick Robins multi-racial tour of South Africa. (*Peter Stanford*)
Left: Lord's, 1967. (*Sport & General*)
Right above: Over the hills . . . with Skipper I as pacemaker. (*Associated Newspapers*)
Right: At home with Vivienne, Lynn and Skipper I.

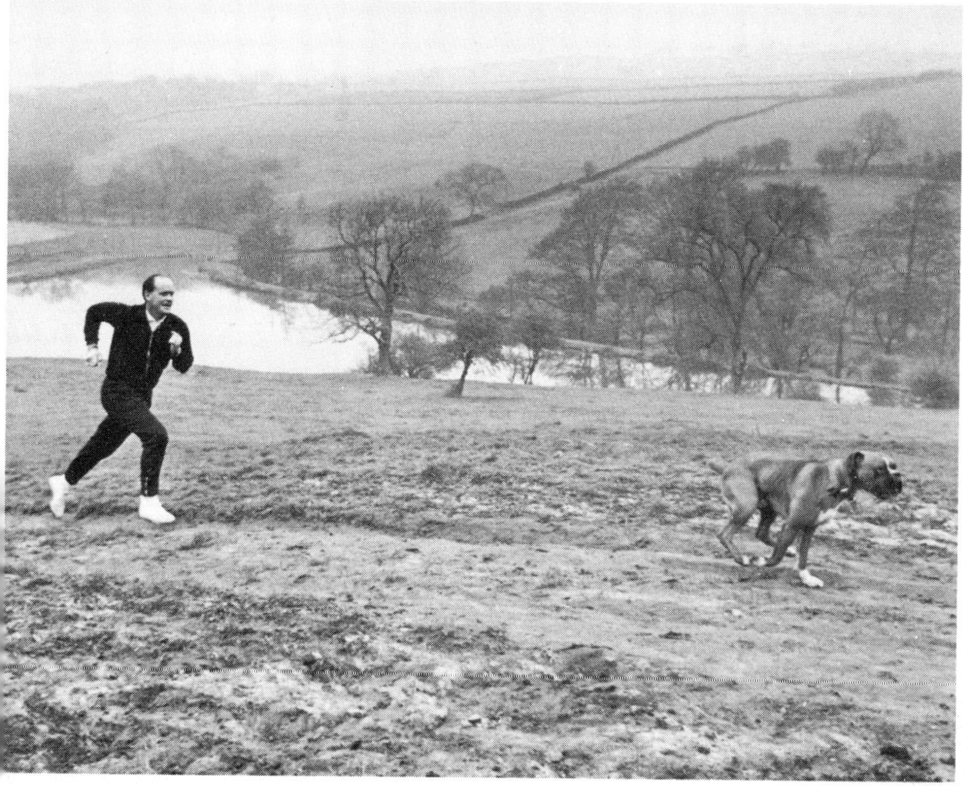

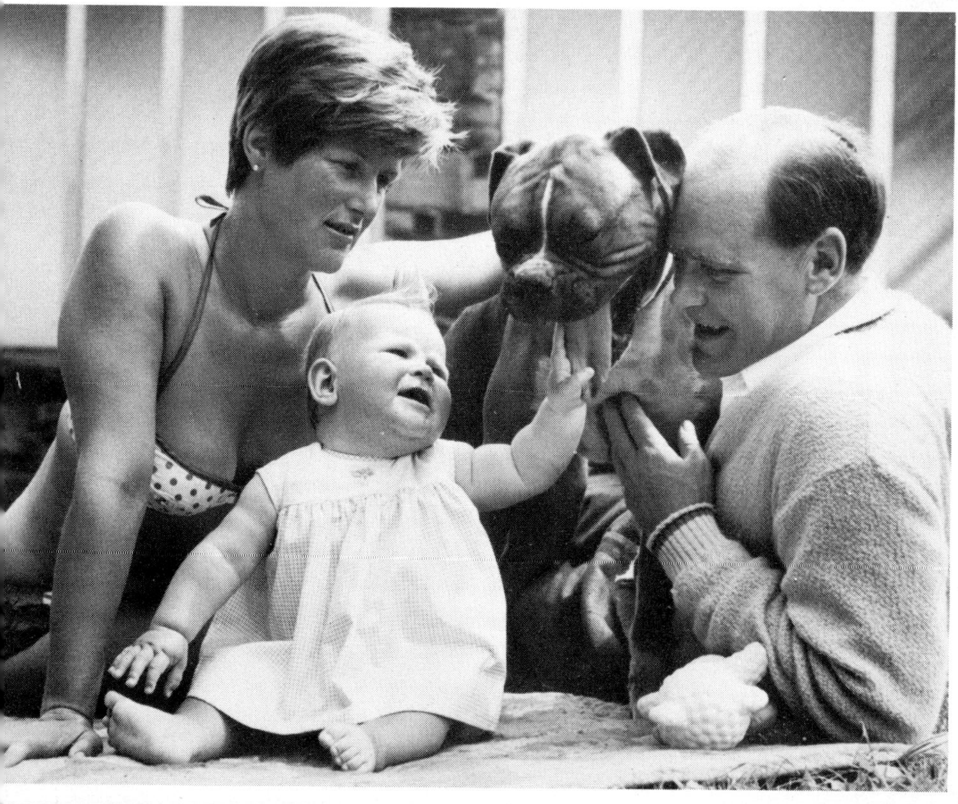

Brian Close CBE – with the
family at Buckingham
Palace, 1975. (*Westminster
Press*)

getting too many opportunities to do his stuff, such was the strength which preceded him. He wanted, really, to go in at number four, the stroke-maker's position. But he wasn't, then, a genuine stroke-player. His strength was founded on resolute, implacable defence. The theory was that if he stayed there long enough he would inevitably make runs. But he couldn't do that at number six and I didn't fancy him at four in view of the time he took to make his runs. Geoff had come into the side the previous season after a great run in the Colts: 126 not out and 11 not out; 32 and 87 not out; 39 and 104 not out; 56; but only one of those matches had been won, the rest drawn, so he had already achieved a certain reputation for selfishness. I reasoned that his characteristics were better suited to opening than batting anywhere else. In normal circumstances, the more solidly you play for yourself as an opener, the better the job you are automatically doing for your side. Boycs didn't like the idea of opening. He liked it even less when he was out for two against Sussex and for nought and two in the next match against Surrey. I had to talk to him. I had discussed the matter with my senior players and we were generally in agreement that Boycs would make a good opener.

He had terrific powers of concentration. His restricted range of strokes meant he took fewer chances. He believed in building an innings on a secure foundation. He was a 'safe' sort of batsman. But success was vital to him, so after failures in two games he was in the depths of despair. Geoff had a fixation about Jackie Hampshire, too. They had both grown up in roughly the same area of South Yorkshire and had developed as contemporaries, but whereas Jackie was an exciting stroke-maker who hit the ball very hard, Geoff was basically a defensive batsman who needed time to build an innings. Hampshire, too, was a gregarious, out-going sort of lad, fond of a pint, a joke, a sing-song; Boycott was introspective, broody, obsessed with an ambition to score more runs for Yorkshire than anyone had ever done. Hampshire got into the Yorkshire Colts before Boycott, got into the first team before him, was capped before him. Geoff brooded. And when he was tried as an opener his partner was J. H. Hampshire. Against Surrey, while Boycs was bowled by Loader for a duck, Jackie scored 120 out of 246. Boycs brooded again.

He really was upset. He took his cricket very much to heart.

It was the breath of life to him to succeed. Nobody likes failing and he took it very badly indeed. So I had to make it very, very clear to him that what he liked was not as important as what was best for the team. 'You are the ideal bloke to do this job', I said, and I think it began to dawn on him for the first time that cricket is not an individual's game. 'You have the technique to make a success of it', I went on. 'Now the next time you are asked to open get stuck in and learn all about the job.'

So off I went to the Fourth Test, with F.S., and off to Cardiff with Yorkshire went Boycott, now with Ray Illingworth back as captain. It was an eventful match. Padgett was back in the side so Boycott dropped down to number five and watched Jackie Hampshire score a choice 81 on a beautiful wicket. Everyone made runs and Boycs, trying desperately to top Hampers' score before the declaration came, fell ¡ust one run short. Glamorgan, bowled out for 84, were made to ollow on and when they batted much more staunchly in the second innings, some impulse prompted Illy to give Hampshire a turn with the ball. Now Jackie could bowl a very useful leg-spinner in the nets but rarely if ever was he called upon to bowl in a match except in a meaningless situation like that one at Taunton a few weeks previously. Now he proceeded to run through Glamorgan late on the Thursday and on Friday morning polished them off with seven for 52 by a quarter to twelve.

That was 26 July, 1963, and to this day that remains Jackie Hampshire's only real set of bowling figures in first-class cricket! To Boycott it was like the kiss of death. 'What do I do now', he lamented on the way to Worcester for the next game, 'learn to bowl slow left-arm?'

That finish caused a problem in another quarter. The *Daily Express* representative in our personal press following never arrived at a game until after lunch as a matter of rather obscure principle. That day he arrived to find that not only had the game finished long ago, but even the ground staff had gone home. He had to wait until the mid-afternoon edition of the *South Wales Echo* was on the streets to find out what had happened and then found he had missed one of the most astonishing performances of the season – Hampshire, seven for 52. Perhaps he thought Peter Richardson had written the story for the *Echo*!

Defeat at Worcester was followed by victory at Scarborough against Warwicks and Boycott, back as opener, scored 62 and 28. He followed this up with 113 and 20 not out in the return Roses match, and so joined the select band of players who have scored a century in each of one season's Roses games. Peter Marner hit 83 against us at Old Trafford. What a player he might have become! He hit the ball harder than almost anyone I have ever seen.

Against Derbyshire at Headingley I had another little joust with the pain barrier. On a rain-affected wicket, Derbyshire won the toss and batted. At first the wicket was slow, but as it dried and more pitch marks were made, it became quite nasty. We bowled them out for 123 and watched the 'top come off the wicket' as we did so. By sheer accident, Les Jackson took a knock on the elbow from Freddie (it wasn't a bouncer; it just reared from a length on a mutilated pitch) and couldn't bowl. We knew it was going to be difficult for us too, but with Les Jackson unfit, we would only have to contend with pace at one end. However, it was the very genuine pace of Harold Rhodes and he very quickly had Boycs and Sharpie caught off balls that flew. Having seen them go within the space of a few runs, it was obvious that Dusty's end was the danger one. They had only spinners to bowl at the other, namely Derek Morgan and Edwin Smith, both off-spinners. I made up my mind to stay and take Dusty for as long as I could, and told the incoming batsmen to tackle forcibly the off-spinners. I took 88 out of the next 96 balls from Rhodes in what seemed like an action replay of the Lord's Test. I was black and blue and I scored only 20 runs. But I got them in twos or fours so that I stayed at 'my' end and we managed a first innings lead of 31 which proved priceless because we rolled them over the second time for only 85 – and still lost three wickets knocking off the runs.

The final Test meant I missed the drawn game at Clacton, where Trevor Bailey kept Illy and the boys at bay which didn't please my first lieutenant. He was even less pleased however, on the long trip north to Scarborough. Richard Hutton had joined the side on completion of his summer term at Cambridge and drove Illy's car on the first stretch up the A1 whilst his captain slept. Let Raymond tell the story himself. 'I was awakened by a strong smell of burning rubber and Richard's dreamy voice saying, "I say, Illy, your brakes aren't very good." Looking up I found we were approaching a roundabout at about 70 m.p.h. How we got to the other side of it is a bit of a mystery but when we stopped I found that Richard had driven from Clacton with the hand-brake on!'

Then they had to find a garage which would open up for them, which isn't easy in Stamford (Lincs) after ten o'clock at night, and they got to Scarborough in the small hours. After a minimum of sleep, Illy's temper was not improved by losing the toss and having to field when he would have liked to get his head down in the dressing-room. However, Hutton made some amends by helping to bowl out Leics for 124. With 165 not out from Boycott, Yorkshire won by an innings and 111 runs. Illy himself took five for 13 in the second innings. Scarborough was very much a happy hunting ground for him. It was usually an easy-paced wicket but later on in the second day it tended to dust a little and almost as a matter of course Ray would finish off games by taking five or six second-innings wickets. But he didn't let Richard drive him again in a hurry. In fact no one was very keen on allowing young Hutton to get his hands on any car. He was an entertaining character, and not a bad cricketer at all, but he was gloriously vague, especially when he was at the wheel (he hadn't a car of his own at that time, being an impoverished undergraduate). I remember sitting near the window of our hotel in Nottingham once and watching as he drove Don Wilson's nice new Ford towards the entrance, while in earnest conversation with the owner beside him. With studied care Richard drove straight into a traffic sign outside the door. His friendship with Wils stood the test, however, and the two of them with Philip Sharpe formed a trio who were not only very close but a constant source of entertainment, in one way and another, to all of us. Richard was one of the very few people ever to have the last word with F.S. Fred was regaling us one evening with tales of his greatness. It went on, it seemed, for hours (Fred had a lot of greatness to talk about!) until Richard cut in to ask, with that slow, almost drawled delivery and dead-pan expression, 'Fred. Would you describe yourself as a modest man?'

From Scarborough we drove back with Leicestershire to their own headquarters, where we beat them again. Thus we had won the championship in my first season as captain. It had been a golden summer.

*   *   *

The next two seasons were not good championship seasons for Yorkshire. Bad weather hit cricket all over the country and it seemed to hit us more than most. Worcestershire got off to a flying start in 1964 and won the title by 39 clear points which made them very worthy champions. They had always been a good bowling side. Now, with Tom Graveney playing with all his immense ability, their batting had been strengthened immeasurably. Not only was Tom a great stroke-maker but he was a player of such class that he could get runs in just the way his captain asked of him. Worcs won 18 games, four more than their nearest rivals, Northants, and we had to be content with fifth spot. But it was good to watch the development of Boycott who again topped the averages, scoring 1,427 at 59.45 and getting his first Test cap against Australia at Headingley in July. He got his first century against them for Yorkshire at Bradford in early August, then went straight to the final Test at The Oval and took another off their bowling. It was interesting to see in 1977 that thirteen years later he was still the man whose back the Aussies were happiest to see.

I didn't get back into the England side which was more than a little disappointing for me. In 1963 I had played in all five Tests, almost exclusively as a batsman, and scored consistently if not heavily, to total 315 runs at 31.50. We had lost that series and the captaincy was in question when 1964 dawned. I felt I had a pretty good chance of leading England, not simply getting a place as a batsman who could bowl if necessary. In the event, I was not selected at all and it was only sometime later that I heard a truly remarkable story. Richie Benaud, who led the Aussies on their previous tour, had now retired from Test cricket and was concentrating on cricket journalism which included writing in this country for the *News of the World*. Before the 1964 season began he confided in one of the best-known cricket-writers in this country, 'The only way Australia will lose this Test series is if Brian Close captains England. I am going to make sure he *doesn't* by writing that he *should*.' Now that sounds incredible, but

91

think about it for a moment. For years it had been said that the Aussies persuaded the English selectors to play men who would be cannon-fodder for the tourists by (a) making sure they performed well in matches which didn't matter and (b) dropping a word here and there about how much they respected so-and-so. You don't have to be a genius to look through Test sides and find men who should never have set foot on a Test field against Australia. So here we had a former Australian Test captain, and an excellent captain at that, writing in Britain's biggest-selling newspaper that I was the man to prevent Australia winning the series. Plot and counter-plot. Anyway, that's the story as told to me by the man who dined with Richie as he hatched his plan. He knew there was no way the England selectors were ever going to do what an Australian had told them they should.

We had one or two memorable matches – not always happy memories – in 1964, notably a defeat by Warwicks at Edgbaston where we were annihilated by the West Indian doctor from Scotland, Rudolph Valentino Webster: 12.4-7-6-7. I met him in Melbourne during the Centenary Test celebrations – he lives in Australia now. I'll never forget that bowling performance against us. It bowled us out for 54, replying to 210, and we were made to follow on. This time we scored 286, which put us right back in the game. We had Warwicks on the hooks at 66-6 until the two Smiths, A.C. and M.J.K., put on another 68 to win the game – a fine cricket match. Against Notts at Scarborough we encountered Keith Gillhouley, who had been our slow left-armer for most of 1961 and he took five for 102, but Illy (as ever at North Marine Road) did his stuff in their second innings, 7-82.

The previous season we had at last found the regular opening partner for Fred who had been sought for ten years or more – a medium fast bowler of big out-swingers called Tony Nicholson. He had been born in the West Riding, taken to Rhodesia by his parents and had grown up there. When he joined Yorkshire (the family had returned to England) he hadn't lost his native accent! In 1962 he had played in three or four games. In 1963, in fact, he had been at the pre-season nets but seeing no real prospect of getting into Yorkshire's first team he had taken a pro-ing position in the Central Lancs League. By June of that year he was recalled and he finished the season with 66 wickets at 16.87. Nick, as he was quickly known to everyone, had a heart as big as a pumpkin. When he had developed the ball which cut back off the seam from the off, as a variation to his stock outswinger, he became a very useful bowler indeed, especially when there was just a bit of damp in the wicket or a humid atmosphere. He quickly became an enthusiastic member of the Rabbits section of our golfing fraternity, too. This consisted not only of players, but included the scorer, Ted Lester, and certain members of our press corps. Whenever a game finished early there was a quick check round for the nearest golf course.

Nick played his golf with a fine disregard for strict interpretation of some of the Rules – while his acquaintance with the etiquette of the game was not particularly close. But he was a great enthusiast and played at every opportunity. (Once, during Vic Wilson's captaincy, he went out at 7.30 a.m. to play eighteen holes before the day's cricket began, on a beautiful wicket at Worcester. The skipper found out and sentenced Nick to a full day's hard labour with the ball!) His needle matches with Mel Ryan were a constant topic of hotel and dressing-room conversation because Ryan, the gentlest and mildest of personalities, became an absolute tiger on the golf course. By virtue of business interests outside the game he was probably the wealthiest member of the side but if he lost half-a-crown playing golf, he was inconsolable. Nick used to whale the ball all over the place and whenever it went into the thick of a wood he would wander off after it; as his partners reached the green, Nick's ball would come whistling out . . . 'for two'. It seemed that in the thickest of forests, Tony's ball was always found sitting up nicely in the middle of a clearing. Finally, Ryan reached such a state of dementia that he would not let Nick play any kind of shot unless he was standing next to him. To this day, in Yorkshire cricket/golf circles, a ball hit into the middle of any kind of enclosure is said to have 'a Nicholson lie'.

Nick took seven for 32 in the Headingley Roses match of 1964, a game in which the smiling head of Sonny Ramadhin reared itself in opposition once again, with eight for 121 off 50 overs. The overs that fellow bowled! And in 1978 he is still trundling 'em down in the Northern Leagues.

The next year, 1965, brought more bad weather, a second successive championship for Worcs, a Test series win for South Africa, leadership of the Yorkshire averages again for Geoffrey Boycott, and our first Gillette Cup. And before the season was more than a fortnight old we had been bowled out for 23 by Hampshire at Middlesbrough. We had lost by 10 wickets before lunch on the second day and that had not happened very often in Yorkshire's history. Consequently the match does not rank very high in my prouder memories of skippering Yorkshire, but in tribute to some superb fast bowling by Butch White it has to be recorded. The wicket wasn't what you would call a very good one. We were bowled out in the first innings for 121 of which F. S. Trueman made 55 at number nine (we were 47 for seven when he went in). Hampshire replied with 125 and we greeted the end of the first day thankfully.

On the second morning we had eight down for 13, Don Wilson at number 10 was top scorer with seven not out, and we had lost by 10 wickets at one o'clock. Butch White took six for 10 off 10 overs, seven of which were maidens, giving a magnificent display of genuine fast bowling. He was a lovely character (not especially on that occasion, but in general!), strong as a bull, and it's a bit surprising that he played only twice for England. That morning he went through us like a whirlwind.

We finished fourth in the championship but we won the third-ever Gillette Cup Final in rather unusual circumstances. At Bradford, the previous July, we had lost a championship match to Surrey after declaring our second innings at 283 for three with both Jackie Hampshire and myself getting not out centuries. The damage had been done by our first innings dismissal for 147, so we never really had enough room for manoeuvre – the work of David Sydenham, the left-arm fast-medium bowler, who took seven for 32. The memory of that performance went with us into the Gillette Cup Final two months later, and so nearly cost us the Cup.

In the first round we beat Leicestershire comfortably enough by four wickets. The start of the second round at Taunton was delayed for a long time by rain and when I went out to have a look at the pitch with Colin Atkinson, the Somerset skipper, I expressed all sorts of forebodings . . . 'it won't be fit to run about' . . . 'the fielders will be slipping and falling all over the place . . .' This, I'm sure, prompted Colin to bat when the umpires at length decided we had to start. The thing to do, of course, was to put the other side in. With moisture around the pitch was going to be sharp and nasty to begin with. If the game went over into the next day the side batting second had a reasonable chance of getting a wicket which had dried out considerably. Even if the game was crammed into one day, it could only mean that the side batting first had been bowled out cheaply and it's much easier to thrash for a given target. No, the only sensible thing to do was to field if one won the toss, but I think I convinced Colin that it would be a disadvantage. Anyway, he won it and decided to bat. In 34 overs Somerset were all out for 63 and Merv Kitchen, who played damn well, was not out 39. With Boycs acting as sheet anchor we knocked them off for the loss of three wickets. The semi-final at Edgbaston was a tense affair. Warwicks had five seamers and they got us out for 177 – not a big total and it would have been a lot smaller if it hadn't been for some dedicated grafting by Illy, Hutton and Jimmy Binks. Our seamers couldn't make any impression at all – Freddie, Hutton, John Waring – and in no time Warwicks were 60-odd and the only wicket to fall had been a run-out. Desperate diseases call for desperate remedies. I thought, 'I'll try the spinners. It's not going to turn, but I can deploy more fieldsmen in run-saving positions and I'll hope to bog Warwicks down.'

It was, I suppose, muck or nettles, as they say in Yorkshire . . . but it worked. On a non-turner, the batsmen were contained so effectively (or allowed themselves to be put on the defensive) that Don Wilson bowled 13 Gillette Cup overs for 15 runs (and got a couple of wickets) while Ray bowled his 13 for 29 and suddenly Warwicks, from being so firmly in the driving seat, were right behind the eight-ball. They panicked. Billy Ibadulla had been run out early on. He was now followed by Dennis Amiss, Jim Stewart, Tom Cartwright and Rudi Webster – all run out going for impossible runs because they had got behind the clock. We won by 20 runs and there was a tremendous satisfaction in having fashioned a win out of nothing. At 60 for one, Warwicks had only to cruise to victory with no problems at all. Put simply, we had beaten them in our thinking.

So on to Lord's for our first Cup Final. We won by the massive margin of 175 runs and it could so easily have been a very different story, as I said. After 12 overs we had scored about 15 runs because

Boycs and Ken Taylor were completely bogged down by Geoff Arnold and Sydenham. The memory of his 7-32 at Park Avenue was clearly haunting both batsmen and they couldn't get the bowling away at all. I was due to bat number five, with Doug Padgett at three and Sharpe at four – but as the overs dribbled away and the scoreboard scarcely moved, Duggie said, 'Why don't you go in at three? You will be better trying to force it than I am and that left-arm over-the-wicket stuff may not be so difficult for you as for the right-handers.' It was good thinking, good cricket sense.

I padded up very quickly and almost at once Taylor was caught by Ken Barrington. (He would probably have done Surrey a great favour by dropping it!) I went out and said to Geoff, 'Come on, Boycs. We've got to get this score moving. Start looking for the ones.' And we started taking singles all over the place. Nothing upsets a fielding side more. It plays havoc with field-placing and unsettles everybody. Gradually we loosened the grip and then I told Boycott, 'Right, we've got things moving. Now start to put some force into your shots.' Immediately he cracked a beautiful four.

Phase three of the campaign opened with the instruction: 'Bloody marvellous. Now hit everything.' And no one had ever seen anything like it from Boycott. He was hitting the off-spinner over mid-wicket and long-on. *Over* mid-wicket and long-on. How often do you see Geoffrey hit shots like that, twelve or thirteen years later? At that time no one had *ever* seen him do it. It was a side of his character no one had seen. From being 22 for one with nearly a quarter of our overs gone, we were 214 for two when the next wicket fell (I was caught off David Gibson for 79) and there was still time for Trueman to smash 24, Hampshire 38 not out and Wilson 11 not out. And Boycott – 146. Arnold and Sydenham, who had each had a remarkably economical opening spell, finished with one for 51 and one for 67 respectively . . . Barrington five overs, one for 54; Tindall three overs for 36 runs. It was a slaughter. They had tried everything, to no avail.

At 317 for 4 in our 65 overs I could have bowled Duggie Padgett at both ends and Surrey wouldn't have got the runs. But what a different story it might have been. The complexities of Boycott's character baffle people even to this day; I suppose they always will. I spent ages talking to him in the evenings because I always want to know what motivates a player . . . to understand completely what makes him tick. Geoff's trouble has always been a selfishness which, somehow, he can't help. Yorkshire have never won a thing under his captaincy because he does not pull out all the stops to help other players to become *better* players. In some strange way he seems to be jealous of ability in others. It is not a wilful strain, not a deliberate thing. In his heart he would like his players to do well, yet he does not appear to want them to do as well as him. He has got to be the best. I didn't mind this single-mindedness, this self-centred approach, on most occasions when I was his captain because I was able to use it to the team's advantage. He would ask, 'How many do you want?' . . . by lunch . . . by the close . . . or whatever. And if I gave him a target he was good enough to get it. He has always been clinical in his calculations, at least insofar as they have involved him personally. That is why he has not yet proved to be a good captain of Yorkshire. He is, always has been, a fine player whose personal philosophy was basically unsound. He has learned tactics, knows the game well, knows the players in it. But his single motivation appears to be self-promotion and that, in a team-game, is self-defeating. He discussed tactics with me for hours on end, wanted to know why I had done this and that during the day's play; but he never discussed a philosophical approach, because that was firmly established in his own mind from the start: he had to be the best . . . to score more runs than anyone else . . . more centuries than anyone else. It is a philosophy which, among the people who work and play with Geoffrey, has won him few friends.

Ironically, he would like to be liked. He has never been able to see that greatness in playing ability is not a means to that end, at least not in itself. Cricketers everywhere respect his ability, admire his technical excellence, but few want to sit down and have an evening's relaxation with him. Geoff is not a relaxing person! It was, I am sure, his obsession with greatness in every aspect of batting which started his hooking phase against the 1973 West Indies team. He made a fine start to the series – 97 and 30 at The Oval, 56 not out at Edgbaston where he twice retired hurt in his only innings. Then, at Lord's, England were faced with a West Indian total of 652. It was a game they could not possibly win and consequently Boycott was in the ideal position to demonstrate his immense powers of concentration and his inexhaustible patience. He was in a position to bat for three days if he wanted to (and if he could, of course). Instead, he was out hooking, critically before the end of the second day, for just four runs. In the second innings, he tried again and failed again to establish himself as the master batsman in all circumstances and with all the shots – all because of a stupid article he had read. I rang him up and told him not to be a mug. He was the hardest batsman to get out in the whole world and there he was, making them a present of his wicket.

Psychologically, Geoff has always needed a lot of sorting out. But, by golly, he can bat.

11

ILLY

When I became the England captain in 1966, the first thing I did was to get Ray Illingworth back into the side. When I asked for him, Doug Insole, then the selectors' chairman, said, 'No, Ray's had his chance and he's failed'. 'He is a good county cricketer', I replied, 'he's failed because he's never been captained properly.' And that was true.

In those days we often went in with two off-spinners and invariably Ray was given the 'other' end. He was never given the star treatment, so to speak, never looked upon as a bowler who, more than any other, might do an absolutely top-class job if he were handled properly. Insole claimed that Ray had no variations in his attacking skill. 'Where have you been watching him from?' I asked. 'From the pavilion, of course. In Tests', he replied. I came back: 'Well if you can see a bowler's variations from 70 or 80 yards or so, a batsman 20 yards away can pick them up instantly.'

It took me a long time to convince the four selectors that Illingworth was good enough. The fact was that over something like ten years, since he had become established in the Yorkshire side, Illy had developed into a marvellous bowler. Throughout the sixties he was a superb practitioner to have as a senior player and leading collaborator. No one would ever suggest that Raymond and I were in the least bit alike, either in character, temperament or approach to cricket. But in a marvellous way we seemed to complement each other.

A man who knows us both well was once asked which of us he would rather have as an officer in war, if an attack 'over the top' was due to be made. He replied without hesitation: 'Illy, every time. He would ask for three intelligence reports on the strength and disposi-

99

tion of the enemy, six Met reports for the next twenty-four hours, an expert soil analysis on No Man's Land, plus a detailed breakdown of our own forces, then he'd decide the attack was not feasible at all. Closey would pick up a crowbar, or anything which was lying handy, shout, "Come on, then", and chase off without checking whether we had any cover or support.'

That may not be a *strictly* accurate assessment of our different personalities but it's near enough for the purpose of illustrating how we could work together so closely and, frankly, so successfully. It was Illy and I who worked out the use of a silly mid-off as a counter to that curse of modern batting, the bat-pad defensive cover-up – and it was spectacularly successful against a man who is regarded as one of the great post-war batsmen, Colin Cowdrey.

I have mentioned Colin's century against Yorkshire at Headingley in 1959 as being worthy of note because he so rarely got runs against us. No one doubts that he was a fine player, but he was not a good starter. When he played against us, if possible I used to introduce Illy as soon as Colin appeared, posting myself at silly mid-off. You won't find that ploy in any coaching manual but it's elementary when you think about it. He liked to spend twenty minutes to half an hour having a close look at the bowling, working out the pace and bounce of the wicket. Once Colin had established himself as a top Test batsman, he had developed this habit of playing himself into anything but the really quick bowlers by pushing forward with bat and pad together. Because for many years he was regarded as a great player, he was not used to being crowded in front of the bat. Let's face it, if a lesser player or a young lad came in and proceeded to play with his bat and front leg together, fielders would immediately appear from nowhere and squat down in front of him waiting for the slightest mistake and the possible ricochet of the ball from bat and pad. If this is done to ordinary players why not the good ones too?

Playing bat and pad together originated to cut short legs out of the game if the ball was spinning or even seaming in from the off-side – the pad covered the leg edge of the bat and the batsman only had to worry about the other. That gave him a degree of latitude in which to play defensively. However, in this play there is always the chance the ball might do just enough and strike both bat and pad, and bob up in front. One of the drawbacks of a batsman setting himself up to play this way is that he doesn't have the free movement of his hands and wrists to cope with the movement of the ball particularly from the off (unless the ball is wide and he has plenty of room to play a shot). If, because of the pressure the close fielders put on him, the batsman decides to use a bit of force, he will 'telegraph his intentions' in enough time for the fielders to take evading action.

I remember one match at Gillingham when Cowdrey came in to bat and I put Illy on at once. Philip Sharpe was at slip, Jackie Hampshire and Doug Padgett round the corner at short leg, and I was at silly mid-off. I knew he wouldn't try to knock me out of the way until he was settled and knew exactly what was happening on the wicket. But being crowded as I have decribed upset his composure. As he pushed forward, his bat a little behind his pad, I tensed on my toes ready to move forward. He played a couple, then complained to the umpire that I was moving as he played the ball. The umpire disagreed with him and I remember muttering something like 'If you played with your bat properly instead of your pad, I wouldn't need to be here.' Colin kept pushing forward, but now having to consider Ray's spin – he dare not risk the nick on to his pad with two of us in front waiting for the chance of a catch. Then Illy drifted one away, it nicked the outside edge, and Sharpie took the catch at slip – one of Cowdrey's many failures against us. Colin was a great player if he was allowed to play himself in in his own way. We didn't let him.

The great thing about having Ray bowling in a situation like this was that I knew I could rely absolutely on his accuracy. I knew he wouldn't start experimenting with more ambitious stuff whilst I was so close to the firing-line. He was the complete professional. Between us we were giving the batsman something extra to think about; sometimes we made him desperate and forced him into a shot he wouldn't think of playing in normal circumstances; at worst, we put doubts in his mind.

I have never been shy of daring to try something similar, even with bowlers of less ability when we needed a wicket – Viv Richards, for instance. He can't turn the ball to save his life but in the 1977 season when I was getting to a stage where I badly needed a wicket against Warwickshire, I put Viv on, placed two short legs, and watched with interest from a couple of yards away. Rohan Kanhai of all people played for the spin and saw it go straight on, played again for the spin and got his off stump flattened. Admittedly everyone else had turned it considerably. But Kanhai couldn't believe Viv could go through the motions of spinning on that wicket, and yet make the ball go straight on instead.

But bat-pad batsmen have always irritated me. You should hear Sonny Ramadhin on the subject of that stand of 411 by Peter May and Colin Cowdrey at Edgbaston in 1957. Sonny isn't exactly a garrulous man, but mention the subject of May and Cowdrey and their pads and he will regale you with some bitterness for anything up to half an hour. Remember, he had taken seven for 49 in the first innings. May and Cowdrey, who couldn't 'pick' Ramadhin, decided to play him with their pads until he bowled a loose one. (Remember the lbw law was not as favourable to the bowler then as it is today.) Result: Sonny bowled 98 overs in the second innings, took two for 179, shouted himself hoarse for lbw and at the end of the day collapsed on his hotel bed stupefied with fatigue and frustration. Mind you at no time did John Goddard set out to give the batsmen something else to think about by crowding the bat. In that mammoth record stand there were innumerable bat-pad snicks that went begging in front and on the leg side – either because there was no West Indies fieldsman there, or else because he was too deep. I'd guarantee that an English side would have caught them. But the thinking of West Indian captains has never matched the brilliance of their players' natural ability – at least not in my time.

Ramadhin was a fascinating bowler and he's still taking wickets up in a League on the Yorkshire-Lancashire border where he has kept a pub for many years. The ball that looked most like an off-spinner was in fact, his leg-spinner. The one that looked like a leg-spinner was the off-spinner. Peter and Colin's bat-pad play broke Sonny's heart over those two weary days at Edgbaston in June 1957. To a West Indian, it wasn't cricket.

Since we are exploding a few myths, let's talk about Mike Procter – a fine player with a reputation of being a good player of off-spin. He is – when he's got settled in but not early on. He tends to play himself in with bat and pad together, but because he is such a superb striker of the ball, seldom does he have to worry about a close fielder in front of him. They're all too scared to go there.

When I went to Somerset I found that Brian Langford was mesmerised by Procter and would do damn near anything to avoid bowling at him. Mind you, Proc'y had murdered him several times in earlier matches, so he had reason to feel that way: though he had never bowled at Procter early in an innings, always when he was 'in'. I had to show Langers that by getting at Procter early and pressuring him, we could worry him into hitting the ball before he was ready, giving us a chance.

After that Brian got Mike quite cheaply on the odd occasion and, equally important, got rid of his complex about him. It was a pity that Brian Langford retired soon after I took over the captaincy of Somerset. He was a good bowler – I might have made him even better! More and more is cricket a game of *thinking*, trying to be one jump ahead of the other chap, trying to give him problems which are difficult to solve. Natural ability is a blessing, of course, and one is lucky if one has it. But thinking can make an indifferent player into a good one or for the lack of it, a good one into an indifferent one.

I like to think Illy and I occasionally improved things by careful thought during our years of partnership. It is true that we are entirely different characters. We used to be partners in a regular bridge-four when rain stopped play, and nowhere was our basic difference in approach shown up better than in those sessions. At times our partners were treated to snatches of dialogue like this:–

Illy (returning to table after a walk-round whilst he was dummy): 'Did you get those four spades?'

Close: 'No, we were two light.'

Illy: 'Two light? TWO LIGHT? How the hell could you go down? It was a stone-cold certain contract.'

Close (a little diffidently): 'I was distracted and lost interest in the middle of the hand.'

Illy (apoplectic with fury): 'Lost interest? Don't bloody well lose interest with MY MONEY.'

We were playing for a penny-a-hundred! But that's my Illy. Basically he would rather have bowling figures of 15-8-22-1 than say, 10-0-40-3 which would be my choice. At times I used to think

103

he would rather save a run than take a wicket. We argued, we called each other a lot of things, but we have remained friends for a long time. We have each known what the other could do when it was necessary. We have always had a wholesome respect for each other. And I am sure we were a great combination.

12

THE CHAMPIONSHIP
ON A PLATE

We started 1966 with six wins (two of them in two days) and two draws in our first eight matches because a change of rule that season handed Yorkshire the championship on a plate. We had become used to having to bowl sides out twice to have any chance of winning at all. We expected to have to do it as a matter of course; our cricket was geared to it. That season, first innings were limited to 65 overs and one of our worries was automatically eliminated. Like most amendments of this kind to the Laws, it was well-intentioned. The idea was to achieve more clear-cut results and have fewer drawn games. We had won the championship often enough when it was obligatory to bowl the other side out twice; now we had no need to do so.

Ours was still a splendidly-equipped all-round side with batting in depth, top-class close fieldsmen and athletes for the outfield and bowlers for all types of conditions. In our first win over Gloucs at Middlesbrough, five bowlers – fast, medium and slow – shared the wickets in the first innings; Wilson and Illingworth took all 10 between them in the second and so it went on. Someone always came off. It wasn't until 20 June that we lost a game – to Sussex, by 22 runs – on the second evening of a rain-affected game at Headingley.

We were winning without having a settled opening pair of batsmen, too. Hampshire had decided he didn't like the job and he much preferred to go in at number four where he could play his shots with greater freedom. I did quite a bit of opening that season with either Ken Taylor or Geoff Boycott. Doug Padgett opened with Taylor, Philip Sharpe with both Boycott and Taylor, while for the last month we settled for Boycott and Sharpe. It was really a matter of making the pieces fit. Batsmen who get into a bad seam as openers sometimes like to drop down the order for a while; others prefer to work it out. Sometimes you will find numbers four, five and even six yearning to have a crack at opening, especially in a strong batting side where opportunities are limited. With a first innings limited to 65 overs our number six didn't get many first-innings opportunities. However, the summer was very wet, affecting many games, so there were some marvellously tight finishes.

We lost to Northants at Headingley in July and it is interesting to reflect how many times in the fifties and sixties we did lose to a county who, before the war, expected crushing humiliation from Yorkshire as a matter of course. On this occasion it was that great trouper Albert Lightfoot who took seven for 25 in our first innings. What a great service Albert gave to Northants – and still does, as something like a one-man ground-and-social-staff at Northampton.

But, inevitably I suppose, we could not go through the season without hitting the controversial headlines – at least I couldn't – which duly happened in the Old Trafford Roses match at the beginning of August. One way and another it was the complete opposite of the traditionally dour encounter. Rain interfered on the first day and washed out the second. At lunch on the Tuesday I declared our first innings at 146 for seven. The first indication we had that Lancashire were going to throw down the gauntlet was when Keith Goodwin and Tommy Greenhough, two tail-enders, came out to open their innings. After just two deliveries from Trueman (which brought one run to Goodwin), David Green called in his batsmen. It appeared that after a dressing-room conference during lunch, David had discussed the situation with his players and decided they might as well go for full points (ten) as for the two which were awarded for first-innings lead; and it was well enough known in cricket circles that Yorkshire would make a game of it with anyone, so long as there was a chance of an outright win.

As we came off the field I remembered a new regulation which was in existence that season but which no one had yet used – a team could forfeit its second innings. I checked with the umpires that I could do this and told Green. So ten minutes later, Lancashire were batting again, this time in more orthodox formation – and what a superb afternoon's cricket it was. The majority of the Lancashire batsmen made a few runs each, without anyone ever threatening to run away with it, but we won by 12 runs off the very last ball of the match with Ray Illingworth returning figures of 27-14-33-5. Immediately there were cries of 'collusion', so let me set this particular record straight. At no time did David Green and I ever discuss anything which concerned the way the game was conducted. In fact I have never in my whole career as a captain talked about that sort of thing with an opposing captain. Some newspapers chased up Don Kenyon, captain of our main challengers, Worcestershire, to see what he had to say about the forfeiture of an innings and I am glad to say that Don told them I was perfectly within my rights.

Elated by this win, we drove off to Portsmouth where we were again dogged by rain in that miserable summer. After declaring at 280 for nine we bowled them out for 64 and made three quick inroads into their second innings before a storm left the ground completely waterlogged. On the final day we could see the groundsman was virtually on his own and had a hopeless task to make the square and outfield fit for any further play, so we found blankets and went out – every man-jack of the Yorkshire team – to help with mopping-up operations. The Hampshire team sat in their dressing-room window laughing their socks off at us but we *did* make a re-start possible. However, after getting one wicket, Danny Livingstone and Richard Gilliat held out into the extra half-hour. During this stand Gilliat belted a slow long hop from Don Wilson straight into my forehead – and it rebounded far enough across the soaked outfield for them to run three. The blow knocked me over, the only time I have ever gone down. But I did bowl the next over from the other end!

We lost to Surrey at Bradford by 21 runs when Jefferson had 11-100 in the match and Storey 8-89 – oh yes, and Close 8-69 . . . something of a seamer's wicket. In the return game at The Oval I came as near as I have ever done to a hat-trick. After the opening bowlers had had no success in the first 10 overs or so, I took over at the Vauxhall end to find out myself whether it was still worth persevering with swing and seam, or whether the spinners should be pitched into the battle early. John Edrich nicked one to Sharpe at slip. Ken Barrington came in and did exactly the same thing, first ball. Next came Mickey Stewart to be put down by Jackie Hampshire at leg slip first ball, and off the next he was caught at second slip by Padgett. Three in four balls, but what a hat-trick of England players that would have been . . . Edrich, Barrington, Stewart.

The championship finally came to us at Harrogate where we beat Kent by 24 runs in the last moments of the day – and that despite Underwood's 11 for 135 on a wicket tailor-made for him.

A good season was made even better for me by my recall to the England side and, for the first time, the captaincy. England had lost at Old Trafford, drawn at Lord's, lost at Trent Bridge and Headingley. Both Mike Smith and Colin Cowdrey had had a turn at leading the side. At last, at The Oval, my turn came. I don't know whether, in the circumstances, the selectors expected me to be grateful and therefore pliable but I dug my heels in for the players I wanted, especially Ray Illingworth. It took me three-quarters of an hour to talk them round.

Their argument was that Ray had had his chances and failed and that he was a good county player but not Test class. Mine was that he was far better than the run-of-the-mill county player and had never been skippered properly. The first selector to accept my argument was Don Kenyon, then Peter May came round and the last to yield was Doug Insole. But Illy played and he did a damned good job. He bowled 15 overs (seven maidens), two for 40 in the first innings and he bowled with all his skill and intelligence at Kanhai and Sobers when they were threatening to cut loose. We had Bob Barber bowling leg-spinners before lunch on the first day of a Test match which I suppose was regarded in some quarters as adventurous to the point of madness. But we won. Tom Graveney scored a brilliant 165 and what a tail we had – 166 for 7, 527 all out (J. T. Murray 112 at number nine, Ken Higgs 63 at number 10 and John Snow 59 at number 11 – 128 for the last wicket).

West Indies were 225 all out in the second innings and we won by an innings and 34, dismissing Gary Sobers for a duck. Prior to the match we discussed the relative merits of the opposition individually and collectively amongst ourselves. We knew that Gary was a helluva good hooker of the ball once he was established – bowling bouncers at him then would simply be presenting him with runs. We decided that if the quick bowler was around and fresh when Gary came in, he would try him with one before Gary had worked out the pace and bounce of the wicket. John Snow was bowling when Gary appeared at the crease. We made no alteration to the field to give the West Indies captain any inkling of what was to come. He probably thought we wouldn't waste the first few balls by bowling to one of his strengths. Sure enough Snowy let him have a bouncer first ball – and Gary hooked. I'm sure he was somewhat surprised . . . he was late on it and the ball didn't bounce as high as he thought it might do. The ball hit his glove and I very gladly took the catch at short leg. The innings didn't end without a bit of chat. Charlie Griffith had evidently been distinctly unpleasant during that tour and I don't mean always as a bowler. He had shot his mouth off at Headingley in terms which might well have interested the Race Relations Board and at The Oval he started again when he took a shortish ball on the finger, playing forward. I told him, 'Get on with the bloody game, Charlie. You're ready enough to dish it out but when it comes to taking it it's another tale altogether.' I think I made him understand what we were about.

*   *   *

In 1967 my career moved from the autumn of mellow fruitfulness to a winter of discontent in the space of ten days. We won the championship and for that a great deal of credit goes to Freddie Trueman who skippered Yorkshire for something like half the season whilst I was on Test duty. Three matches with India, three against Pakistan followed the previous season's last Test match success against West Indies. By the end of 1967 I had been captain of England in seven Tests, six of which had been won and one drawn. The championship was won by ten points from Kent and I finished second in the batting averages, but the season didn't start in the most spectacularly success-ful manner because we were bowled out by Kent for 40 at Bradford in the second game. Rain washed out a definite result, as it had in the first game with Glamorgan, and there was no play at all on any of the three days in the Leicestershire match at Headingley. At Hull, how-ever, we found enough time between the showers to beat Worcester-shire by five wickets – and even then we were 37 for five when we did it. More rain . . . not a ball bowled in the Roses match . . . but another miserable summer was affecting most of the counties and we still had to win the last game, against Gloucestershire at Harrogate, to be sure of pipping Kent for the title.

I had been sacked by England a fortnight previously (see *Incident At Edgbaston*), and this had been followed by a television confrontation on a north-south basis between Michael Parkinson, as an outspoken voice of the North, and Peter West, representing the urbane South – the way it seemed, the spokesman of The Establishment. Peter has not an ounce of malice in him and I am sure the whole programme made him more than a little uncomfortable, but as a professional broadcaster – one very close to cricket – it was not unreasonable for him to take part in such a programme when he was asked to do so. Yorkshire supporters in the game at Harrogate did not see it the same way. To them, he was part of the effete southern-based conspiracy to hound their county captain out of his England captaincy. When Peter arrived at Harrogate to cover the match for *The Times*, (unfortunately for him, just after the game had started, with the spectators in their seats) he was subjected to chants and ironic applause all the way along the front of the stand to the press box, which was at the opposite end of the ground. The match was won in two days largely because of the fantastic bowling of Ray Illingworth whose figures were 23-8-58-7 in the first innings and 13-9-6-7 in the second, plus some brilliant catching close to the wicket.

It seemed that the whole team was keyed up to support me with a really spectacular performance. I am a soft and very sentimental person at heart, believe it or not, and I was really proud to be a Yorkshireman and the county captain in that game.

The season brought another 'first' to Yorkshire because our opening Gillette Cup game, against Cambridgeshire, was washed out at Bradford on all three days set aside for it. So bad were the conditions in Yorkshire that it was impossible on any of our first-class grounds even to stage the 10-overs-a-side game on the third day, which was the method laid down in the rules for settling such a problem. On Monday, 24 May, 1967, our officials were frenziedly ringing all round the county in an attempt to find a ground fit for even a 10-overs knockabout ... Headingley, Harrogate, Scarborough, Sheffield ... all in vain. Finally word came that it was possible to play at Castleford, a Yorkshire League club ground. At lunchtime we all chased off the twelve miles or so to Castleford, and just as we arrived there, another storm broke! But this time everyone agreed that the show must go on. 'Show' is right. The sky was as black as night, the rain poured down, thunder rolled and lightning flashed across the sky as we put Cambridgeshire in and saw their opener, David Fairey, hit Fred's first ball straight out of the ground! In impossible conditions they struggled to 43 for eight in their 10 overs and Johnny Wardle, playing against his old county, was bowled for a duck by Tony Nicholson. We saw that with some relief. In such circumstances he could have been an extremely dangerous opponent. We lost four wickets in knocking off the runs and Fairey again made an impression on us by taking two for nine after his 22 out of 43 with the bat.

(I suppose it could only happen to me, but the next Gillette Cup to be so hounded by bad weather was the 1977 semi-final between Somerset and Middlesex and there, this time in a 15-overs farce, we lost the game because we lost the toss. We had to accept the situation, of course, but it was a bitter disappointment for me. I would dearly have loved to sign off for Somerset by leading them to their first-ever trophy and title.)

However, the Tests of 1967 occupied my attention for a large part of that season. I had the job I wanted and, frankly, I didn't see any reason why I should lose it until I was ready to retire.

I had faith in my own knowledge, experience and ability; I knew we had enough good players around to give us a side to beat anyone if it was properly selected and organised. I refused to be meekly quiescent if the selectors sought to do something I considered wrong, because in the last analysis it was my job to get the best performance possible out of the team. I could not prevent their dropping Geoff Boycott for taking too long over his 246 not out in the First Test at Leeds but the case of Robin Hobbs was different. The selectors wanted to drop the Essex leg-spinner for Lord's after just one Test. He took three for 45 and one for 100 at Headingley but I insisted: 'You can't just pick a bloke for one match and then discard him. If you thought he was good enough to be picked in the first place you have got to give him a fair chance to show what he can do.' So Hobbs played at Lord's but didn't get on in the first innings when our seamers bowled out India for 152, and it was the off-spinners who did the damage in the second. We won all three Tests against India without undue trouble from any of them apart from the Nawab of Pataudi and, in one case, Wadekar. The Pakistan matches promised to be a bit tougher.

I did not agree with the selection of Colin Milburn for the First Test. It is not supposed to happen, but the selectors were experimenting with a few people for the winter tour to the West Indies. Colin was an exciting stroke-player – extravagant would probably be a better adjective – and he had his uses as a seam bowler but he was far from being a good fieldsman unless he was in a particular spot, in Colin's case, forward short leg. My views on the value of fielding were well-known and in the five days of a Test match, with a variety of circumstances to face, his limitations could very well turn out to be a liability to the side. I was overruled, Geoff Boycott was left out and Colin opened with Eric Russell. We scored 368 and had them wobbling at 139 for seven. Hanif, who had taken root, was 51 and tried to half sweep, half hit an outswinger which Basil D'Oliveira started on line with the legs, drifting in across the batsman. Specifically for this ball he had a man stationed at deep backward square leg. Our man there was Ollie Milburn. He only had to move in a few yards to swallow the catch but he started too late and put it down. Hanif went on to make 187 not out. Instead of having a first-innings lead of around 200 we had one of 15; much more important was the time that Hanif's innings enabled Pakistan to use up, and the match was drawn.

The missed chance was crucial because the batsman at the other end was a youngster new to Tests in this country. His name was Asif Iqbal. With Hanif gone he would have been struggling in the extreme but with his captain at the other end to guide him through his innings – and he had much advice from the other end – he stayed to make 76 on his Test debut at Lord's in a stand of 130. It cost us a win. Even after that stand had eked out the first innings as far as Monday afternoon, I still had the selectors breathing down my neck to go for a result – a lead of 15 and less than one-and-a-half days to go! How in the world could I think of getting a result? But the instruction to me was: 'Come on, we've got to make a game of it.' So, in turn, I gave instructions to my batsmen, 'Go out and look for runs – not idiotically, but take them where you can.' Russell went at 33-1,

Milburn tried to hook Majid Khan and nearly holed out at long leg. Hanif put another man there, making two. Majid bowled another short one. Apparently without even thinking about the double danger, Colin duly obliged and sent a catch soaring down to Asif. Now I like Colin Milburn. He's a great lad – a wonderful character and a fearless cricketer. I am dreadfully sorry that his injury put him out of first-class cricket prematurely, just when he was at his best. He was an extremely popular man on the county circuit. But in *that* Test match he didn't fulfil expectations.

Barrington was bowled by another newcomer as far as we were concerned – Intikhab Alam – and when Graveney went to Asif we were 95 for four just after tea. It was quite on the cards that we could easily go down the swannee if we lost any more wickets that night. The hour or so that I spent with D'Oliveira that night at the wicket, just holding out, was one of the hardest pieces of grafting I have ever had to carry out in my whole career. It was vital that neither of us got out. If we had, anything could have happened, and the most likely prospect was defeat. By next morning we were able to start to force the pace and to declare at 241 for nine. There was never time to bowl out Pakistan a second time but I don't think about that Test as one we didn't win – I remember it as one we could have lost because of interference by the selectors. You can lose a game against any opposition if you don't do the job right. And it is difficult to do it right if you have pressures from outside, from the men who put you there to do the job in the first place.

For the Second Test at Trent Bridge more pressure was put on me – this time to have Colin Cowdrey back in the side. Although I had done nothing wrong – except to put my own (absolutely valid, I felt) views on certain points, this was the beginning of the end of my captaincy, I am certain. Don't ask me exactly why because I can't tell you. I could see no justification for a change, either on results or the way the team had played, but I had a feeling from that moment . . .

Ken Higgs and Geoff Arnold bowled very well indeed to dismiss Pakistan for 140 and Cowdrey had to open because there was no other position in the order for him. Pakistan's dismissal had taken most of the day and we were just going out for a few overs when a thunderstorm broke and flooded the ground. On Friday the ground was soaked and when we finally got under way we were soon in trouble at 92 for four. Ken Barrington and I got stuck in when the wicket was seaming and lifting like mad. Things were so difficult that we scarcely dared play a shot – and the first time I permitted myself the luxury of playing back, I was out. But at least we had taken the total to 187 for five and we ended with a first-innings lead of 112. When they were out for 114 in the second innings we were left to score just three to win, but it wouldn't have been possible without that grafting, heads-down stand of 95 for our fifth wicket. It can't have been pretty to watch but to those who understand their cricket it would, I trust, be perfectly clear that the stand was vital and its value immeasurable. From those who don't understand their cricket there came a quite irresponsible knocking of Barrington for his patient and utterly invaluable innings of 109 not out.

I have always been willing to make a game of it with anyone. This can involve a spectacularly exciting session; it can equally involve one which is grim and tensely fascinating. You cannot, in any genuinely competitive fixture, simply go out and provide colourful entertainment for its own sake. It is an insult to the intelligence of everyone concerned and it is madness to throw away a game which could be won. Trent Bridge, 1967, was a classic example; anyone who could not appeciate it does not understand the game and all it involves.

We won at The Oval by eight wickets to take the series two-nil with one drawn; but that was ten days after the county championship match at Edgbaston, and the storm-clouds which had been gathering now broke over me.

13

INCIDENT AT EDGBASTON

Three years before my dismissal by Yorkshire came the loss of the England captaincy, something which hit me as hard but in a different way from the later blow.

Yorkshire hurt me deeply and personally. They turned sour the dreams of my youth. They wrecked a career which was my whole life. It was not so much professional pride which was touched as private emotions, sentiments, affections. I loved every minute of my life as a Yorkshire cricketer. It was exactly and precisely the life I wanted – a labour of love rather than a job of work.

My dismissal from the England captaincy struck right into every professional instinct I possess. It was England's top cricketing job and I was perfectly satisfied, when appointed, that my qualifications were adequate. England won six of the next seven Tests and drew the other, and after that I felt those qualifications might now stand up to any reasonable critical scrutiny. I liked being England's captain because I enjoy leadership, because I enjoy doing a job as well as I can and because it brought prestige to my country and to my family and myself. Let us have no hint of hypocrisy about this: I enjoyed, too, the feeling that being England's cricket captain was not going to be a disadvantage when it came to finding a good job to take me through the years when I had finished playing. I certainly didn't ever dream of the sort of financial benefits which sprang from that job only ten years later, but I did think about the type of job it might help me to get after retirement. I don't regard that as selfish or self-seeking. I regard it as a perfectly natural reaction of a man in his mid-thirties with a wife and a home, and, in prospect, a family.

At the same time, I by no means regarded the England captaincy as a means to an end, or as a vehicle specifically to take me along the road to financial security. It was an end in itself, another marvellous dream come true. There were fringe benefits, it is true, and I was confident, quite frankly, in my ability to retain the captaincy until I was ready to retire from cricket.

I never tire, nor shall I ever tire, of stressing the importance of good leadership and this can be most important when you are in command of forces which are, perhaps, of something less than top class. You can still build a winning side given the right basics, the right spirit and the right leadership. Just occasionally there comes a side which has so much natural ability that unless the skipper makes a series of catastrophic mistakes, it is going to win anyway. Look at the West Indies, more so than Australia. Year by year they turn out players of unbelievable natural ability but how many good captains have they produced? One – Frankie Worrell. He has been their only skipper in my experience to think really deeply about the overall strategy and the detailed tactics of a game. He was the only leader, during my years of playing against West Indian teams, who significantly shifted the course of a game by his thinking, as opposed to by changes brought about simply by the natural gifts of the men under his command. Gary Sobers, my very good friend and the greatest all-round cricketer I have ever seen, was far from being a good Test captain. He was a splendid leader by example, but Gary really believed that cricket was a game to be played between two sides in which everyone simply played to the best of his ability. In that case, all things (like the weather and the state of the pitch, the light and the luck) being equal, the better side would win. When you have as much God-given ability as Gary Sobers you can afford the luxury of such uncomplicated reasoning.

It is not, of course, as simple as that. But when I took over the captaincy at The Oval, in 1966, it was to lead a side with a lot of ability, a lot of experience and, most important of all, a lot of cricketing sense. Every member of that side knew what it meant, how important it was, to pull together. The ones with most experience were willing to pool it; the ones with least were not only willing but anxious to learn. And we won the Test after England had not exactly covered herself in glory in the first four of that series. That was because we not only achieved the right blend of players, but we all did our jobs with the team in mind. My career as England's captain had started well.

I was thirty-six when the new season began and I trained, in straightforward fitness terms, harder than I had ever done in my life. First of all I went to a health farm to trim off the extra poundage one normally acquires in a close season. So it was something of an anti-climax when rain washed out most of the first-class cricket scheduled for May. There was virtually no 'form' on which to base selections for the First Test against India at Headingley on 8 June. So we went for known ability. On my way to Harrogate to join the team I called for a look at the pitch and saw it was dry, firm and potentially full of runs. By next morning, to my astonishment it was moist to say the least, and looked as though it would test any batsman, anyway for the first hour or two. George Cawthray, the groundsman, explained that no sooner had the covers been taken off that morning to give the pitch a chance to 'breathe' than a sudden shower had come from nowhere at all before his staff could get the covers back. I gave a lot of thought to what to do if I won the toss and even after winning it and deciding to bat, I still wasn't entirely comfortable when John Edrich and Geoff Boycott went out to open. Edrich was caught behind for one and Ken Barrington, for all of an opening forty minutes in which he was searching for the moving ball, grafted away in the style which made him perhaps the most dependable batsman in the world during his era.

Meanwhile, Geoff Boycott was having a horrible time. Everyone has experienced this sort of thing at one time or another and how Geoff must have hated it in front of his home crowd. He was completely out of touch. But such is his monumental patience and total dedication to the cause of giving no bowler a chance, that he was still there at lunchtime, for 23! When Barrington was out for 93, Tom Graveney took over and the contrast between his fluent stroke-play and Boycott's continued struggle for survival was more pointed than ever – especially to those who didn't or couldn't appreciate the psychology of what Boycott was going through. He scored 43 runs between lunch and tea when we were 156 for two.

On paper – in terms of figures, that is – the situation was right for England to start applying the pressure. During the interval I suggested to Geoff that, without doing anything ostentatiously foolish (unnecessary advice, really!) he might try to play a few shots. He ought, in general terms, to have been seeing the ball and timing it well by this stage. But, and I do wish people would appreciate this sort of thing, the opposition captain was just as aware of the situation as I was. The Nawab of Pataudi set an entirely defensive field and with bowlers who were not exactly the world's worst at their trade, it was difficult for Geoff to get his shots through the field. He could have tried to hit over the top and many batsmen – many in that side – would have tried it. But at that stage of his career it was, and still is, a cardinal sin to graft for hours to establish yourself, then throw it all away in one quixotic gesture. No batsman in history, I suspect, has dealt out more self-punishment on dismissal than Boycs. In those first years with Yorkshire we had watched him come back to the dressing-room, silent and grim, whether he had scored two or 200, slump into a corner with a towel round his neck, and sit for an hour or more without a word.

At Lord's in 1963, rain washed out play on the Saturday; and on Monday, on the sort of rain-affected wicket for which the ground is famous, Yorkshire were bowled out for 144 of which Boycott, an opener, scored 90. It was a truly wonderful innings and from a young player in his first full season it was little short of incredible. The ball was standing straight up from a length, shooting, fizzing and when Geoff *was* out it was to the original unplayable delivery. Alan Moss bowled one that took off and went away, and it would have taken even greater genius than the then-flowering talent of Boycott to get the bat out of the way. He came up the stairs with tears streaming down his cheeks and brushed straight past a man near the door who said, 'Well played, son'. Geoff so badly wanted a hundred on his first appearance at Lord's that he never even heard that rare tribute from his hero, Sir Leonard Hutton.

Now perhaps that helps a little to understand the mind of the man who was battling to find his touch in that First Test of 1967. Graveney was caught on the boundary for 59 and in came Basil D'Oliveira, in such opulent vein that once again the partner could not help but

118

emphasise Geoff's laboured progress. I went on to the balcony to try to indicate that now he had to get a move on, but so profound was his concentration that he never saw me. To make matters worse, from the spectators' point of view – and, by this time, the team's – he began taking singles at the end of overs which certainly helped his growing confidence but kept the strike away from the in-form D'Oliveira. By the end of the day he had scored 106 not out.

Next morning the headlines thirsted for his blood. Ken Barrington had been dropped two years previously for a long innings against New Zealand; so now must Boycott's head roll. It made good, snappy copy. It provided a tailor-made talking point for those newspapers who prefer a succinct (preferably critical) theme to a detailed description of play. Even the more reasoned/considered views of the serious newspapers were disapproving.

It all depends how you look at these things. I didn't ask Geoff what he thought of his press next morning. I knew. He had been out of form and he had played himself back. He had had a struggle and he had won through. He had batted through the first day of what was, after all, a five-day game and he was not out with a ton under his belt. England were in a strong position and from his point of view it was going to be an unassailable one by the time he was out (if, indeed, Geoff ever considered the possibility of being out – I don't honestly think it ever comes within the compass of his thinking when he starts, or is playing, an innings). The pitch was infinitely better on the second day; so was G. Boycott. He went to 200 in half the time his first 100 had taken. He batted beautifully. He was back in form and he obviously revelled in it because he loves batting. He was 246 not out when I declared at 550 for four. We missed five catches and a game we might have won in three-and-a-half days went deep into the fifth. The Noob spent six hours scoring 148 and we had to bat again and make 126 for four to win by six wickets. Geoff Boycott was dropped for the Second Test at Lord's.

After explaining to him that the selectors felt they had no alternative, I stayed with Geoff whilst the press descended on him and I have never wavered in my admiration for the way he handled the situation. One false move, one resentful word of bitterness and a developing Test career could have been nipped in the bud. His statement for publication was this: 'Batting for me is largely a matter of confidence and I felt I needed to build mine up after a series of low scores. I was never conscious of the time factor on the first day. When you are in bad form you never seem to get the half-volleys and when you do play a shot it always seems to find a fielder.' Every batsman who ever lived will know what that means.

We won the Second Test by an innings and 124 runs. The Third was at Edgbaston and, as if as a foretaste of the part that ground was to play in my career, I was in trouble again. We scored 298 and bowled India out for 92. Clearly we had a chance of winning by an innings in a record two days – if I enforced the follow-on. I did not. This wasn't because I was playing to orders or because I wanted to give the spectators who had paid in advance for Saturday a run for their money; but because I knew the selectors, while picking the best possible team for that summer's Tests, wanted a chance to weigh up form for the winter tour to West Indies. As I saw it, here was a chance for men like Colin Milburn, Robin Hobbs and Dennis Amiss to show that they had real Test class. Why should we grind India into the ground in two days? We had won the series and this Test had not given any of those three players a proper chance to show what they could do. Of course, I should have known I couldn't win. I was accused of not being ruthless enough! The same people who wrote that, would in a couple of months time be eternally damning me for being totally ruthless in a county championship match! You absolutely cannot win against a press which shifts its ground as rapidly, as regularly and as paradoxically as that.

We won by 132 runs and as it happened, on a very difficult pitch. Not many players enhanced their reputations but Amiss did score a good 45 and laid the foundation for the entirely justifiable reputation he had achieved as a good grafter who would get his head down and work. In the First Test against Pakistan we were held up by an innings of immense concentration from Hanif Mohammed who carried his bat for 187, scored in nine hours. No doubt Geoff Boycott reflected that no one in Pakistan would advocate dropping him for the next game! That game was drawn. We won the Second Test after yet another public debate about a slow-scoring innings from Ken Barrington and my defence of it, and we won at The Oval despite a dazzling innings by Asif which earned me another salvo from the armchair critics. I had, it seemed, made every possible mistake in my seven-match career as England's captain – but somehow we had won six and drawn the other. Yet I was never to lead my country again.

The sacking by England was not so shattering as that by Yorkshire because I was forewarned. That made it no more palatable, but it was less of a shock. Yorkshire's action left me feeling inexpressibly sad; England's left me bitter because it was so totally undeserved. Looking back on the game which brought it about I say quite firmly and un-equivocally, ten years later: if I had that time over again, I would do exactly what I did against Warwickshire at Edgbaston in August 1967. I would say exactly what I said at the time. I would refrain from saying what I was urged on all sides to say – i.e. 'I am sorry'.

I am not sorry for any single aspect of my captaincy in that game. I started it by trying to win and I ended it by trying to prevent the other side winning. That is the way I have played my cricket all my life and as far as I am concerned it is the only way to play the game. And what made it all so damned illogical was that game against Warwickshire had nothing whatsoever to do with the England team or how I skippered it. Probably the whole secret lay in something I had been told a month before, by a newspaperman, and it may perhaps indicate the sort of influence these chaps can have when you know the sort of 'information' they acquire. He had said to me, 'For God's sake, Brian, keep your nose clean because they are just waiting at Lord's for a chance to prevent you leading the side in the West Indies.' Good, comforting stuff for an England captain!

Yorkshire went into that Edgbaston game needing to beat Warwick-shire so that we could take over at the top of the table from Kent. They bowled well and we were out for 238. In Warwickshire's first innings we didn't bowl very well, and we missed at least four chances in the field. I was not in a particularly good temper as we came in for lunch and I was, in fact, deep in thought about what to say to my players during the break. The county championship has always been of vital importance to Yorkshire and as far as I was concerned we had gone a fair way that morning towards chucking it away. As we passed through the Warwickshire members' seats I heard a remark directed at me which was more than unpleasant. In normal circumstances it would have been a bit easier to have ignored the remark, but I was hot, sticky, worried and short-tempered. I went along the empty row of seats behind the man I thought had spoken and asked, 'Excuse me, was it you who said that?' I had put my hand on the shoulder of the man to whom I was speaking. He turned, put his hand on my arm and replied emphatically, 'No, I did not.' I said, 'I'm terribly sorry', and went in to lunch. That was all that was said, but it's a bit unusual for a player to challenge a member of the public – disgusting as the remark directed at me had been – so I saw Leslie Deakins, the Warwickshire secretary, and told him what had happened. 'Don't worry', he said. 'I'll let you know if anyone complains. Until then, forget it.' In point of fact, the supporter and I had a drink together later and I assumed the incident had been forgotten.

At the time it was upsetting, especially coming on top of a sub-standard morning's play by my side. Perhaps I was wrong to challenge the man I thought had tossed the jibe at me but it was a particularly nasty remark. Anyway, I hadn't found him. I had committed a *gaffe*. I had apologised for it and the apology had been accepted. So now to get on with the job I was paid to do.

Warwickshire led us by four runs on the first innings. We made 42 for one on the Thursday and, in between showers, were bowled out for 145 on the Friday. Mike Smith's boys had to get 142 in 102 minutes to win and it was up to Yorkshire to make them fight for every one of those runs. The way we made them fight, allied to the conditions which slowed things down drastically, cost me the England captaincy.

As I have said, I did or said nothing in that afternoon's play that I would not do or say again – every time, given the same circumstances. The ball was wet; it needed drying frequently. Warwickshire were taking quick singles to make me change a defensive field; I changed it frequently. At no time did I instruct our bowlers to take their time about bowling an over. At no time did I take any action I wouldn't have taken if we had been at the bottom of the county championship table.

At that time a bowler was obliged to dry the ball under the super-vision of the umpire. In this case my three faster bowlers – Trueman, Nicholson and Hutton – carried a cloth in their pockets to speed things up. A point was made that we bowled only two overs in the last eleven minutes. But in Freddie's last over he bowled two no-balls – that certainly extends the time the over takes but it gives the opposition a run plus another chance of scoring. And the fall of Alan Smith's and Dennis Amiss's wickets took up time, too, even though the new batsmen rushed to the middle. No, I did nothing for which I felt, or feel, it was necessary to apologise but that is what some newspapers demanded and even some of my friends advised. But why? It is held to this day in many quarters that if I had publicly apologised for deliberate time-wasting I would not have been deposed from the England captaincy. No one at Lord's officially asked me to apologise, mind you, though they did officially drop me from the captaincy. But even if I had been asked officially I could not have done so. I had nothing to apologise for. But the press (or at least one newspaper) had not finished with me yet. Nine days after the game at Edgbaston had finished *The People* ran this story:

'The truth about an amazing scene involving England and Yorkshire skipper Brian Close can be revealed for the first time today.

'Two highly-respected cricket supporters have confirmed that at lunchtime during the now notorious time-wasting county match at Edgbaston, Birmingham, Brian Close dashed into the members' enclosure, seized a spectator by the collar and shook him angrily.'

That classic piece of muck-raking – from a newspaper whose cricket columnist was my senior player, Freddie Trueman! – appeared at the time the captaincy for the West Indies tour was being discussed and I don't think there can be any doubt that it cooked my goose. For the benefit of the people who researched, wrote and published the story of the two 'highly respected' but anonymous cricket supporters, *and* for the benefit of the authorities who accepted it, let me offer the following statement, volunteered to me by Mr Doug Nicholls, of 87 Lichfield Road, Walsall Wood, Staffs:

'I was sitting in the members' enclosure about four rows from the front and a few yards in from the gate leading on to the field. As the players were coming off for lunch I heard a voice from somewhere behind me make this personal remark directed at Close.

'The next moment Close was coming through the gate and along an empty row behind me. He put his hand on my shoulder. I was a bit shocked. I wondered what was coming next and half rose up. I told Close: "Take your hand off me." Said Close, "Did you say that?" "No, I didn't", I replied. "Oh, I'm very sorry to trouble you", said Close, who turned away and went to the dressing-room.

'That was all that took place. Nothing more. Some people suggested that I should complain but Close had done nothing. He had apologised for the incident and it was closed as far as I was concerned. There was nothing for me to complain about.'

Mike Smith was the Warwickshire captain in that game. At the end of it, as we shook hands, I said, 'You deserved to beat us but we could not in all fairness give you the game. We had to make you fight.' Mike replied, 'We understand. It was a great game, anyhow.' And at the end of the season, when we had won the championship, he sent us a telegram which read simply, 'Congratulations. The best team won.' I'm very glad I have that telegram.

On Wednesday, 23 August, five days after the Edgbaston match, I went to Lord's to face a panel of former county captains to answer complaints about Yorkshire's tactics against Warwickshire. Naturally enough, I turned things over in my mind again and again as I drove southwards. The more I thought about the game the more convinced I was that I could not be reproached, legally or even morally, for anything I had done or not done. I had already sent a written statement to Lord's, which is reproduced verbatim here:

'There has been a lot of publicity in the Press re Warwickshire 2nd innings and our bowling rate. For the record, may I state every point which has a bearing on the matter. First of all the first 25 minutes of their innings it was raining lightly and we did not object although we might easily have done, and in my judgment it was sometimes heavy enough to leave the field – at no time had Yorkshire a chance of winning. However, this rain meant that my bowlers had to wipe the ball every time it rolled much across the ground. Because the Warwickshire batsmen were playing very well, I could not place fieldsmen near enough to the wicket to stop sharp singles and many times when the ball was pushed down in front, the bowler had to follow through nearly to the other wicket in order to save singles. This again was a contributing factor and could not possibly be helped. Even amongst all this we were bowling our 16th over when the hour came along and 70 odd runs having been scored.

'A little later it started drizzling again. This not only handicapped the bowlers but also the fielders who were sliding around. I made an appeal which the Umpires rejected and as we took our places again it started to throw it down. We all raced off the field. Evidently whilst we were in the dressing room and the Umpires had not quite got off the rain stopped suddenly. As soon as this was pointed out we returned to the field with the last 10 minutes to go. At this point I put Freddie Trueman on to bowl. His next over along with cleaning the wet ball included 8 balls (2 "no" balls) and one wicket. It took 6 minutes to complete but, in the circumstances, was not unexceptional. The last over was bowled by Richard Hutton who was bowling at the scoreboard end for the first time. Richard had a practice run up as he always does when starting at a new end – if this was wrong, then David Brown (Warwickshire) does this very same thing every new spell he comes on for. The first ball of his over bowled A. C. Smith and this more or less made it certain that this over was the final over. During the latter stages of the match I shouted at the top of my voice to fieldsmen instructions where to go as the tempo of the game changed. Unfortunately, there was so much noise around the ground from the crowd that my voice was at most times lost in it. This obviously caused slight delays trying to get the instructions through to my players but was no fault of mine or the Yorkshire Team. At the start of the last over, I had to run across to Richard Hutton to give him instructions to bowl straight because if he got a wicket it would ensure that it would be the last over. At this point Mr. Elliott (Umpire) spoke to me "Get on with it". I might point out that I only had to run across to Richard Hutton because he had not heard my instructions, which had been shouted several times, because of the volume of noise from the crowd. When we left the field certain members of the crowd tried to kick and trip our players and one young fellow raised an umbrella as if to crown Freddie Trueman over the head. He saw him and pushed him away turned to go into the dressing-room and this bloke tried again – fortunately someone restrained him.

'I think that this puts the record right from Yorkshire's point of view. Obviously at no time do we *give* a match away but we did nothing unusual or different from what anyone else would have done against us to save it in the circumstances. I consider that my players conducted themselves very well in view of the abuse and behaviour of the crowd.'

At Lord's I put my case to Arthur Gilligan, who was at that time president-elect of MCC; C. G. A. Paris, of Hampshire; D. G. Clark, of Kent; and E. J. Gothard (Derbyshire). Brian Sellers was there, with Doug Insole, the chairman of selectors, as observers, but they had no voting powers.

If that committee of inquiry had been a jury in a criminal court I could have objected to two of them on the grounds that their judgement might be something less than impartial. Clark had recently published his committee's report on the future of cricket and, when the press had telephoned for the views of various players, I had offered some comments which were critical. I couldn't expect him to look at me with an entirely unjaundiced eye. As for Mr Gothard, he came into a room that summer where someone had got me going a bit – it was in a London hotel during the Lord's Test – on the subject of that overworked cliché, 'brighter cricket'. A crowd of us were there and Mr Gothard – a stranger to me – joined in. I asked him: 'Whom do you support?' and he replied 'Derbyshire'. So I told him: 'You are the worst team in the county for defensive attitudes.' He got up and walked out and it was then that I was told that he was the *President* of Derbyshire. So I didn't really expect Mr Gothard to have a particularly favourable view of me. Nevertheless I did not expect the verdict of the committee:

'We came to the unanimous decision that the Yorkshire team had used delaying tactics during the second Warwickshire innings and that these tactics constituted unfair play and were against the best interests of the game.

'Furthermore, the committee held the captain, Brian Close, entirely responsible for these tactics. They have, therefore, severely censured him and this decision will be conveyed to the Yorkshire County Cricket Club.'

I just couldn't believe it. I still don't understand how the committee could reach that decision. I thought about a game at Bradford the previous season when we needed to score 173 in two hours to beat

Surrey. Mickey Stewart, a shrewd and experienced captain, slowed down the over-rate and placed his field so that we got ourselves out trying to win. We didn't complain. And Mickey Stewart was not severely censured at Lord's. But then his name wasn't Brian Close.

I was boiling when I came out of that meeting. What, I asked myself, was I going to do if a similar situation cropped up? Should I ask spinners to bowl with a wet ball in case we didn't get through enough overs? Was I expected to ask my side to *run* to their fielding positions? A dozen different thoughts were swirling round in my mind and pretty near the front of them was an intention to go to The Oval and say to the England selectors: 'I can't skipper the team against Pakistan.' I think that is what I would have done but for the fact that Brian Sellers followed me out of the meeting and caught me up halfway down the stairs. I said, 'How can I captain a side now?' He replied, 'Come on, forget about this. You've got a job to do.' If he hadn't done that I could very well have gone to The Oval and said 'Find yourselves a new captain.'

So the day after my censure I had to lead England, and I shall always be grateful not only to my team but to The Oval crowd because not once did I hear a mention of the Lord's verdict. I had that on my mind for starters; I had the dreadful fear that I was going to be deprived of the captaincy for the winter tour; so it needed something to put the finishing touch to my anxieties. It came, of course. During Saturday I was approached to make a statement about that story which was to appear in *The People* the following day, headlined: 'Brian Close Sensation. He Attacked Man in Crowd.' So one way and another, I played that Test with a few things on my mind. On Sunday my wife and I were at Ken Barrington's home trying to keep out of the way of the press. They tracked us down but Ken put them off. No one could keep them off when I went back to the England team's hotel on Sunday night. Viv went in the front but I had been advised by Doug Insole not to make any statement. So I went round to the back and lay on the floor, hiding behind a pile of sand bricks as one or two of the pressmen chased round there, until the night porter opened the back door to let me in. It's not always a dignified job being England's captain! And amidst all this I was trying to win a Test match. We did win it, and with it the series.

127

Ironically, it was from the Pakistan skipper, Hanif, that I got the first hint of the bad news to come. In The Oval pavilion he whispered, 'I've heard rumours they haven't picked you for the West Indies.' I said I hadn't heard anything and Hanif added, 'I sincerely hope you get it.'

Half an hour later Doug Insole asked for a word with me. We went into the empty England dressing-room and he said, 'I'm sorry to have to give you this news but you will not be leading the side in the West Indies.'

I had then to go to a reception, to smile at people, to accept congratulations on winning the series, to make a speech, to make polite small-talk with the hierarchy. And all the time I was bleeding inside. I may not bruise easily, but I do bleed. It was all so bloody, horribly unfair.

So Colin Cowdrey was recalled as captain and, in the West Indies, slowed down the bowling rate so ostentatiously that it is the only time I have ever seen Gary Sobers really angry! One law for Close . . .

14

BOTHER AT T'MILL

At least I was still captain of Yorkshire. After four county champion-ship games of 1968 I left Freddie out of the side to play Warwicks at Middlesbrough. It wasn't something I did lightly, not without a very great deal of thought. He had been a truly magnificent bowler over more years than anyone had any right to expect. He had bowled thousands of overs and rarely missed a game through injury or illness. His strength, stamina and sustained hostility had been little short of miraculous. But in 1968 he was thirty-seven years old. He could still produce periods of savage speed but more and more he was having to spend time 'coasting' – and he was not in the side to do that. Fred saw himself developing into a medium-pacer, using all the accumulated experience of twenty years' bowling, all his knowledge of pitches and players. But he was by temperament totally unsuited to the role. The genuine medium-pacer expects to be hit for four from time to time and when it happens to say to himself, 'I strayed fractionally in line or length there. I have to make sure it doesn't happen again.' The whole essence of that type of attack is wearing down the batsman, and keeping cool and unruffled if he counter-attacks. Freddie's attitude in his thirty-eighth year was the same as it had been in his nineteenth – if anyone hit him for four he wanted to knock the bats-man's head off. That is fine, it's right, in the genuine fast bowler: an essential part of his make-up. On particular types of wickets (that Headingley Test which caused the Australians so much anguish, for instance), that vast experience and knowledge of how to use the ball could be invaluable at medium pace. But as a way of life it just wasn't Fred. To some extent it was encouraged by Yorkshire officials going round in winter and saying at dinners, 'Fred can go on for years yet. He'll make a fine medium pacer.' And because he adored the lime-light and hated the thought of leaving active participation in cricket, Freddie began to believe it was true.

Now over the years he had stored up for himself a fair bit of hate. He had not only dismissed batsmen; he had made clear his contempt for them. And that again was fine. It was a potent weapon in his armoury to have a psychological advantage over batsmen. We had all watched, over the years, young and inexperienced players come to the wicket literally shaking with nervousness and apprehension at their first encounter with Fiery Fred. There was an awful danger now that he might start to be regarded as Friendly Fred. Batsmen who wouldn't have had a price against him five years previously now drove him for four. Goodish batsmen, who previously hadn't been quite good enough to cope with him, now started to get runs and to take revenge for the humiliations of previous years. Tony Nicholson had deve-loped into a fine partner for Fred and he could bowl long spells of medium-fast if asked to do so. Ken Taylor could bowl little seamers: so could I if it was necessary. Just beginning to come along was a genuine opening bowler called Chris Old. No, I knew what I wanted from Fred and if he couldn't or wouldn't deliver the goods, there were going to be times when he had to be left out. This was one of them and he wasn't pleased. However, we beat Warwicks by an innings, with Boycott scoring a masterly 180 not out, Nick taking the wickets in the first innings and Illy in the second.

Fred came back for the Roses match – there was never any question or his not giving everything in *that* game – and took five for 45 and three for 17. Part of Freddie's strength was his sublime belief in his own greatness. He firmly believed to the end of his career that he was better than any bowler who had been called up by England since he left the Test scene four years earlier and, privately, he was not without support for that view in the Yorkshire camp. We all had the most tremendous respect for his ability, particularly his consistent delivery of the goods over so many years and we would have hated to see him 'collared' by batsmen even (whether he believed it or not) more than he would. We learned to live with his cryptic catch-phrase: 'I'm still t'quickest in t'world when I want to slip missen', and, indeed, from time to time we saw definite evidence of its truth. Fred was always a truly great player; sadly he was not always a great colleague.

On 31 May we drew a marvellous game with Gloucestershire at Bristol with our last pair at the wicket (Chris Old, who had tonsillitis and did not expect to bat, had to change hurriedly and go out and hold the fort with Illy for two-and-a-half overs to save it when the newly-arrived Mike Procter scythed through us), and I suffered an injury which kept me out of the next half-dozen games. F.S. took over as captain and he did a good job. The win over the Australians at Sheffield was, I think, one of the high spots of a great career. He treasures the memory, and rightly so. He loved being captain and I can understand that. *I* loved being captain. But let me take you back a matter of weeks . . . just for a moment.

One of our most devoted supporters was Mrs Betty O'Neill, a South Yorkshire lass by birth who ran a business down in Cornwall. She used to pop up to see us when we played in Somerset and occasionally at other grounds. Every season she used to send a fiver to our first match for the lads to have a drink on her. (Oh yes. A fiver comfortably bought a drink round the whole team in 1968.) Her letter that year arrived at a ground just after we had left. It was re-addressed to the next game and missed us there. Then it went the rounds for the first few weeks of the season until it finally arrived at my home on the morning of 19 June.

That brings us back up to date. I was still out of the side but planning to go to **Headingley** to watch the game and to have some treatment. The previous evening I had had a telephone call from the secretary, Jack Nash, to ask if I was coming. I was wanted at a meeting of the cricket committee on the afternoon of the 19th. I went in and encountered an atmosphere reminiscent of The Inquisition. Now I cannot claim that the summons to the meeting was entirely unexpected because two days previously I had had a telephone call from Crawford White, of the *Daily Express*, who – to my complete astonishment – said, 'They tell me you are in a bit of bother with your committee.' I had no knowledge at all of this and told him so. Crawford said, 'Well, forewarned is forearmed. It's going round that you are in trouble. And if you do leave Yorkshire, Leicestershire would like you.' He mentioned a salary which was nearly twice as much as my Yorkshire pay! So I knew something was in the wind though I hadn't the faintest idea in the world what it was.

Brian Sellers soon told me. It seemed that I had 'misappropriated funds intended for the team'. That sounded a serious charge and for a moment I couldn't understand what the chairman was talking about. Then Mrs O'Neill's cheque was mentioned. I had it in my pocket . . . the letter which had arrived *that morning*. I took it out of my pocket and threw it on to the table, the envelope black with re-addressings and postmarks. The chairman read it, said: 'Oh well, that's that then.' No apology. Just brief, brusque acceptance that what he had said to me was horribly, totally false. But there was more to come.

The committee had been told that I was absorbed in horse-racing to the detriment of the team's cricket; and one further charge, that the senior players were not satisfied with my captaincy. Well, it has never been any secret in cricket that I love horses and racing. I think the racing stride of a thoroughbred is one of the most beautiful sights one can see. I have a lot of pals in racing. I love a day at the races. Racing had long been my hobby, and I spent time in the dressing-room reading the *Sporting Life* just as Sharpe and Hutton did crossword puzzles and Fred went to sleep. Everyone does his own thing in a dressing-room where hours are spent each week. But 'to the detriment of Yorkshire cricket' – absolutely not. That was my seventh year as captain; we had won the county championship in my first year, 1963, the Gillette Cup in 1965, the championship again in 1966 and 1967; so I felt I had not exactly been letting things slide. 'Dissatisfaction amongst the senior players'? Well, that was news to me and I was in pretty close touch with my players.

I knew there was a certain amount of dissatisfaction with the committee, and that at times we felt we were winning things despite the committee rather than with their backing. We had even formed the impression that there was some jealousy because we were heading towards our seventh championship in ten years which would equal Yorkshire's pre-war record. Incredible though it sounds, we sensed an 'anti' feeling from our own higher echelons. But where had these tales about me come from? Only one man in the team was in close touch with the committee in my absence – the acting captain, Fred. I said so. One of the committee, Ronnie Burnet, very quickly said, 'It hasn't come from Fred.' He said it just a bit too quickly. I was sure I was right. And the meeting finished in no time at all after that. Brian Sellers told me, 'You are the captain. You'd better go and find what the trouble is all about.' I went up to the dressing-room, caught Fred's eye and threw Mrs O'Neill's note and cheque on to the table, telling him: 'Fred – there's that cheque I've spent.' No comment. At close of play I went for a drink with the lads and sure enough my two most senior players, Ray Illingworth and Jimmy Binks, echoed my thoughts: 'The stirring must have come from Fred.' I saw Fred and told him, 'If you want my job so badly you can have it.'

We all knew Fred well enough, of course, yet it still came as a shock to find this attempt (which I was sure had come from him) to sabotage me had been made whilst I was out of action. When one thought about it, however, it was not difficult to work out his probable reasoning. He was over the top as one of the great fast bowlers of all time but he did not want to go out of cricket – yet. He could try his hand at medium-paced seaming but the only way he was going to be able to command a regular place for any length of time was as captain.

The following day I sought a meeting with Brian Sellers and told him: 'You have two courses open to you as I see it. Either you let me go and let Fred take over, or Fred retires. The atmosphere in the dressing-room is not going to be particularly happy with this sort of thing going on.' The support I got from my chairman was: 'It's your job as captain to sort it out. Go and get on with it.'

I missed the draw at Northampton and Fred's famous victory over the Australians and, still a spectator, I saw the side lose by playing terribly badly against Glamorgan at Sheffield. I came back (with a duck) for the drawn game against Kent at Bradford and then we got back on the championship trail with wins over Glamorgan in Cardiff, Worcestershire at Sheffield and Surrey at The Oval. The dreadful weather of the holiday season then saw us draw four consecutive games in July and early August and against Somerset at Scarborough we had a glimpse of a young Australian called Greg Chappell. He had so much natural ability, and on English wickets he added to that a great deal of technique. Finally, at Hull in the last days of August we had to beat Surrey to win the championship for the third year in succession. Without Boycott we scored 327 for nine, bowled them out for 189, had a quick thrash to 112 for seven and left ourselves enough time to bowl them out, all things being equal. We had stoppages for rain and bad light but things went well enough through the early part of the afternoon until we had Surrey at 121 for seven. It looked nice and safe, until Younis Ahmed and Arnold Long got together and we just couldn't shift them. For one-and-threequarter hours they held us at bay until there were only ten minutes play left – perhaps four overs at the most. Younis, now confidently in his stride feeling that the crisis was past, was beginning to open up. He swept Don Wilson round to leg and the ball cracked me straight on the shin at forward short. It rebounded to hit Jackie Hampshire on his ankle. He was hopping about but Don Wilson was pointing out the blood spurting through my flannels and running down into my sock. I snarled at him to get on with it because time was running out and crouched a foot closer at short leg. Next ball I saw Younis wind himself up to have another go and I was too close to do anything about it. So I clenched my teeth and set myself to take whatever came. The ball hit my body, then my arm, ricocheted up in the air and Jimmy Binks took the catch. Younis stood there open-mouthed until the umpire told him he was out. Eight minutes left. Robin Jackman came in, Wilson ran one right through him and he was lbw. Another two minutes ticked by as the last man (Mike Selvey, later to make his name with Middlesex's championship-winning side) came in but he could only watch as Tony Nicholson had Long caught behind with the last ball of his over. We had won the championship with five minutes to spare. It had been a 'funny' season but at least we had done what we had set out to do. In the dressing-room a doctor looked at my shin and sent me to hospital to have it fixed. By the time I got back all the celebration champagne had vanished! They don't stand on ceremony, these Yorkshire lads.

15

THE BREAK-UP
OF A GREAT SIDE

During the winter of 1968-69 Fred Trueman announced his retirement, Ray Illingworth had tried and failed to persuade the committee to break with tradition and to give him a contract which provided some long-term security and had joined Leicestershire, Ken Taylor had taken a teaching and coaching position in New Zealand. These were grievous blows.

Yet with Chris Old developing into a fine opening bowler and the ever-willing Nicholson in support, plus Richard Hutton, we had a more than useful front-line attack. Don Wilson was now a player of twelve years experience who had toured New Zealand and India – and to back him up in the spin-bowling department there was the promising Geoff Cope, with me in reserve to do a bit of whatever was necessary. The batting had experience and depth: Boycott, Sharpe, Padgett, Hampshire, Hutton and myself, with Colts like Chris Balderstone and Barrie Leadbeater waiting in the wings, and promising youngsters Colin Johnson, Andrew Dalton and John Woodford all knocking on the door. But the start of the season was marred once again by wretched weather. We accumulated only 22 points from our first seven games, only one of which was finished, and it was not until 20 June that we registered our first win – over Gloucestershire at Middlesbrough. The next three games were drawn as well, always with interference from the weather, and in the third of them – at Bristol in the return match with Gloucestershire – I pulled a calf muscle. It was one of those days when all the bowlers seemed to have problems at once. Old bowled seven no-balls, Hutton four no-balls and a wide, Woodford two wides . . . even Nick, who was almost mechanical in his

135

rhythm, was no-balled . . . so I had to do quite a bit of bowling myself. In the middle of it I felt the muscle go . . . ping. I had to bat with a runner and Jimmy Binks directed operations in the field. We lost by five wickets in the very last minute of the game but that should never have happened. Mike Procter holed out at deep extra cover from the first ball he received from Wilson, something like a fifty-yard carry, but to the astonishment of the bowler and field he stayed where he was. When they appealed, the umpire said it was a bump-ball. If it was, it was the biggest one I have ever seen. Procter was not out 51 when the winning run was scored.

I was out of the side with my injury until late August and Jimmy Binks had to lead a side which was still trying to re-establish itself after the loss of three Test players.

The championship had been put virtually out of reach, anyway, by that terrible start to the season. The weather, and our luck, did not improve and we finished thirteenth in the table with only three wins. Jimmy Binks was playing, too, with a deep sense of resentment which ultimately led to his retirement at the end of the season. Jimmy, as I have said, could be stroppy at times because he was a highly-intelligent lad and he never suffered fools gladly. In mid-May, when we went to Norwich for our opening Gillette Cup game against Norfolk, the game took two days to complete (more rain) and as I was staying with Lord Mackintosh, an old friend, I missed the incident which led indirectly to Jimmy's resignation. He went out for a drink with Jackie Hampshire and they ran into two Yorkshire committee-men and Cyril Washbrook, the adjudicator of the man-of-the-match award. The evening was spent talking and arguing cricket as usual and no doubt the committeemen said something which sounded stupid to Jimmy. Neither of them had ever played for Yorkshire and J. G. Binks was never a lad to shrink from speaking his mind. But it was an off-duty occasion; it was cricket-talk by five blokes all intimately associated with the game over a beer or two.

Jimmy quite openly said the players felt, at times, that the committee seemed to have done their damndest to stop the team winning. It was the sort of thing we had all felt and said amongst ourselves many times and by telling two committeemen in a strictly informal and off-the-record context Jimmy felt he was doing no more than voice an honest and justified opinion. Next morning he forgot about it and got on with the job of polishing off Norfolk, but sadly, our two committee men were too small-minded to see it in the same way. The minute we got back to Yorkshire he was hauled before the cricket committee – on the mat for criticising them! That upset Jimmy deeply and I entirely sympathise with him. For an off-duty conversation over a beer to be made the subject of an official reprimand was absolutely disgraceful. Good God. If I had been sensitive enough to react like that to some of the things the lads said to me over the years I wouldn't have had a team at all. Talking cricket was one of the strengths of the Yorkshire side. There was always total freedom to express views in the frankest (and often the most colourful) terms. That was the way we learned from our mistakes, the way we all grew to understand each other intimately. It was immensely helpful to the way we played our cricket. The dreadful over-reaction of those two committee men emphasised the yawning gulf between their approach and ours.

At the end of the season, when Jimmy received an offer of promotion with his firm which required him to work for them on a full-time basis, he took it – not without a lot of heart-searching, I'm sure, because he knew and loved his cricket. But the full-time job offered him security for the future. What did the feudal attitude of the committee offer him?

At least he was with us for the remainder of 1969 and although we had a bad time in the championship, we won the Gillette Cup again. In the second round at Old Trafford we kept the Lancashire opening pair so quiet for so long that their innings never had a chance to develop. In fact when Hutton got Barrie Wood out for three after goodness-knows-how-many overs we gave him a rollicking – and it wasn't entirely a joke! They totalled 173-8 in 60 overs and Boycott and Sharpe made it easy for us by scoring 137 for the first wicket. In the next round at The Oval we lost Sharpe before a run had been scored and we lost the next wicket just before lunch at 159 as Boycott and I gave Surrey a reminder of the 1965 final. With 272 on the board we had no trouble in containing them and won by 138 runs. I missed the semi-final, against Notts at Scarborough, because of my calf-muscle injury and Jimmy Binks took us through in a relatively low-scoring game: 191 against 123. It was a big day for Peter Stringer, the seamer who later went to Leicestershire, who finished Notts off with 4.5-1-4-3.

And so to the final, against Derbyshire. In our previous game, against Sussex in the championship, Snow had hit Boycott on the hand and broken a bone and young Leadbeater had taken a blow on the thumb but that was not broken. He had to play, painful or not. Now both injuries had been well publicised and I had a feeling that Derek Morgan had been toying with the idea of putting us in to bat. Then he would use his battery of quickies and seamers whilst there was some life in the wicket early on. On the other hand, I wanted to bat first, having been to 'the big occasion' before and having sensed the atmosphere and tensions that could be created by the Lord's ground and a huge crowd. Perhaps in a sense we didn't really need to toss – but then people can always change their minds at the last minute. Derek and I approached the toss tight-lipped and tense; we tossed and he won. Suddenly it occurred to me that on this brilliantly sunny morning, he might back down and decide to bat first after all – so I tried a bit of reverse psychology on him. Instead of giving him too much time to think about his choice, I didn't hang around waiting for him: I turned and walked straight back towards the pavilion, as if to imply that by getting out of his way quickly, I certainly didn't want Yorkshire to bat. Whether my action had anything to do with it or not a moment later Derek chased after me, catching up before I'd gone twenty yards, and invited us to bat. I hope that my face didn't betray the relief I felt inside. I turned back, ordered the roller, and then went in to tell the lads.

Leadbeater and Woodford put on 39 for the first wicket. I went in at number three again, primarily because I was a left-hander. It often upsets a bowling attack when a right- and a left-hander are in together, particularly in limited-over cricket. At that time Yorkshire had only two left-handers, the other being Don Wilson.

Barrie Leadbeater and I took the score quietly up to 50, and then in one of our mid-wicket chats I said: 'Come on Barrie, let's quicken the tempo.' The lad was feeling the pain from his thumb, no doubt at all about that. I saw him take one hand away several times as he played a shot and he lamented, 'I can't hit it.' 'All right then', I replied, 'if you can't score quickly, then get yourself out. You've done your job. It's no use wasting overs with the others to come.' Sharpe,

Padgett, Hampshire and Hutton were waiting and Wilson could give it a slog too. Somehow Barrie swung his bat, grimacing whenever he connected with the ball, but he produced some good shots and had the odd fortunate strike. He scored 76 of our total of 219-8 which wasn't bad against their six seam bowlers. The only time we were not in command was during their opening partnership but once we had broken that we were able to control the game and won by 69 runs. At the man-of-the-match ceremony, Colin Cowdrey, the adjudicator, said, 'It should go to you' (I had scored 37, taken three for 36, held two catches and directed operations) 'but I am going to give it to the youngster.' Momentarily I could have knocked his head off, but it was too wonderful an occasion to spoil with selfish feelings. Here was something to enjoy together, to share whilst victory was with us – with our members, our public, our *Yorkshire*. There isn't a thrill in the world that beats being a part of a team and being successful. 'All for one and one for all' . . . in a way, I've had more than my share of glory. I'm not grumbling.

16

THE WORST DAY OF MY LIFE

The worst day of my life was 25 November 1970.

I was working for an automatic machine company during the winter at that time and when Mr John Nash, the Yorkshire secretary, had 'phoned the previous evening to ask me to go to county head-quarters next day I had to switch round a few appointments. I assumed it was some sort of routine matter connected with the team – but I had no idea at all what the meeting was going to be about as I drove the ten miles or so from my home in Tong Park to the county offices at Headingley.

So it was just a bit of a surprise to find no committee in session but just Mr Nash, sitting across the table from me, and away to the left, at the end of the table, Brian Sellers. The Crackerjack. Mr Yorkshire Cricket himself. The man who had skippered that marvellous York-shire team of the 1930s and ruled with his iron rod a side which included such tremendous personalities as Herbert Sutcliffe, Len Hutton, Ticker Mitchell, Maurice Leyland, Hedley Verity, George Macaulay, Arthur Wood and Bill Bowes. The side which had won the championship in 1931, 1932, 1933, 1935, 1937, 1938 and 1939 and then again in the first year after the war. The side on whose greatness and whose legends I had been brought up in an atmosphere of total hero-worship. To this day, despite all that has happened, I not only address him as 'Mr Sellers', I think of him as 'Mr Sellers'. That was the extent of my respect for the traditions of authority in York-shire cricket.

I was still extremely curious about the reason for my being sum-moned, and the circumstances as much as the atmosphere made me just a bit apprehensive. But nothing in the world could have prepared me for the shock that was about to hit me. Brian Sellers looked along the table and said, 'Well, Brian, you've had a good innings.' As soon as he said that I knew something *very* funny was going to happen but I still wasn't prepared for the next bit. The committee had had a meeting, said the chairman. They had decided that my services were no longer required and that I had to make a decision whether to resign or be sacked.

Well, just how do you take an announcement like that? How is the poor brain, which has spent its formative years hoping to be good enough to be picked for Yorkshire and its relatively mature years working day and night to win matches and honours for Yorkshire, expected to absorb such shattering news?

The bottom had suddenly dropped out of my world and yet I still couldn't entirely take in what it all meant. My consciousness told me that the greatest, most overwhelming disaster of my life was taking place, yet my mind simply couldn't grasp the enormity of it all.

Try, if you can, to imagine the starry-eyed, ingenuous delight with which I had first gone into the Yorkshire team, which I have described. That had never left me. I might be Closey the old hand who had played for Yorkshire and England over twenty years or more, but inside I was still capable, every time I played for my county, of feeling the schoolboy thrill of wearing the white rose sweater, of sitting in the dressing-room where Sutcliffe and Hutton, Leyland and Verity had sat and all the immortals before them. I might be the hard man who had taken Wes Hall and Charlie Griffith on the chest and refused to acknowledge the pain or the bruises, but I could still be hurt in another, far more poignant way. And, by God, whatever was happening to me now was hurting. It was really hurting.

Yet I was still in some sort of daze about it all. It had happened too swiftly. I had been bludgeoned. Through the blur of battered emotions I heard myself saying,

'How long have I got to decide because I'd like a word with my wife?'

'You've got ten minutes', replied Brian Sellers.

'Before you leave this office we want to know. We have prepared two statements for a public announcement and whatever you decide will decide which statement is issued.'

Ten minutes. Ten minutes to decide how the cricketing world would learn that *my* world had been smashed into little pieces. Just ten minutes.

John Nash said the county were going to issue their statement at two o'clock and it was then some time between half-past ten and eleven. I tried to sort out my thoughts and the first reaction was that there was going to be one hell of a row when the news broke. Brian Close was going to be in the middle of yet another controversy and everything within me shrank from the thought. I had had enough rows in my life and I didn't want to have another. The two prepared statements were read over to me and I decided that resignation was the lesser of the two evils.

I can't honestly say I thought it out very clearly . . . not in ten minutes. You think about sacking and you think about resignation and you think one seems to have a bit of dignity while the other suggests nothing but stigma. The consequences of both are awful but somehow you think there won't be so much of a shout about resignation. You don't, in a moment like that, think about 'wrongful dismissal' in either the legal sense or the moral. You just think, 'I'm sick. What *is* this bloody terrible thing that is happening to me? How can I avoid some of the mess that is going to follow?'

So I said, 'I'll resign'. And at once the tension went out of the atmosphere in that room. Well, it went out of John Nash and Brian Sellers, anyway. Vaguely I realised I had taken the pressure off them, but I hadn't taken any off myself. All I wanted to do was get out of that room, away from Headingley, and to talk to Vivienne. I drove away with my mind still in a whirl. I wanted to cry. As I drove along Kirkstall Road my vision misted up so much I had to stop. And then I was sick, there at the side of the road.

When I got home Vivienne was out, collecting Lynn from play-school, so I sat there thinking over all my memories of my days with Yorkshire . . . the moments of success, the laughs, the men I had played with and against, and gradually realising it was all over. There would be no more of those golden days to store up in the memory. Have you ever had toothache and pushed against it with your tongue to make the pain sharper? I suppose you do it to stop the pain creeping up and taking you by surprise. So I did that. I went over those days as a schoolboy when I never dared let myself hope I would play for Yorkshire. I could dream, but hope was being too pre-sumptuous. I went over that first day, joining the great men in City Square and driving to Cambridge.

I recalled championships won and Gillette Cup finals at Lord's. I thought of the Sundays playing golf when we were on the southern or the West Country tour. I thought of the evenings, talking cricket with the most knowledgeable and deeply-involved band of cricketers in the country. When my mind faltered I forced it to come back and think again about those days . . . days which were now finished, would never be again.

There had been no preparation for that. When you decide that a particular season is going to be your last, you have a whole summer to work up to retirement. Even then it is going to be a great wrench. Very few first-class cricketers go out of the game without regret and I am certain none goes out without spending at least the following season yearning for life 'on the circuit'. But at least they have a chance to prepare. This had just hit me like a sledgehammer. The thought of joining another county just had not occurred to me then. If I had thought about that I could have told myself that other Yorkshiremen had had to face it – during my own career I had seen Willie Watson go to Leicestershire, followed years later by Ray Illingworth, Brian Bolus go to Notts, Jimmy Binks and Freddie Trueman go into retirement, Johnny Wardle into League cricket in another spectacular Yorkshire dismissal. But you just don't think it is ever going to happen to you. In my case I hadn't even started to wonder, at that stage, 'why'? All I could feel was an appalling sense of loss; all my emotions were bound up in a sense of misery – total and absolute.

Vivienne came in, took one look at me – I must have looked ghastly – and asked, 'What on earth is the matter? What's gone wrong?' I told her, and then said that of the two alternatives, I had chosen to resign. She thought about it for a minute and then said, 'Don't you realise that by resigning you have done all their dirty work for them?' It was then that I began to realise just how it would look to all that loyal band of Yorkshire supporters who had just supported my benefit. I had taken their money and just walked out on them. More than that, forgetting the benefit, it would look as though

144

I was letting the side down when it was beginning to enter a transitional stage. Jimmy Binks, Freddie, and Ken Taylor had all retired in the last few years; Ray had gone to Leicester. There were a lot of good young players coming on but they weren't all completely ready. Geoff Boycott was going to be an obvious choice as the next captain, but *he* wasn't ready then, either.

One of the greatest strengths of Yorkshire cricket over a century has been its sense of tradition and that involves, vitally, a sense of continuity. In a couple of years time Geoff – who had always thought deeply about his cricket in the real Yorkshire tradition – would be ready for the captaincy. I had even mentioned to the committee that when it was time to hand over I would be willing to spend a season playing under his captaincy so that there was a helping hand if he needed it. That continuity was going to be destroyed and quite honestly there was no need to indulge myself in false humility – I feared for the effect on Yorkshire cricket. The supporters deserved something better than this. They had been, for more than a century, the most loyal, the most devoted, the most staunch and the most steadfast supporters of cricket anywhere in the world. It mattered to me a great deal that they did not think I had slunk quietly away in the close season and resigned.

But most of all it mattered what might happen to the team. It was *my* Yorkshire as much as the committee's and the chairman's. Brian Sellers had given the greater part of his life to Yorkshire cricket but then so had I. He believed in it and loved it with tremendous passion – but so did I. He had led the county with outstanding success for nine years, but so had I for eight, and was a senior professional for four before that with captains who were not exactly in the Brian Sellers mould. For the first time I began to feel anger as well as sadness. This is not the right way, I thought, for my career with Yorkshire to end. I permitted myself enough pride to feel that I deserved something better than to go out like that. I telephoned Roy Parsons (who had organised my benefit) and he said, 'I think Vivienne is right'. I telephoned Jack Mewies (who apart from being my solicitor is a personal friend who loves cricket) and he went further. He said, 'I wonder if we can stop the committee from issuing that statement and find out why they have done this?' I said I doubted it because of the deadline at two o'clock.

145

It was still only just after noon. It seemed ten years since I had started out for Headingley and that ten-thirty meeting. I tried to 'phone the county office but it was twenty minutes to half an hour before I could get through. They were evidently very busy on the 'phone about something! When I finally made contact I said, 'Mr Nash, it's Brian Close here. I have changed my mind and decided to take the sack instead of resigning.' I am afraid this came as a bit of a shock to the Yorkshire secretary. He stammered and spluttered for quite a time and the first coherent sentence he uttered was to say that he had already issued the statement that I had resigned. It was twelve-forty-five. I said 'But you told me the statement was not going to be made before two o'clock. You had better 'phone everyone you have told and change it.' I put the 'phone down, had a cup of tea and started to pick up the pieces of my life.

The appointments I had changed from that morning still had to be kept. I still had my winter job to do and I try to do every job as well as I can. I still had a wife and family to think about. Life had to go on. My first appointment was in Wakefield and while I was in the office there – less than an hour after leaving home – I had my first intimation of the row that was just beginning to brew, the row that in the first place I thought might be avoided by resigning. My agent rang from London to say, 'Can you come to town? David Coleman wants you to appear on *Sportsnight* tonight.'

I went. I was conscious that I was leaving Viv with the mess because Brian Close has always been an object of some interest to newspapers. And the hordes were gathering at my home.

Over the years one gets to know cricket writers pretty well; some become personal friends. One is accustomed to talking to them. But this sort of mess brings down the newshounds. Now I am sure some of them are perfectly nice chaps with homes and families of their own but their approach is very much an impersonal one. In a context of this kind they have no personal friendships to damage, no professional contacts to alienate. And they all of them have news editors back in the office who don't easily take 'no' or 'no statement to make' for an answer. They simply say 'go back and try again', or 'keep at it until someone says something'. I had rung Viv to tell her that I was going on to London, she had told the news reporters gathered at my home and they, presumably, had told their news editors. The result was an *impasse* at Tong Park. The reporters were parked in my home and there they stayed.

One even wandered upstairs and looked in our bedroom. He came back down and announced to the others, 'He is not away for the night; his pyjamas are still under his pillow.' So they stayed, bolstered by their belief, no doubt, that D. B. Close possessed only one pair of pyjamas! Finally Viv rang my agent to ask his advice and he said, 'Make just one statement to one of them.' I heard it on my car radio as I drove from Wakefield to London. The storm I had dreaded had broken.

A number of Yorkshire members formed an action group aimed at reforming the committee and changing the way things were run. There were meetings and more meetings. Everywhere I went I was asked why I had been presented with the ultimatum and I knew no more than anyone else. But gradually the county were forced to make bits of statements, while pressmen dug more bits from various committeemen until a picture began to emerge. My services were no longer required, it seemed, for three reasons: one, I did not encourage and 'bring on' the youngsters sufficiently; two, I was not fit; three, I criticised one-day cricket. Let me answer each of those allegations in full for the first time – the first time I have had an opportunity to do so.

Among the players I 'did not encourage or bring on' during my captaincy of Yorkshire were Geoffrey Boycott, Jackie Hampshire, Chris Old, Barrie Leadbeater and Geoff Cope. My predecessor as captain had told the committee that Boycott was not good enough and said he should be released! This was put to me in *my* first year as captain and I replied, 'Let me have a season with him before you decide something like that.' They did, and Boycott hasn't turned out to be a bad player, has he?

In April, 1968, I was accused by a Very Great Man on the Yorkshire committee of not giving Geoff Cope a fair chance in the previous season. I was told I had not given him sufficient bowling opportunities to get the experience he needed to become Ray Illingworth's successor. This didn't seem to make sense to me and I thought about it. Suddenly it came to me. I asked the chairman for permission to refute the allegation, and pointed out that during 1967 I had captained

147

England in six Tests against India and Pakistan. That meant I had been away from Yorkshire cricket for thirty days and it was only when I was an absentee with England that Geoff played for Yorkshire, so it was a bit hard to blame me for not bowling him. But – d'you know – Herbert Sutcliffe never ceased to insist that I was unfair to Cope that season!

Chris Old and Jackie Hampshire developed into England players and Barrie Leadbeater was capped by the county and won a Gillette Cup final man-of-the-match award, so I don't think I really held up their progress very much.

Allegation number two – 'not fit'. At the beginning of 1970 I was 50 not out in a championship game at Middlesbrough on the Saturday, then came to Bradford to play in a John Player League game on the Sunday. I had to dive full length to avoid being run out and as soon as I hit the ground I knew something had 'gone'. I got up and found that I could not use my right arm, so I took no further part in either match. After hospital treatment, my arm was put in a sling and I didn't play again for about seven weeks. Now let me make the point again that a captain can have an immense influence on the performance of a side, not just in terms of total scores and the final bowling-out of the opposition but by his use of individual talents. For example, by encouraging those talents when necessary and giving them a rest when they need it or the situation demands it, by relating one talent to another, by having the right fieldsman in the right place at the right time, by having the right bowler operating for a particular batsman, by using any of a hundred subtle ploys in the course of game. I had a pretty fair ability at this sort of thing and if anyone regards it as immodest of me to say so, I'm sorry. But to me it is futile to be self-effacing about something as important as this. The simple fact was that by the middle of the season, after I had been off for seven weeks, we were doing so badly that I had to come back even though – the committee were correct but made their criticism for the wrong reasons – I was far from a hundred per cent fit. I was, in effect, playing with one and a half arms. I couldn't bowl and I virtually hung on to the bat with the right hand, rather than gripping it properly.

At the beginning of July we were down near the bottom of the table. By the third week in August we were in contention for the championship. I'm sure we would have won it too, but for England taking away Chris Old and Don Wilson (bowlers whom I had coaxed and guided nearly to the top of the first-class bowling averages that season) for the international series, England *v* Rest of the World, when political issues so tragically, for cricket, prevented the South Africans from touring. Since we were very short of replacements, their departure left our bowling attack looking pretty sad in some games. I remember one match against a full-strength Northants side that August, when, with Tony Nicholson injured, we took the field with only Richard Hutton, Geoff Cope and a young Colt, Mike Bore, as bowlers. We still made Northants follow on, but the second time round we hadn't enough resources to press the advantage home. At that time, too, Cope was wandering through a nightmare of allegations that he was a chucker.

The committee were right to the extent that I had not been fully fit for most of the season. But I had *become* unfit whilst playing for the side, not through neglecting my fitness, and I played whilst unfit to do what I could to stop the slide. I am more than content to be judged on the results achieved that season when I was playing and when I was not.

Thirdly, one-day cricket. I do not, cannot, never have complained about the financial benefits it has brought to the game. I do not, cannot, never have accepted that its effect upon county championship and therefore Test cricket has been anything but seriously damaging. Whatever criticisms I was accused of levelling at one-day cricket in those days have all been voiced since by just about everyone concerned with championship and Test games, notably the chairman of the Test selectors.

I was told that the committee's resign-or-be-sacked decision was unanimous. Some time afterwards I found myself at a dinner, sitting next to one member, Ted Umbers, who said, 'I am sorry; I did not agree with it.' Another, Desmond Bailey, told me, 'I am sorry. I voted against you but I wish you all the best.'

I said, 'I will tell you this – whatever you were thinking about at the time, it couldn't have been Yorkshire cricket. In the next ten years you will realise your mistake. And you'll know who *was* thinking about Yorkshire.'

It affords me no satisfaction at all to be proved right.

21

VILLAIN...

All through his playing career, Freddie Trueman was credited with making remarks which he never made at all . . . 'Pass the salt, Gunga Din', to a high-ranking West Indian official . . . 'I see you've got your colour back, Colonel', to an Indian manager. At half the cricket dinners one attends, these stupid legends are trotted out as gospel truth by people who have never met Fred in their lives. Lord knows there are enough good, perfectly true stories involving the colourful F.S. to remove any need for inventions. In terms of cricketing crises, I feel a little the same way. If Brian Close was ever in the vicinity of a disaster it was his fault and his alone. If ever there was any question about where blame should be placed, my shoulders provided the most appropriate place for it to be deposited. And, just as with Fred, legends grow, and are repeated over and over again until they become accepted fact. How many people, recalling Old Trafford, 1961, today nod sagely and say, 'Oh yes. That was where Close made an idiot of himself'? A hell of a lot.

Let me take you back now, and tell you about Old Trafford. There I watched a pattern of play develop, analysed it, and, when the opportunity came, tried to do something about it. Let me tell you in detail what I set out to do and why. Let me explain why it didn't come off . . . because the margin between success and failure in a situation like that is so slender. In this case it was about two inches.

The Australians came to Old Trafford at the end of July with the series standing at one-all with one drawn. After a two-year absence, I was back in the side for the Fourth Test and saw our quick bowlers demolish Australia for 190. We gained a first-innings lead of 177.

Geoffrey Pullar started us off with 63 and the middle order all batted well. I had scored 33 when I nicked a ball from 'Garth' MacKenzie on to my pad and was given out lbw. Even Wally Grout sympathised, and Australians are not much given to sympathy in the middle of a Test match! In their second innings the Aussies batted much better, but at 334 for nine they had a lead of only 157. For some reason best known to himself, Peter May took off David Allen (who had taken the last two wickets) as soon as he was hit to the boundary. The wicket, while still in good condition, was turning a little and one couldn't see the last-wicket pair holding out for long in such circumstances. But the quicker bowlers were brought back and Alan Davidson and McKenzie put on 98 for the last wicket. We now needed 256 runs to win, a very different proposition, especially as we now had to fight the clock as well as the opposition.

Ramon Subba Row, who opened with Pullar, was not exactly an exotic stroke-maker at the best of times, and as he had been out for two in the first innings he made an extra careful start. Noddy Pullar scored 26 out of the first 40 and then was caught by O'Neill off Davidson. Ted Dexter came in to play a truly magnificent innings, spraying a series of brilliant shots all round the field. Subba Row was still more or less pushing up and down the line but I suppose at that stage it could be argued that he was playing the sheet-anchor role. Richie Benaud put himself on to bowl at the Stretford end to try to stem the flow of runs. He bowled round the wicket to Subba Row into the fast bowler's rough outside his off-stump. After nearly five days play, this was quite considerable; most of it had been caused by Freddie Trueman's wonderful, flowing, follow-through.

Now at that time, a no-ball was judged off the bowler's back foot alone, and consequently his *front* foot was coming down well in front of the batting crease, and his next two follow-through strides caused patches of wear pretty close to the line of the left-hander's off stump. This was a painful fact of life to any left-handed batsman at that time, and is so even now, though to a lesser extent.

Playing with Yorkshire, Freddie Trueman's follow-through, for instance, caused such problems that I once went something like two years without attempting a cover drive. But back to Old Trafford. Benaud's deliveries leapt out of the rough at Subba Row, coming at all angles, some stopping, some turning, some going on. Subba Row hardly dared to play at the ball, he just shoved his front leg down the wicket to cover up. Meanwhile, normal – over the wicket – deliveries to Dexter pitched on the true surface; Benaud could not stop Dexter making shots at all. Sitting in the pavilion, watching the innings develop, I said to Peter May: 'If we get two left-handers together we could find ourselves in trouble.' He didn't say anything.

Unable to check Dexter's charge (his innings was really getting England back into the game with a chance of winning), Richie suddenly decided to try bowling round the wicket to him too. Richie's record as a Test bowler in England is not particularly impressive, but I hope no one doubts that he was one of the most accurate leg-spinners of all time or that he was one of the shrewdest captains ever to lead Australia. Knowing how captains think, I am pretty sure that he went round the wicket in the first place as a defensive measure. He certainly put the brake on now. Not only was the line of the bowling a difficult one for Dexter but once the ball pitched into the rough it was jumping, turning, rearing and then occasionally shooting straight through. Any shot with the ball pitching there was risky. When Subba Row had the strike he dried up completely and simply took the ball on the pads.

All this time I was watching every ball and again I said to the captain, 'If we get two left-handers together the innings could come to a grinding halt.' He just murmured 'Mm – mmm' but made no further comment and it became increasingly obvious to me that if this happened someone would have to try to manhandle Richie – presumably me. I supposed that if we were still going for a win, we had to work out our own destiny. Mine was that I had to get after Benaud. The chance came fairly quickly. Dexter got into a tangle as Richie pitched yet again into the rough and was caught at the wicket for a brilliant 76. May went in and was promptly bowled round his legs trying to sweep. At 150 for three I was out in the middle and we *had* got two left-handers together. We still needed another 106 and the rate required was 72 an hour. Where did we look to get our runs? Benaud's first ball to me turned and hit the pad, the second turned and lifted and I thought, 'Christ! It's not safe to play a shot at all.' I watched with a certain amount of astonishment as Subba Row

153

pushed back a maiden over from Slasher Mackay. It looked very much as if he was playing for himself. Now that's what I would have liked to have done myself. I had been in and out of the England team five times up to then, playing consecutively in only two of the five Tests. Benaud was the only problem bowler, and if I was thinking of my wicket, I didn't have to play at him so long as I covered properly with my pads. But if I did that, England would lose the slender chance of winning given to us by Ted Dexter's innings. Yes, if I finished the game with a few runs not out, I might even get picked for the final Test. I would have done no wrong. However, my whole upbringing in all sport had been that if you had any chance to win, you pursued that chance to your utmost until it had gone. I thought that if my effort failed, there were still six wickets left. So I made up my mind I was going to attack Richie, and had a very careful look round the field. There was a slip, a square cover, extra cover and deepish mid-off. On the on-side there was a leg-slip, a deep long-leg backward of square, mid-wicket, deep mid-wicket and a deepish mid-on.

Now bear in mind one important factor: the laws at that time limited the number of on-side fieldsmen to five, only two being behind the wicket. Richie had them – the leg slip and the long leg. That was where I decided the runs should come . . . by lapping from outside the off-stump into the ninety-degree area between square-leg and the wicket-keeper. If I had thought I could spare a quarter of an hour or so to settle in and look at things, I would most gladly have done so. But at 72 an hour there simply wasn't time to do that and have any chance of winning. The run-rate would be even higher by that time and, Lord knows, 72 an hour is high enough in a Test innings. I had decided on my policy; now to put it into operation.

If that policy is still not clear, let me make it clear. Offside shots were too risky altogether with the ball lifting, turning, kicking, stopping. If I got across to lap him on to the leg side, behind square, I could not be bowled, I could not be lbw and it was unlikely that I was going to be caught because even if I mis-hit and got a top edge, leg-slip was out of the picture and it was not going to carry far enough to the second fieldsman who was back on the edge. It was a free shot and would get me at least one, perhaps two, or even maybe the odd four.

Richie bowled. He bowled not into the rough but on to the true part of the wicket. I went to the pitch of it, timed it well and it went over the long-on boundary for six. That was a bonus. Richie wasn't going to drop many there. I still had to base my policy on scoring round the corner. He bowled; I played at a couple and got rapped on the pad. That didn't matter. I couldn't be lbw and I wasn't going to be bowled. He bowled again. I got a top edge. Safe. And two runs. (Let me just interrupt myself there to say I know the lap doesn't look a graceful shot even when played well. It is an improvisation. It's a shot for use when more orthodox strokes are out for one reason or another. But it is a very useful shot and one that I have played probably more times than anyone else in the game. All right, I've been out from it. But I've also scored a lot of runs and won matches with it.)

Benaud, naturally enough, saw what I was about and thought about his counter-move. It was like a tremendous game of chess; move and counter-move; my brain against his; my knowledge of cricket against his. He moved his long leg in, almost to the point where he was saving the one, and moved deep mid-wicket a little squarer. Remember, he couldn't be behind square; there were already two fielders in that arc. That was Richie's move. The old brainbox started ticking round again and I reasoned that the ninety-degree area was still my best bet for runs. Only two men covering a big, big area. If I hit it well it would clear Norman O'Neill (who had been brought in); if I got a top edge it would drop fine of him and still clear of leg slip. Benaud bowled and I lapped. I hit it all but well. It was clearing Norman O'Neill when he leapt high into the air, right arm upstretched and stopped the ball with just two fingers. It stuck; I was out for eight. By such slender margins are reputations made or marred. The highest point O'Neill could possibly reach was with those two fingers and the ball stuck. Another fraction of an inch higher and it would have been four; another fraction of an inch nearer the meat of the bat and it would have been four; another yard squarer of the fieldsman (Richie has since said that was actually where he wanted O'Neill) and it would have been four. If I could have done this a few times Benaud would have had three alternatives. One, continuing round the wicket and making more field-changes, e.g. moving back leg slip for the top edge and O'Neill deeper to the boundary, which would have made it safe for me to tickle singles round the corner. Two, going over the wicket and having to bowl on to the unworn part of the pitch – more shots available to the batsman. Three, taking himself off and bringing back a bowler who could not exploit the rough in the same way. Any of those moves would have meant I had won the battle. Norman O'Neill's two outstretched fingers, however, meant I had lost it. But my *policy* was right. It was based on the most careful thought and drew on all my experience.

I can understand members of the public thinking it looked naive and that is why it becomes doubly important for people who should understand such situations to explain them to the lay watcher. Not for one second would I expect a chap who loves cricket but watches it as a straightforward contest between a man with a bat and another with a ball to start going through all the thought processes which I applied. But a batsman doesn't just look round the field in an idle way. If he is doing his job properly he considers all the factors I had to take into account there . . . the condition of the pitch and more particularly the part where Richie was focussing his attention and his attack; the placing of the field in relation to this bowling; the crying need to score runs somewhere and, if possible, to blast Benaud out of the firing-line – that most of all.

I don't regard myself as some sort of unique character in this respect. I expect England captains to think about them, too. I expect former England captains to think about them when they are explaining a situation to millions of listeners all over the world on radio. I specially expect thoughtful appreciation of a tactical situation from a former England captain who is also a former Yorkshire captain and the man in charge of the team where I first began to learn something about the first-class game. But Norman Yardley told BBC listeners that after that shot I ought never to be picked for England again. That hurt and dismayed me most of all. I expect that from people like Jim Swanton (he didn't want me in the England team in the first place) and one doesn't take much notice of that sort of thing (except to deplore the influence men like that are allowed to wield). Norman Yardley's castigation was something entirely different and to this day there must be millions of people whose view of me is based on his spur-of-the-moment judgment which *cannot* have been made with any thought for the problems and requirements of the situation.

Years later Norman wrote a newspaper column saying that if he ever had to pick an England team I would always be his captain. Not many people would see that article. Certainly nothing like the number who heard him on 1 August 1961.

Looking back to Old Trafford, and thinking of the stick I took (as well as disappearing from the Test scene once again) I am moved to ask a few questions:

1. Was Subba Row playing sheet-anchor or playing for himself? I think I know the answer to that one . . .

2. Why were we ever in a position of struggling to win after Australia, with a lead of only 157, had nine wickets down? McKenzie and Davidson wouldn't have continued indefinitely to hit the turning ball from David Allen.

3. Why did no one find it even remotely reprehensible that Peter May should be bowled round his legs playing some sort of upright sweep while it was 'irresponsible' for me to be caught trying to score the runs we needed?

4. Six wickets fell after mine. Had they nothing to do with our defeat?

5. And finally – the most incomprehensible bit of all – why in God's name am I blamed for *losing* the Test? I can understand blame for not winning it but to be held solely responsible for losing it is a bit much, even by the high standards of public pillorying I have come to expect.

Watching our later batsmen play some strange shots and get out I thought, 'No one knows whether we are going for the runs or playing for a draw or what. No one has set any guidelines or laid down any policy.' At least I knew what I was trying to do.

18

...OR HERO?

So after Old Trafford I was out in the wilderness again. Before that Test I had had two years of exile after scoring 27 in my only innings against India at Headingley, taking one for 18 and four for 35 and holding four catches. I can't remember any special accusations levelled against me on that occasion. I was just dropped after a pretty reasonable all-round performance.

Now it had happened again in more spectacular circumstances. How long would it be before the next recall? As it turned out, it was two years – or two seasons, at any rate, until the West Indies arrived for their 1963 tour. They were led by Frankie Worrell, had a very strong batting line-up (apart from trouble finding the right opening partner for Conrad Hunte) and an attack spearheaded by Wes Hall and Charlie Griffith. Let us get that partnership into perspective right away. Wes Hall was a great fast bowler and would have been in any era, but apart from Lord's, all that year's Tests were played on slow wickets and he constituted no particularly terrifying threat. He was good; he bowled well; but he didn't really come into his own except at Lord's. Charlie Griffith was a medium to medium-fast bowler who, it was believed, chucked the yorker and the bouncer.

On a faster wicket with bounce like Lord's that made him a problem. As Lord's was grappling, at the time, with the controversial issue of its 'ridge' there were problems all round. Without any notice until his delivery stride Griffith snarled at you a delivery which was three to four yards faster than the one before. Bowling in his usual way, he had the semblance of an out-swinger and that was all. You felt that you could put one hand in your pocket and play him comfortably. The one he seemed to throw went a bit against the arm and it came roaring at you from a quite different angle. Wes, in contrast, had all the characteristics of the classic fast bowler. He was good to watch with those long strides, accelerating from God knows how far back, arms swinging, and while on the four slow wickets that summer he was not impossible to play comfortably, he did produce one or two beauties. At Old Trafford I remember Colin Cowdrey moving inside the line and losing his leg stump. As a pair, Wes and Charlie were quite a combination.

I had been brought back, I am sure, and played in the whole of that series, because of the influence of Ted Dexter – and, of course, because of the presence of Hall and Griffith! I don't think Dexter and I were on the same wavelength but we had a professional respect for each other. Anyway, I started at Old Trafford on a disappointing wicket. For two days it was flat and uninteresting and the West Indies scored 501 for six declared. Then the pitch started disappearing. Wes and Charlie knocked the top off it and Lance Gibbs cleaned up – five for 59 and six for 98 as we lost by 10 wickets. He got me in each innings (for 30 and 32) and I swore, 'This fellow will never get me out again.' He didn't either, until nearly ten years later when he was with Warwickshire and I was with Somerset. I was trying to knock him out of the game and got one that didn't bounce.

We went to Lord's one down in the series and a serious selectorial mistake resulted in Brian Statham being dropped. Here we were on the one Test wicket with real pace and lift and to partner Freddie Trueman we brought in Derek Shackleton. Shack was a fine bowler of medium-pace seamers – none better – and in the county championship he was one of the most respected opponents throughout his whole career. But Lord's cried out for two great fast bowling partners in harness. We had let the West Indies off the hook before we started.

They won the toss, as they had at Old Trafford, and scored 301. Freddie toiled for 44 overs and took six for 100: Shack toiled even longer – more than 50 overs – and his three for 93 included the last two batsmen. We ended the first innings just four behind after a horrible start in which we lost Mickey Stewart and John Edrich to Griffith for a total of two. West Indies scored 229 in the second innings (Trueman 5-52, Shackleton 4-72) and we needed 234 to win.

We had three down for not very many and Colin Cowdrey in the dressing-room with a broken forearm, fending off a flyer, when I went in. Everybody in both innings had been getting out to balls which flew off 'the ridge' – chest high, shoulder high. But, if the ball pitched just *over* 'the ridge' it was liable to shoot through low. Batting, you might say, was not easy. And then there was Charlie.

In these circumstances, with Hall rather in his element, your first consideration as a batsman was simply survival. With the ball rearing as it was it required intense concentration to keep the bat and hands out of the way of the balls which flew – and there were plenty of them. In the first innings I hit Wes for a cover-driven four and he gave me the stare. We both knew what was coming next and I got into position for the bouncer. Sure enough it came, but it came at a speed which was shattering, climbing like lightning. I was coming through for the hook when suddenly I realised, 'You'll never get there in time.' And then, almost as a terrifying afterthought, 'God, it's coming straight between my eyes.'

I swayed my head away. I'll never know how I got it out of the line in time but I felt the ball tug at my right eyebrow as it went on and up, over Deryck Murray's head to land far, far behind the wicket-keeper. That was Wes Hall on a wicket with pace, bounce and the ridge. At the other end was Charlie. We had problems. As if they weren't enough in themselves, there were several interruptions for rain and bad light with the result that the batsmen had to settle in over and over again whilst every so often Wes and Charlie could put their feet up, have a rest, and then come roaring at us again.

For a time I batted with Ken Barrington who was so often glorified as England's saviour in Tests. He didn't like it much in this one. He backed away, swished at air, carved over the slips and I said to Sid Buller, the umpire, with a wry grin, 'If I batted as badly as Ken is doing now I'd never play for England again.' But he stayed to get 60, somehow or other, and when he was out we were 130 for four. A win was still on, but the difficulty of scoring runs, plus the interruptions, made it something of a tall order. After tea we were not only fighting the opposition but the clock as well. Something had to be done. I decided to try to upset Wes.

Now walking down the pitch to him may have looked a bit dramatic

161

but it wasn't unthinking bravado. Far from it. By getting a long way down I was countering to some extent the effect of the ridge but even more important, I made Wes lose his rag. In he came, all power and fire and fury, and just as he was getting into his delivery-stride he saw me coming towards him. His eyes popped like chapel hat-pegs. He screamed to a halt, clutching his back and groaning. It took a lot of consoling and coaxing and soothing by Frankie Worrell to get him back to the end of that long, long run and start all over again. I had won the round. After that he wasn't quite the same. He was looking for me coming at him. His line and length suffered. But he was still fast and he was still hostile. Only an idiot would imagine that it was going to be easy, even after that. I was hit. I was hit a lot of times. And there was still Charlie lurking around, awaiting his recall. But I scored runs and kept on scoring them until a glance at the clock told me we had about eighteen minutes to score 16 to win. Jim Parks had come and gone for 17, Freddie Titmus for 11 and Freddie Trueman for none and David Allen was with me, doing a fine job of keeping one end propped up. I couldn't expect him to get the runs. He was doing enough simply by staying there. Cowdrey had a broken arm and I didn't know whether he would come out or not. That left only Shack. I had to get those runs.

Eighteen minutes would give us four overs at most at their bowling rate, probably only three. And here came Charlie now. During the whole of that series, whenever a stand looked like developing, on would come C. C. Griffith to break it. It happened time and time again. Still, I had coped with him through the afternoon and I could do it again. What I had to concentrate on now was where to score those 16 runs. Worrell was one of the most astute of all West Indies captains so I had to out-think him as well. I had to break up the pattern of the bowling and find gaps in the field. Most of the fielders were back when I had strike and it wasn't going to be easy to score four an over, especially as I had also to keep in mind shielding Allen from as much of the bowling as possible. I noticed that Rohan Kanhai, who was at mid-wicket, came in a long way to cut off the single so that decided me. If I could pass him as he moved in and get a four through there we could push for the rest. In came Charlie from the Nursery End, the same casual, easy run-up, and then suddenly it was

162

the bouncer. Not only that, but it came up the hill as well like an off-spinner . . . a very, very fast, bouncing off-spinner. I'd set my body in line with the ball so that if I missed it, it would hit my body. I hadn't reckoned for the movement up the slope. The ball just caught the bottom edge and squeezed through between my arm and my body as it screamed up. Murray took the catch twenty yards back and I was out for 70.

Of course that ball was thrown. No one on earth could have bowled at that speed from that approach. We only managed a draw when Cowdrey came back to bat one-handed. But at least I wasn't an irresponsible idiot in the eyes of most sports writers . . . not that time.

19

WE COULD HAVE BEATEN WEST INDIES

The morning of Sunday, 30 May 1976, was a beauty, like most mornings during that golden summer. It felt rather good to be alive as I came downstairs in our hotel in Portsmouth on my way to the ground for the John Player League game with Hampshire. At that moment I had forgotten the Test team was being announced, although I had been thinking about it during the previous few weeks. Just as I was going through the door I was called back to the telephone. It was Brian Scovell of the *Daily Mail* ringing to ask how I felt about being recalled to the England side.

It felt great.

Despite all that had happened I had never really given up hope of being called up again but I didn't expect to be chosen simply as a player. I felt that with a lot of unsatisfactory series and results since Ray Illingworth had been made to pay for, really, just one Test when most of his players let him down, I could be called on to skipper England again. I had never lost a Test as captain and I hadn't a bad record all round as a leader so I always thought there was a chance.

Then, in the past few weeks, particularly since I had made runs against the West Indies at Taunton, there had been a great deal of speculation about my being given another run. Most of it, however, was either disapproving the idea or damning it with faint praise. For some reason which I have never understood one of the pet hobbies of certain newspapers is putting up their own Aunt Sallys so that they can knock them down!

In the meantime Dennis Amiss had been to see me for a bit of advice on how to play really fast bowling and two of the selectors had

165

consulted me on the best way of getting Vivvy Richards out, so it seemed that people really close to the game felt I had something to offer. I felt I could help some of the younger players with advice.

Dennis, for instance, has always been a good player; but he had begun to bat with his arms a little too tightly positioned close to his body, with the result that he was restricting his own freedom of movement, and not getting into position early enough to play his shots, defensive or offensive. We had a long natter and I like to think it played some part in his double century at The Oval, although I noticed there that he had actually exaggerated the movement back and across which I had suggested and, in fact, it got him out in the second innings. But that was *after* he had made a couple of hundred in the first, so it wasn't a bad Test comeback.

Then, the matter of getting Richards out . . . well, it isn't easy at any time but Viv had sort of grown up with me in his first-class career in this country and I felt that if he had a weakness I had a fair idea what it was. So I told the two selectors: 'Get your best left-arm quickie who bowls over the wicket and swings the ball back in at the right-handed batsman.' Well, if you look around English bowling that doesn't leave much margin for error in selection but obviously they didn't take a blind bit of notice. Ken Barrington, however, made damn sure he took John Lever with him to India and there wasn't a batsman anywhere near Viv Richards' class to bowl at there!

Yet I still thought if I was brought back it would be as captain and when Tony Greig was appointed I thought that was it. So it was something of a surprise to see myself in the twelve as a player, but no less a thrill. No matter how many times I have been picked for England, or discarded, it's still a thrill, the anticipation of taking part in the greatest of cricketing occasions.

Generally, the press reaction was either lukewarm or downright critical, so the pressure was on. Once again I was on a hiding to nothing. If I succeeded it would be regarded only as a temporary measure for this series and one which had been introduced only because I didn't get out of the way of fast bowling. If I failed . . . I honestly dare not think of it. I so desperately wanted to do well – desperately, awfully, terribly. My career had to end shortly and after all those years of knocking this was my chance to go out at the top.

No one will ever quite know just how much it meant to me to do well but I think a few people have some idea.

So these were a few of the things going through my mind when the second wicket fell at Trent Bridge; the things I had to clear out of my mind when I took guard. You cannot afford to have intrusive thoughts cluttering your mind when you are batting, still less when you are about to take the first ball from one of the world's fastest bowlers in a Test which means virtually cricketing life or death to you. Have you ever watched a top golfer hover over a vital putt, then walk away and stroll about a bit to clear his mind? It's like that.

So in came Wayne Daniel with the first delivery of my seventh Test comeback, to project a ball a distance of about 20 yards at a speed of more than 90 miles an hour. Work out how much time that gives you to computerise its line, length and ETA, and then transmit the answer to your muscles and reflexes!

Right. Here it comes. Its line is straight, perhaps very slightly middle-and-off, its arrival point is a normal fast bowler's length. My eyes send the message to my brain and that moves arms and legs and hips. I get across, the bat comes down.

Chrrrrist! The ball isn't there. After pitching it has exploded like a rocket off the seam towards the slips. One thought goes through my head: that is one of the three best deliveries I have ever received in my life. The next two weren't bad, either. In fact, after all his trouble with his run-up on the tour, young Mr Daniel managed, for me, to string together three of the best balls he'll ever bowl in close order in his life. I got off the mark and then came another of those magic balls which Fate reserves for me. I had a very close look at it on television that night because I couldn't understand how I missed it (I'd got a touch and had been caught – that's missing it) and it moved so late and so fast that I could scarcely believe my eyes.

But I'd gone, and that meant there was just one chance left.

It was about half-an-hour before lunch on the final day when we lost our second wicket in the second innings, not the best time for a crisis-torn player to face another crisis. I walked out thinking 'This really is it. I can't afford to fail.' Everyone, it seemed, was after my blood. They hadn't wanted me to be picked in the first place and this was a golden chance to gloat. I mustn't fail.

167

And – I could scarcely credit it – Andy Roberts bowled me a ball which, if possible, was even better than the one Wayne Daniel had saved to greet me in the first innings. I froze and somehow avoided following it.

Up in the television commentary box, Jim Laker was enjoying himself with snide remarks which didn't come particularly well from someone, who, great bowler though he was, didn't exactly have the biggest heart of anyone who ever played. In the radio box, Trevor Bailey was saying (with an understanding I didn't really appreciate at the time) that one simply could not expect the reflexes of a man of forty-five to be as smart as those of a chap in his twenties. On reflection I think I was a bit irritated at what I thought was a suggestion that I was not fit, because I was proud of my fitness and how I had come in after almost two days in the field.

Having survived that first one, and I can put it no higher than that, I got off the mark and then things clicked into place. It was a grinding job of saving the game and I don't pretend it was much fun for any-one to watch. But I never missed a ball after that and suddenly it was summer.

At teatime I suggested to the captain that we might play a few shots but he replied: 'No. Get stuck in and stay there.' So John Edrich and I stayed and the Test was saved – not with any great distinction to England, but we hadn't lost. And I had survived another personal crisis.

*   *   *

We could have won the 1976 series against West Indies. That may seem a bit far-fetched in view of the hammering England took in the end, followed by a complete whitewash in the one-day inter-nationals for the Prudential Cup. But let's look, first, at what hap-pened in the five Tests in broad outline. We were never going to win at Trent Bridge after the first day but as it happened, we saved the game fairly comfortably in the end. We had the West Indies on the run at Lord's and if it hadn't rained all day on the Saturday we could certainly have beaten them and, one up in the series, the last three Tests would have taken on an entirely different complexion.

Tony Greig's notorious remark about 'making 'em grovel' turned out to be a sort of battle-cry for the West Indies and their supporters *once they had got in front*, as they did from the moment they won the toss at Trent Bridge. Viv Richards told me, 'That's what made the West Indies into a team for the series. Up to that point we were simply a collection of individuals – but once we had heard about Greig's remark, there was no way England were going to beat us.'

But it could all have been so different. Greggie's remark, taking political and historical considerations into account, turned out to be particularly unfortunate but who am I to talk about unfortunate remarks? Everyone in cricket knew what he meant – that if you get on top of the West Indies the odds are that you will stay on top. It's as simple as that and cricketing history proves the point. The astonishing thing was that Tony, having made his point, made no attempt to drive it home once he got on the field.

According to the newspapers, England had picked a 'defensive' team. The selection of myself, and of John Edrich, was said to be the main evidence for this assertion. Poppycock. I certainly don't regard myself as a defensive batsman and a fair proportion of the criticism that has come my way in Tests has arisen from my *attacking* policies. They can't have it both ways.

In the event, both Edrich and myself were required to play defensive roles on the last day at Trent Bridge, but that was what the situation demanded. That didn't make our selection 'defensive' in policy.

For any side to build a big score in a Test match, someone has to play a long innings. Sometimes a long innings has to be played merely to get a respectable score, or one that is relatively a big score, as we saw Dennis Amiss doing more than once on the 1976-77 tour of India. There was much talk about the need to recall Geoff Boycott when first the Australian, then the West Indian, fast bowlers were scything through the England batting, but surely no one thought this meant we would have seen batting of the Compton-May-Dexter type? Geoff would have been there, if he had been recalled in those two series, as a man capable of playing a long innings against genuinely fast bowling.

That, surely, was the original thinking behind asking John Edrich to open and me to bat at number four against the West Indies. We both had a lot of experience and we both had a fair record against top-class quicks. And we neither of us would get out of the way of their stuff. No. It was on our first day in the field at Nottingham that we went defensive. All right, when Viv Richards is on his way to 200 you are struggling a bit. But he has got to get on his way first, hasn't he?

I've already mentioned the sort of bowler I felt we ought to have had to try to unsettle him early on, but once we had gone into the First Test without John Lever we had to try something else. We didn't. From the moment the West Indies had started to build a big score we went defensive and in no time at all we were ultra-defensive. You don't get world-class stroke-players out by spreading the field and waiting for something to happen. And has anyone yet thought up a better way of curtailing the run-scoring rate than by getting the batsman out?

From early on that first morning we had no close fieldsmen and so, free from any worries about the consequences of a false or edged stroke, the West Indies were always going to have a birthday.

I have always believed in improvising, in trying to make something happen. I believe implicitly in trying to 'pressure' batsmen, whatever the situation. Give batsmen like Richards and Lloyd and Greenidge the freedom of the field and you've had it – in technicolour with stereophonic sound! Pressure them, give them something to think about, and at least you are in with a chance no matter how good the wicket. I can't think of any bowler in the world who wouldn't rather bowl at Clive Lloyd than Geoff Boycott for the first half-hour of his innings. In that period Clive will invariably give you a chance; Geoff will give you none at all.

When young batsmen are trying to establish themselves they have to expect an extra slip and always a short leg to be posted. They know they are being tried and tested. But an established, world-class player doesn't always expect to be crowded. And he finds himself thinking, 'Now what's all this about? I haven't had to cope with this sort of thing for the past five years. What's on?' Once you have got him thinking something *might* be happening that he has every right not to expect, then you've established the bridgehead. In Yorkshire, Ray

Illingworth and I (together with Jimmy Binks as the best man to know what was happening with every ball) used to spend hours working this sort of thing out, and particularly in relation to a specific batsman in action. We would post one fielder, and sometimes more, on the opposite side of the wicket to the one where the ball would go, except by accident; if for just one ball the batsman allowed himself to think one *might* go the wrong way, we were in with a chance. A batsman's experience and knowledge would tell him that it couldn't happen; it was our job to sow the seed of doubt in his mind that it just might. Then he would be thinking irrationally and we had won.

West Indian batsmen especially do not react rationally to pressure. They are natural stroke-players and they love to – seem impelled to – do what comes naturally. We didn't make them think or worry on that first day at Trent Bridge. We gave them the freedom of those wide open spaces and we paid for it.

I was disappointed in Greggie that day. He's a likeable chap; he's a pretty dynamic sort of personality; and I thought that if he was not frightened of getting stuck in and attacking we had a chance of shifting the West Indies for a score which was reasonable from our point of view. As it was, it took me a day and a half to persuade him to put some fielders in close-catching positions. And then eight wickets fell rather quickly.

I was a bit disappointed at not getting a bowl myself, as a matter of fact. Almost everyone else had a go. Just in case I was asked, Alan Knott and I had worked out a little ploy designed, we hoped, to shift Viv Richards – based on the fact that I was his captain in Somerset and that I had been in close touch with him since he first came into English cricket. We reasoned that he would probably treat the first ball with respect, either as a gesture to his skipper or perhaps even with a touch of irony, but would then set out to knock the second one into the middle of the Trent. I was then going to bowl a quick one just outside his leg-stump – not the easiest ball to hit by a batsman advancing to paste you – and Knottie would be waiting for it to catch Viv out of his ground. Well, that was the theory of it. Whether it would have worked we shall never know but it was the sort of thing which, as I have said, was worth a try.

Yes, Greggie disappointed me, but he was learning, as we all go on learning something every day we spend in a cricket field; at Lord's we attacked.

But for that rain on the Saturday – and what a disappointment that was because there is no sight in cricket like Lord's bulging at the seams – we would have won. If we had scored a few more runs on the Monday morning and scored them a little quicker, I think we could still have won. At least with 60 runs under my belt in the first innings and 46 in the second I felt I had now won a personal battle and justified my selection to even the most jaundiced of my critics.

In fact there could have been many more runs. I was feeling really good, feeling happy, enjoying my cricket and Van Holder pulled off a rather startling catch in both innings. Even though the sense of disappointment was great I didn't think twice about hoodoos and jinxes at that point. I suppose I did allow myself the luxury of a feeling that if a fielder brings off one brilliant catch in a day it has to be me on the receiving end. But all in all I thought I'd done a fair job in both playing a longish innings and getting some runs. Little did I know what was to come at Old Trafford. (See first chapter – *The End . . . and The Beginning.*)

20

THE BALL OF FIRE

Wisden 1950 records that in a match at Cambridge University the previous season 'Yorkshire gave a trial to three young players: Lowson, an opening batsman; Close, an all-rounder; and Trueman, *a spin bowler.*'

I have tidied up *Wisden's* deplorable punctuation in this particular passage but the slight error of fact remains to delight posterity. Freddie, I'm sure, can never have seen it or libel writs would have been flying thick and fast. To call him anything in the world but *a fast bowler* would be to him the ultimate heresy. And no one who knows him would argue with that. Fred, from the first moment I set eyes on him, radiated the hostility, the disregard for the views or comfort of others, that were his trademark throughout an incredibly long (for a fast bowler) and historic career. There will never be another like him, not only because the game has changed so much, but because I cannot see any county – not even Yorkshire – producing a bowler who combines natural strength and fitness with a perfect delivery stride and action.

For much of my career with Yorkshire I had a love-hate relationship with Freddie. He was a truly great bowler when he wanted to be. For sheer artistry in moving the ball at tremendous pace I can rate only Ray Lindwall with him and Ray didn't have Fred's 'beastliness'. There was a ruthlessness, a callousness about his permanent warfare with batsmen which underlay all his clowning and his wisecracking. No matter how much chat went on between the overs and in the dressing-room, once he started on that smooth, accelerating run to the wicket, he meant business. And his business was getting batsmen out: when he wanted to do so.

Peter Parfitt tells how, as a young batsman with Middlesex, he tried to hook Freddie, but ended up splattering his own nose and most of his mouth all over his own face. After retiring to the dressing-room for repairs his captain sent him out again at the fall of the next wicket. As he approached the middle, he was surprised to find Freddie approaching, and, with the appearance of solicitude, asking: 'Are you all right, son?' 'Yes, thank you, Fred', replied 'Parf'. 'Why do you ask?' 'Oh, it's just that they don't usually come back when I've hit 'em', said Fred, before retiring into the middle distance to release a bouncer at the wounded warrior.

Peter Wight, the Guyanan batsman who played with Somerset and is now a first-class umpire, regularly used to score 2,000 runs a season against every bowler in the country – except F.S. He'd score centuries off men like Peter Loader, who was not the most pleasant of customers when he wanted to be unpleasant; off Brian Statham in his heyday; off Trevor Bailey, Terry Spencer, Butch White. But if he got double figures with Fred in action you could be certain that it included a couple of involuntary fours through the slips.

On the celebrated occasion in 1962 when Vic Wilson, Yorkshire's skipper, sent Freddie home for being late on parade at Taunton for the start of our game against Somerset, Peter Wight fielded all day Saturday with ill-disguised impatience. This was his chance to get runs against Yorkshire and he couldn't wait to take it. In fact, he had to wait two days, because we batted all day Saturday on a beautiful wicket and scored 323. On the Sunday – what a good day it used to be before the introduction of the John Player League – Peter went off to a benefit match at Portishead to get himself 'in nick'.

On the Monday morning, our left-arm fast bowler, Mick Cowan, who certainly wasn't slow, removed Graham Atkinson, caught behind for 12 and then had 'Chico' Roe caught at slip for 14. That brought together Wight and Bill Alley. We missed the usual colourful dialogue between Freddie and Bill which customarily continued throughout the Australian's innings, with frequent invocations of the copulative verb, but we couldn't worry much about that as the score went up and up and up. They put on 186 together and as Cowan – like Tony Nicholson, his partner, he had a great big heart – tried harder and harder to pound some life out of the pitch, Peter's high-pitched voice could be heard all over the ground offering advice to his partner, 'Hook him, Alley. Hook him.' The exasperated Cowan snarled at him, 'You hook me, you ———. Let's see if you hook me next time you are down that end.' Peter arrived at the other end. Mick summoned up the last dregs of strength and energy and hurled a ferocious bumper straight at the batsman's throat. It was still rising as it cleared the fences round the ground. Peter Wight scored 215 that day and we trailed by 174 on the first innings. That's what it meant to him to have Fred Trueman out of the Yorkshire side.

The skipper wasn't very popular in our hotel that night. We had won the county championship in 1959 and 1960, but in 1961 we had only been second and that, to Yorkshire cricket-lovers in those days, was failure. So it had become all the more important to win in 1962 and the dropping of Fred, in our eyes, was a major tactical error no matter how great the magnitude of his sins. As a matter of fact Vic Wilson had had a word with me in the morning when Fred was late and said, 'He's been late so many times – I'm fed up. I am thinking of leaving him out.' I told him, 'Well, that's your decision but you should have thought about disciplining Fred when you took over three years ago.'

Nevertheless, I was shortly to find that he could be a real trial to his captain because I took over that job the following season. I had, on many occasions, suggested to Vic Wilson that he was bowling Fred for too long. Ronnie Burnet, his predecessor as captain, did the same thing. They both seemed to think that F.S. was the only bowler who could win matches for us. The result was he had sometimes been bowling for 30 overs in a day on a pitch that gave him no help at all. In short, he had been bowled into the ground on occasions.

Freddie, like the great bowler he was, had learned to bowl within himself and sometimes he was simply running in and turning his arm over. Then towards the end of the day, he would suddenly start bowling really fast. This wasn't just an accident or something brought about by a change in atmospheric conditions. It was that Fred knew there wasn't much point in killing himself by bowling flat out on a slow wicket against top-class batsmen; but when we got near to the end of a day the opposition would be trying to push things along, perhaps with lesser batsmen, and giving more chances. That was his chance to come into his own.

175

Now that is not to say for one second that Freddie just jumped in when there was a chance of easy pickings. Not at all. His fabulous record shows that, and he was better at knocking down numbers one, two, three and four than any other bowler in his day. But a county championship season covers an awful lot of days and on many of those days there are long periods when even the best fast bowler in the world is not going to be effective. That is when a captain has got to try to 'fiddle' something, to contrive something.

It took me nearly a year to convince Fred to accept that he was going to be a better bowler and a more useful bowler to the side if he was used in short spells. Like most bowlers he *liked* bowling and he most of all liked taking wickets. With classic over-simplification he reasoned that he couldn't take wickets if he wasn't bowling. Ergo – Fred wanted to be bowling.

He could, of course, be highly temperamental if he didn't get his own way. He never hid his feelings – he would moan and groan and sulk. We went to Scarborough for The Festival at the end of the 1964 season with Freddie needing, I think, just three wickets for his 100. After The Festival we were all going off to Canada, the United States and Bermuda for a tour which promised to be rather a super holiday for us all. We started at Scarborough by scoring 353 for eight declared against MCC and when they went in, Brian Bolus went for five, Keith Fletcher for one (c Binks b Trueman) and suddenly they were 16 for two. Festival matches are, of course, entirely different from county championship games, and the crowds come in for sheer cricket entertainment. This looked like developing into a follow-on by MCC and no one in the ground on the last morning – if it went that far. So I said to Freddie, 'Have a rest. It's going to be over in two days at this rate.' He blew up. He had bowled only nine overs and was getting into his stride. He had got one wicket and he only wanted two more for his 100. I was the biggest so-and so on earth . . . and so on.

I put on Ray Illingworth and Don Wilson with a brief to bowl reasonably but not to worry if a few runs were scored. By setting non-attacking fields (and on a wicket which wasn't much use to spinners, anyway) we let MCC avoid the follow-on while Fred languished at deep fine leg, expressing colourful views on the captaincy to anyone who came within earshot. At one stage, half the team couldn't field for laughing.

Finally, when MCC had reached 183 for eight I called down to the boundary, 'Come on, Fred. Finish it off.'

'Bollocks', he roared back. 'Stick your so-and-so ball. I'm not bloody bowling.'

'Fair enough', I said. 'Take your sweater off again, Illy.'

Ray came back, fizzed out Don Brennan and Butch White in three deliveries and F.S., still muttering darkly, clumped back with us to the pavilion.

There, the tickets had arrived for the trip to America and I started passing them out in alphabetical order. When I got to 'T' and called to Freddie he blasted back, 'Stick it. I'm not bloody well going.'

There was only one way to deal with F.S. in that mood. 'All right, Freddie. Sleep on it and let me know definitely in the morning, will you? If you are not going I'll have to get a replacement and he'll have to get a visa right quick.'

That evening the Ford Motor Company, who were one of our principal sponsors for the tour, gave a reception at the Grand Hotel and I saw Freddie take Geoff Boycott (who was the most junior player, then) on one side and give him a right ear-bashing. As a matter of fact, Boycs always had his own share of problems of one sort and another so I think they gave each other an ear-bashing which wouldn't suit Fred at all. He always liked an audience to listen with respectful attention, and completely accept his point of view. He came in next morning, and graciously agreed to accompany us. And he got his two wickets.

But what a great bowler. What a great character. In some ways he was at his most entertaining when he was moaning because his terminology was so colourful and some of his claims so outrageous that one just could not help laughing. He loves to tell wildly exaggerated stories about my driving, along with a mutual friend of ours. Most of them are not true but they make such good tales that I actually enjoy listening to them myself. In fact for my testimonial brochure with Somerset I persuaded the two of them to contribute an article incorporating some of the stories.

In his very first game for Yorkshire, a catch went straight to

Freddie and he tried to take it with hands held like a crocodile's jaws. It went through, hit him on the chest and dropped to the ground. At the end of the over Norman Yardley said very quietly, 'What happened to that then, Fred?' Without a second's hesitation came the reply: 'That bugger hit it with a bloody steel bat.'

That is the first recorded instance of a Trueman instant epigram. There were so many more to come over the years, giving as much amusement to his circle as his bowling gave pleasure, indeed delight, to everyone who was not actually facing it.

17

VIVIENNE

It is not generally known that Gary Sobers has played cricket for Yorkshire. He did, in 1964, and he loved it. It is even less well-known that Gary would have liked nothing better than to play regularly for Yorkshire and that when first Lancashire, then Notts were trying to lure him from his club professional post in Staffordshire, he delayed signing as long as possible in the hope that Yorkshire would break with their long tradition of 'home-grown' players and invite him to join them.

During the summer of 1964 I had been talking to Gary about one thing and another and I suggested that he play for Bermuda against us while we were on tour. He grinned, and said 'I'm not playing against you buggers out there on the matting wickets. But I'll play *for* you.' He did – and he enjoyed it. I'm not sure that the ghost of Lord Hawke would enjoy it quite so much but it was not only a privilege to watch a great player like Garfield St Aubyn Sobers in action; it was a sheer delight to take part in a game of cricket which involved him. To dig up a tired old cliché, he was truly one of the great gentlemen of cricket. We have been friends for many years and I have only known him be really upset once – by the delaying tactics of Colin Cowdrey in the West Indies on the 1967-68 tour. The irony of this did not escape me. At the time I was in the West Indies as a newspaper-observer because, as you will remember, I had been sacked from the England captaincy for allegedly using delaying tactics in a game between Yorkshire and Warwickshire!

We started the tour in New York, moved on to Toronto and Vancouver, then down to Los Angeles where we played on the ground named after that epitome of the English gentleman on the silver screen, Sir C. Aubrey Smith. Then it was back to New York and finally to Bermuda, where Gary joined us. It wasn't a pushover because the opposition all wanted to do well against us. They had some useful players and the umpire looked their way once or twice so it was a good contest. But before the cricket started we had a rest day which most of us spent at the Breakers Beach Club. I was a bit weary. It had been a hard season; I had done most of the organising of the tour myself and throughout I was determined that the team would uphold the good name and dignity of Yorkshire cricket, both on and off the field.

I was lounging about the Beach Club one day, relaxing just before lunch, when I met a very attractive BOAC hostess called Vivienne. We chatted for bit and then she said, 'I'm going for a swim. Are you coming?' Freddie Trueman read a bit more into the situation than I did – and indeed more than there was – so he followed us down to the sea. But he's not a great man for swimming, so when we ploughed out, Fred went back to the club.

After the swim, Vivienne and a friend of hers joined the team for lunch. The rest of the afternoon passed cheerfully and quickly – we had had a hectic trip, and a bit of relaxed female company was more than welcome. I had noticed, I suppose with some disappointment, that Vivienne was engaged, so treading carefully I told her that the team had been invited to a reception at the Governor-General's residence that evening, and I asked her if she would like to come along as my guest. She said 'I'll see'. Obviously I couldn't pick her up because I had no car, and in any case I had to lead the team to Government House. But to my delight she arrived during the evening. She mixed marvellously with everyone and she had a tremendous sense of fun. I took her to dinner.

After the meal I said: 'Look, I'm sorry. I know you are engaged but *I* am going to marry you.'

'Don't be so stupid', retorted Vivienne.

Well, I suppose there have been more romantic proposals, and certainly there have been more encouraging receptions of proposals; but by that time I was hooked. She wouldn't give me her 'phone number when she left the Island a couple of days later, and she said that was it. We had had a very pleasant and perfectly innocent acquaintance for a few days in Bermuda but now we each went back to get on with our own lives.

Not me. When we reached London I ferreted out Viv's 'phone number from BOAC and stayed on to watch the Piccadilly Match-Play Championships at Wentworth. I rang her and eventually she agreed to see me. We went to a performance of the Black and White Minstrel show. The Black and Whites have always had a strong link with cricket and many cricketers have enjoyed close friendships with them. Philip Sharpe and Don Wilson, for instance, used to do a whole Black and White's routine lasting about half-an-hour with every word and every gesture (if not every note) an exact copy. After the show Viv and I went to have a chat with Tony Mercer and Leslie Crowther and then to dinner.

After the meal she said, 'Let's be clear about this. It's the last time you see me.' I suppose that was clear enough for anyone. Not me. I sent her an Andy Williams record, *Can't Get Used to Losing You*, and I kept on 'phoning her.

We were married at Viv's home in Ottery St Mary, Devon, in March 1965. That was the best thing that ever happened to me.

Five years later came the worst thing ever – the summary and, to me, incomprehensible, dismissal by Yorkshire – and that led to another of those strange ironies which are scattered so liberally through my career. I joined Somerset and spent my summers largely in Taunton, twenty or thirty miles from Vivienne's home in Devon; while she remained in Yorkshire with our two children, Lynn and Lance, amongst my relatives and my roots. That, together with various accidents of circumstance which have decreed that the name Brian Close should never be out of the headlines for long, has not made life easy for my wife. Very rarely is the telephone silent for long. Apart from all the 'outside' calls, we have conducted most of our life over it between April and September. Never have Viv's great qualities of adaptability been more valuable.

Fortunately – I should say 'thank God' – our friends did not share the Yorkshire committee's disapproval of me and the West Riding remains my home. When my testimonial with Somerset came round I had several offers of help within my native county and they created a problem. Jackie Hampshire was Yorkshire's beneficiary in the same year and naturally I wasn't going to do anything to take one ha'-penny from Hampers. Yet how did I explain this to friends who wanted to help me?

I wrote to Jack and we sorted things out between us, but that did not prevent an intervention of cheap pettiness from the Yorkshire headquarters. I was saddened more than angered.

That Somerset testimonial meant that I was away from home more than ever in 1976. Before cricket started I was organising events; at the end of the season I was going around making personal appearances and trying to thank all the people who had given a hand. And – again, thank God – what a lot of people there were to thank. If 1976 did nothing else for me it made me realise how good it is to have friends and a family.

Retirement has enabled me to have a little more time to do jobs around the house, because as I have said, having a home in Yorkshire whilst spending most of the summer miles away meant seeing very little of my family between April and September. I promptly set out to decorate the dining room and applied three rolls of wallpaper – the stuff with the relief, or roughened, effect. It looked fine and I was rather proud of it. Then it was pointed out to me that I had put it on the wrong way round, or back-to-front!

At least I see more of the children than I have ever done which is important at a time when they are growing up. Lynn is going through a 'horsey' period, potty about ponies and riding, and is generally interested in wildlife and biology so that at various seasons I tend to find tadpoles in the marmalade jar or conkers under my cushion.

I think the most impressionable moment of Lance's life so far has been his visit to Buckingham Palace when I received my CBE in 1975. He was absolutely fascinated by the Guards, couldn't take his eyes off them, and has been a bit military-minded ever since. From the investiture I went straight to Weston-super-Mare for the Cricket Festival, and, after reading the notes which accompany the Order, I told him, 'When anything happens to me, you can have this.' 'What is it?' he asked. 'Well, it shows that I am a Commander of the Order of the British Empire.' So Lance spent that evening going round our friends in the lounge of the Atlantic Hotel, Weston, showing them the cross on its pink ribbon and telling them, 'My daddy's a Commando. And when anything happens to him, this is mine.'

I was proud and delighted to be honoured, yet like most Yorkshire-men I have always felt it strange that Freddie Trueman has never figured in a Birthday or New Year's Honours list. He has been the greatest fast bowler of my time. His performances were fantastic; as an entertainer on a cricket field in every way he had no peer. His 'services to cricket' have been perhaps more substantial than anyone else's in my day, yet they have never been recognised by an award.

22

BLOOD AND TEAS

I have talked about close fielding and its purpose; it does, of course, carry with it certain risks. I didn't spend most of my playing career standing very close to the bat without taking a knock or two. Not all bowlers drop every ball precisely where they (and you!) wish; not all batsmen are willing to be intimidated and driven into their shell. And I suppose that over the years I have taken my share of stick, not only from West Indian fast bowlers but from county batsmen, too. Three or four incidents stand out.

One, which has become an after-dinner joke in many speakers' repertoires, happened against Gloucestershire when Martin Young hit a ball on to my forehead at short-leg and was caught out by Philip Sharpe at slip off the rebound. At Gravesend I took one on the head from a full-blooded clout by Alan Brown, Kent's big fast bowler (who could tonk it a bit) and the ball dropped just short of the boundary. Perhaps the fiercest blow from a cricket ball came at Portsmouth where we had been held up by rain in a match which we badly wanted to win. (Come to think of it, was there ever a game we didn't badly want to win?) We had been helping the groundstaff to mop up so that we could get on with the game but when we finally resumed the out-field was still very wet indeed so there was little or no run on the ball. Naturally, we were crowding the batsmen and Richard Gilliat hit one straight into my face and it ricocheted away across the sodden grass. They ran *three* while it was being retrieved. At Hull, we were in the last half-hour of a game with Surrey and Don Wilson was bowling to Younis Ahmed. He got a juicy half-volley on his legs and swept it with a full flow of the bat and the ball hit me full on the shin. It was painful yes, and I hopped a bit but when I was ready for the next ball and it didn't come I turned round and snarled at Wils, 'Get on with it. We've only a few overs left.' But Don was looking down at my leg. 'What about that?' he gulped. And then I saw that blood was seeping through my flannels and running down into my boot. We got on with the game.

Now this is not bravado. It is not told for any purpose other than to illustrate my whole philosophy of cricket. While there is a chance of winning a game, nothing . . . *nothing* . . . should be allowed to get in the way. I seem fated to be in the flight of a ball of one sort or another. Within a few weeks of retiring from first-class cricket I was playing in a pro-am golf tournament at Cambridge.

My pro partner was Bob Charles, from New Zealand, the world's greatest left-hander, and the four was completed by two amateur left-handers, one of them the captain of the club. I was hitting it well and enjoying myself until we were about seven holes out and I had moved a little ahead of one of my amateur partners who was playing his second shot with a fairway wood. I was walking along the semi-rough, well out of line (or so I thought) admiring the view, when he dragged his shot and the ball hit me behind the left ear from a distance of about twenty yards. Just what is the velocity of a golf ball, struck by a wood from twenty yards, I wonder? It rebounded straight back over the player's head . . . he played his next shot further away from the green. I dropped a shot or two after that and my partners kept looking at me. I suppose they thought I should be dead, but then one or two batsmen over the years have thought that, too.

Against Gloucestershire at Harrogate I was fielding at silly point to Ron Nicholls when Don Wilson dropped one short. (I don't know why I like Wils!) Nicholls square cut hard into the covers. The ball cracked me over the left eye and careered towards third man. As I remember it I played hell with third man for not trying to catch it, and after a few 'friendly' words of advice to the bowler about the importance of line and length I got down for the next ball. But I couldn't see because blood was running into my eye and down my shirt. It must have looked pretty gory from the spectators' point of view because George Allcock, our physio, came dashing out with towels to mop up the mess.

So I suppose I deserved to be regarded as a bit of a character in cricket. I am not going to admit to eccentricity because that depends on one's viewpoint. But I will concede that I am an individualist. My favourite drink when I am really thirsty is a cup of tea – well, a pot of tea. One cup is just an appetiser! 'Closey's pot of tea' in the dressing-room had become a standard requirement on all county grounds by the time I retired and I had just about got them all trained. Playing in South Africa with Derrick Robins' touring side I decided to develop this a bit further by having a teapot and cup brought out during the drinks interval and the idea caught on with some of the side. Graham Roope became very keen on it but I don't think he has managed to persuade them at The Oval yet to let him have tea instead of orange juice when he's playing at home. However, I can tell him it is possible. During my last game in county cricket, two of our players were off the field with injuries and I wasn't especially pleased about it. So I sent a message to the dressing-room: 'Tell those two lazy so-and-sos, to bring out some drinks – and a pot of tea for me.' And I got it.

One of the strongest personalities in cricket in my time was Wilf Wooller, a great Welsh international rugby threequarter and a tough all-rounder who captained Glamorgan, afterwards becoming the county secretary.

Somerset were playing Glamorgan in Cardiff. After a rain-interrupted first day, I decided to bat on into the second afternoon's play. Now that might savour slightly of using a sledgehammer to crack a nut, but it was my job as the Somerset skipper to win the game if I possibly could and in all the circumstances that seemed the best way of doing so. It outraged Wilf, who, as the Glamorgan secretary, seized the microphone and, over the public address system, addressed the crowd thus: 'In view of Somerset's negative approach to this game we are willing to refund the admission money of any spectator who wishes to call at the county office.'

Well, all hell was let loose at once. I heard the announcement with a bit of a grin. I knew Wilf and he knew me. But the press, TV and radio were on to it like a dog after a rabbit. We were both interviewed extensively and that evening, as Wilf and I stood in the bar having a drink together, the newspaper presses and the radio and TV channels were churning out the latest episode in the storm-tossed career of D. B. Close. I had the last laugh twice over (a) because Somerset beat Glamorgan by an innings and (b) because I picked up about sixty pounds in interview fees and Wilf, who had started it all, got, I think, three pounds, because he was and is a regular broadcaster in Wales and he was expected to give the interviews as part of his normal duties! He knew what he was doing when he made the announcement, too. There were only about forty people in the ground and as most of them were county members not many refunds were called for!

But when it comes to personal eccentricities, then once again it must be F. S. Trueman who takes the prize. *Wisden* records that he started his cricketing life with the date of birth: 6 February 1931. That makes Freddie eighteen days older than me, and that's right. At the end of his career, *Wisden* was still recording the year of his birth as 1931. But have a look at your *Wisdens* of the early sixties, and you will find that suddenly Fred was born on 6 February 1932. Yes, in mid-career, Fiery managed to persuade *Wisden* that he was actually a year younger than their records showed, impelled, no doubt, by a touch of vanity which decreed that he couldn't really be the world's greatest when he was getting a bit long in the tooth. If only he could have seen that the continued excellence of his bowling as the years went by made him even greater. He was not, however, able to persuade the Yorkshire secretary that he was some kind of changeling; the year of his birth in county records was inflexibly chronicled as 1931!

23

TOURING

My first tour abroad – to Australia in 1950-51 – brought professional disappointment and personal misery. My second started with boredom, developed into hilarity which provoked, as near as makes no difference, an international incident and ended with a demonstration of the extraordinary influence sport can assert in the most delicate of situations.

When the MCC 'A' team visited Pakistan in 1955-56, the Muslim state which, geographically, was part of the Indian sub-continent, was in the first decade of its existence. It was still struggling to find an identity which was not simply religious and political. It was not the ideal spot for a tour by high-spirited and lively young Englishmen. The Pakistanis tried, and tried hard, to entertain us in off-duty moments. They showed us their new dams and their monuments to national heroes like Jinnah and Liaquat Ali Khan. They took us hunting. But their hotels were not yet up to western standards and the food was strange in the extreme to most of us. The basic facilities which we needed to combat natural home-sickness were just not there.

In consequence, we had to a very large extent to make our own entertainment. This involved a good deal of what, I suppose, was schoolboyish horseplay. Once, we were accommodated in two separate establishments and this led to raids upon each other. We'd find ourselves locked out if we left our quarters unguarded, with precious supplies of western food being knocked back by the opposition whenever they could get their hands on it. Looking back more than twenty years I can still smile at the memory of those juvenile capers because I think of them in context and at the time they were very important to us as a means of keeping up morale. Nothing is better for the flagging spirit than a good laugh and we made sure, in our own way, that the laughs kept coming.

We had our own particular villains and as the cricket part of the tour developed the greatest of these became an umpire called Idris Beg. He seemed to be officiating in every other game we played and there was a never-ending string of strange lbw decisions against us. When he was not 'standing', Idris always seemed to be around, his picture in every newspaper account of every social event. We turned him into a sort of masochistic joke – 'old Idris' became a catch-phrase which was worked into nearly every conversation, no matter what the topic.

Then at a place called Sialkot, our larking about began to take a definite pattern. As a Muslim country, Pakistan was basically 'dry' but in Sialkot our host managed to organise a fair amount of hooch. I remember it was there that I first drank whisky. But the fun really started when Billy Sutcliffe walked up behind Ken Barrington and held a half-pint of beer over his head. We thought at first it was just a gesture, but then Billy slopped the whole lot over Ken. Barrington reacted in an entirely predictable way and from glasses of ale the ammunition grew in volume to buckets of water. In no time at all everyone was roaming the gardens with supplies of water in whatever receptacle he could find, stalking everyone else, and more particularly those who had not yet had 'the water treatment'. Tony Lock had gone to bed, but he was dragged out with the ultimatum: 'Either you come out or you get soaked there.' He got soaked anyway and pretty soon the only two left who had escaped were Jim Parks and myself. I'm not sure how Jim kept clear but I climbed a tree and sat there for about an hour and a half, watching everyone else stalking through the gardens down below, with water being splattered everywhere.

'The water treatment' became an established part of our off-duty routine. When we got to Peshawar it had developed on parallel lines with our irritation directed at Idris Beg. So a little plot was hatched. Two huge cauldron-like vessels were filled with water and placed high in the ceiling, near the sky-lights, and at close of play Idris was invited to our hotel for a friendly drink and chat. He declined, so after a sort of council of war at our place we all set off up to the Pakistani team's hotel (where Idris was always to be found – we felt he even sat in on their team-talks!) in horse-drawn tongas, having a race en route. Once there, we dismissed three of the tongas and retained one and then I don't know what got into us: Idris came out through the door, taking a stroll in the evening air or something, and we grabbed him. With Roy Swetman and I hanging on to the shouting and bawling Idris the tonga careered back to our hotel with the rest of the party running behind. As the circus left the hotel the *chowkidars* (watchmen) rushed out to be greeted by a laughing, shouting, motley collection of tourists (who reassured them 'it's only the MCC' – one shudders to contemplate how this would have been regarded in NW1) and one highly-indignant, and not a little alarmed, Pakistan umpire.

Once inside our hotel we set out to placate Idris, explaining that it was just a bit of a lark and we really wanted him to have a social sort of evening with us.

Idris seemed to be accepting the situation but all the while was gently sliding towards the door. Suddenly he made a bolt for it, pursued by our skipper, Donald Carr, and myself. The skipper it was who flattened Idris with a flying rugger tackle in the gardens. The victim was hauled back into the hotel and placed in the seat designated in advance as his. And again we addressed him with assorted blandishments, the most potent of which was that we only devoted this sort of attention to the really top people – like Frank Chester. As Frank was renowned as the best umpire in the world, this seemed to impress Idris more than anything and he settled down. Donald Carr brought him over a glass of water, explaining the while that Frank Chester had been not only a willing but, indeed, a grateful recipient of 'the treatment'. That was the signal for Swetman and I, up on the skylight. We up-ended our cauldrons and Idris was directly on the receiving end. He was soaked, his hair plastered down, his clothes oozing rivulets of water over the floor. He didn't look too good.

So we weighed in with the tributes: 'You took that well, Idris. You are one of us, now. You and Frank Chester.' We didn't quite give him honorary membership of MCC but it was getting on that way. All would probably have been well if a couple of the Pakistan players hadn't got wind that something was happening. Just when everything was getting nice and matey with Idris, a couple of them came through the door, took one look at their umpire, and burst out laughing. That did it. Idris – shades of Frank Chester or not – had lost face with his countrymen. He stormed off.

Well, there was hell to play. Apparently Idris went back and claimed that he had been kidnapped, beaten up, had whisky forced down him – the lot. The Pakistan newspapers got hold of the story, and as soon as they were on the streets next morning, the MCC party were involved in a state of emergency. Lorry-loads of troops descended on us to guard the hotel. Peshawar is very close to the north-west frontier where the local populace has always been rather independent in its thinking, shall we say, and I suppose anything could have happened. Next day was a rest day in the match and I remember playing golf with some of the other lads, six armed soldiers walking fifty yards behind. Idris played it up to the full, making his next public appearance in a dressing-gown (as if fresh from a hospital bed) with one arm in a sling. He was now a national figure. (If we had only known the furore back home we would have realised he was an *international* figure!)

Even so, we were acutely aware that things were a bit dicey. I don't think many of us realised just *how* dicey. Few of us had spent much time away from England before. Even fewer had spent much time in a new, sensitive, even touchy State. It was difficult for us to realise that indulgence in what was to us perfectly normal, if admittedly boyish, horseplay, had touched the national pride of an entire nation in a tender spot. Frankly, it was difficult to suppress a giggle at being escorted to a cricket match by armed soldiery.

Everything was resolved in the most extraordinary fashion. For our next game we were centred on the Pakistan Air Force College and because it was known that a few of us played football, we were challenged to a game which we won eight-nil. Maurice Tompkin, Alan Watkins, the skipper, and myself had all played football at a decent level and quite a few of the others were useful performers. So we were then challenged by the national champions, Multan. The match was not going to be easy to fit into our schedule, but it seemed to be good public relations because our previous game had re-orientated to some extent the publicity we had been receiving. Idris Beg's injured pride paled a little beside the prospect of the national champion soccer side cutting down these high-spirited visitors. All depended on when our cricket match finished – and in the event it was over just after lunch on the third day. As we walked off, hundreds of coolies walked on. Almost by the time we had reached our coach the cricket ground had been transformed into a football pitch – markings, posts, flags, the lot. So after a short break, out went the football XI in the hottest part of the day. At half-time we looked like the survivors of the Grand National, lathered up to the eye-balls. Without pausing to reflect that it might reawaken memories of recent incidents, Alan Moss and the other non-footballers lined up buckets of water on the touchline and gave us all the water treatment. Never was it more welcome. Thirty thousand cheering Pakistanis saw us beat their champions two-nil and applauded us off the field. That must have been a unique occasion – footballers restoring the prestige of cricket hooligans! We went to Karachi and won our last (cricket) game there . . . I wonder what happened to Idris Beg, folk-hero and martyr?

My next tour was an entirely different affair. In 1967, having lost the England captaincy and thus the privilege of leading the team on the tour to West Indies, I was commissioned to cover that tour for the *Sunday Mirror*, with an article a week for the *Yorkshire Evening Post*, and I was to write a book at the rate of five to six hundred words a day on the cricket as it happened. Also I did a certain amount of writing and broadcasting within the islands themselves. With me went Peter Smith, to hold my hand in journalistic terms. Such an assignment was a new experience altogether and I found it interesting and enjoyable, but at the same time frustrating – because I very badly wanted to be out in the middle.

In the West Indian newspapers I was asked to make one or two predictions about the cricket and the players, and it is with some pleasure that I record only one of those predictions as going wrong. It was made after I had watched Rohan Kanhai batting with new-found concentration and resolution in the First Test in Trinidad. I then forecast that he would score more runs in the series than any other West Indian batsman. I was wrong because Gary Sobers scored a double century in the last Test and pipped Rohan by two runs! The worst part of my job was watching England play such bloody awful cricket and not being able to do anything about it. I played quite a bit of golf with Gary between Tests and I knew just how fed up he was at the way we played, but the worst thing of all was the way we slowed down the games to an absolutely funereal pace. That was dreadful in itself, but to me it was anathema in view of the fact that I had been deprived of the captaincy as a direct result of, allegedly, slowing down Yorkshire's game with Warwicks at Edgbaston the previous season. Our over-rate in that game was greased lightning compared with England's on that tour. And I had to sit in the press box and listen to John Thicknesse, of the London *Evening Standard*, applauding Colin Cowdrey's 'cuteness' in slowing the games down. Thicknesse had been one of my principal critics at Edgbaston only months before!

Because of the wretched way we played our negative cricket we failed to win two (and possibly three) games we should have won, and we damn nearly lost one of those. We won the Fourth Test in Trinidad because Gary was goaded into showing his contempt for our abysmal over-rate. His declaration, setting England 215 in 165 minutes was, by any standards of logic, madly generous because he simply hadn't the bowlers either to break through and win or to slow the game down and put England under pressure – but it wouldn't have been in his nature to win by negative tactics, anyway. I was broadcasting on that game with Crawford White, of the *Daily Express*, and Sir Learie Constantine was doing expert summaries with me.

When the declaration came I denounced it in fairly specific terms – 'If ever a match has been handed to us on a plate, this is it – we'll win without playing a shot in anger.' Sir Learie defended Gary, saying that if we went for the runs the West Indies would bowl us out. As it was, we won easily, yet Cowdrey was not going to go for the runs at all. He was prepared to play for a draw even when the game had been handed to him as I say, on a plate. It was Boycott, Edrich and Barrington who got together and told the captain, 'Look – we can win this.'

Throughout the whole tour, I never stirred from the press box while play was taking place. I was conscious that some of my temporary colleagues were just looking for any chance at all to snipe at me . . . 'he wrote about games he didn't see' – that sort of thing, so I saw to it that they got no chance. I kept clear of the players as much as possible so that no one was put in an embarrassing position and it was Cowdrey, in fact, who approached me. (I think I had written some good cricket sense in my articles for the Island newspapers, and impressed a lot of people – not least the players themselves. So far, what I'd predicted had been right.)

On the morning of the Fourth Test Cowdrey said, 'I was trying to get hold of you on the 'phone last night.' 'Oh, why was that?' I asked. Colin said, 'I wanted to ask you who you thought we should play today – an extra quick bowler, or another slow bowler.' 'Well', I said, 'you've declared your team now so it can't make any difference but I would have told you to play an extra spinner.' Colin said he had, in fact, opted to play an extra quick bowler. 'Then you are heading for a draw', I commented. 'The extra quickie will help you to draw; an extra spinner would have helped you win it.' You have to bear in mind that our over-rate was horrifying – something like eleven or twelve an hour. My view is that people, captains and players alike, should want to play as much cricket as possible, to pack as much as possible into a day. You don't win matches by slowing them down.

I enjoyed touring in a new role. It was interesting, in many ways it was fun. But none of it was an adequate substitute for playing. One major triumph I enjoyed in the West Indies was in theory only. A doctor friend in Guyana was a great one for a bet on the horses and a system out there was that you could pick three horses in the big races in England, and if they finished in the first four in any order, you would get the odds multiplied together divided by six. Knowing that I have a passing interest in English racing, he asked me to pick him six horses for the Grand National so that he could have a flutter – any three from six. I gave him six horses that I thought might do well, when he showed me the list of runners. Next morning I listened to radio commentary on the race with Keith Miller. My six tips finished first, second, third, fourth and sixth – and the last fell. Not only did I not have a bet, but my friend, when I met him at the Test, said he hadn't either!

During the summer of 1973, Derrick Robins approached me to ask if I would skipper a multi-racial side to make a tour of South Africa under his sponsorship. We were to include coloured players in our party and we were to play matches against both black and white

195

South Africans. It was a trend-setting tour; I felt it couldn't do anything but good. It turned out to be a spectacularly successful tour. South Africa had been excluded from world cricket at a time when they were just beginning to enjoy a golden age and the cricket we played and the players we saw served to emphasise the tragedy of it. With Younis Ahmed, of Surrey and Pakistan, in our side and John Shepherd, the West Indian from Kent, we had a smooth and incident-free tour which was wholly enjoyable for everyone. Politicians will tell me it is an over-simplification to say that keeping sporting links with South Africa can help the development of black and coloured players there. They may be right. But at the very worst, cricketing links would never create the bitterness and misery that the politicians heap upon a country with so much potential in every way.

Since then I have led another Robins tour to South Africa and an International Wanderers side to Rhodesia. For me – I set aside political considerations – they are two great countries I would be glad to visit as a cricketer, or just as Brian Close, citizen, any time.

24

RIGHT HAND, LEFT HAND

The 'old' days of the county championship, with each county playing thirty-two championship games, had a lot to commend them from a playing point of view. In the first place they produced real county champions because each county played every other one twice and you reckoned that, given an even break with the weather in the various areas of the country, everyone played roughly the same amount of cricket. With an emasculated fixture list such as we have today it is much easier for some areas to play on a higher proportion of days than others.

Playing regularly six days a week you knew where you were and you settled into a routine of driving from one ground to another every Tuesday and Friday night. In a way it became part of the fun of it all. Calling at the same restaurants, a drink in the same pub, the usual contest about who would be first to arrive. Dave Halfyard, that great character who used to bowl seamers for Kent (and afterwards for a short time with Notts before going on to the first-class umpires' list) used to travel about in one of those little bubble cars and the lads could never understand how he always got to the hotel first! Dave's home is in Cornwall (in fact he still turns out for Cornwall when he is not 'standing' in the first-class game) so for a home game with Kent he had to travel three times as far as for an away game with Somerset.

In some ways the fixture structure of that era helped to promote a better team spirit than the present system where the most lunatic things can happen. You can be playing, say, Northants on a Saturday at Northampton, a wicket where you need two spinners and a batsman who likes to take his time a bit. You'll need them again on the

Monday and Tuesday, but in between, for the Sunday John Player game, you chuck out the spinners and the steady batsman for two inexpert but willing medium-paced seamers plus a slogger and go haring off across the county, sometimes even out of the county.

Before that League started in 1968, Sunday, when you were on the southern or West Country tour, was always golf day. Almost invariably we were invited to a club near the ground where we were playing over the weekend and given the courtesy of the course for the day. Cricketers everywhere were immensely grateful for the kindness and hospitality they found at some of the most famous golf clubs in England and Wales. There has long been a fairly close link between the two sports because cricket has produced more than a few excellent players. Ted Dexter, I suppose, has been the outstanding example, followed by Colin Cowdrey, Tom Graveney, the Bedser twins (those inseparables whose handicaps have always gone up or down in concert with each other), while I became a category one (scratch to three handicap) player myself fairly quickly after taking up the game. Every county side has always had its contingent of enthusiastic hackers, too, and they used to make themselves up into fours and tail along behind, cheerfully taking fifteen from tee to green and not counting the air shots!

In the early sixties, we had in the Yorkshire party for a game at Middlesbrough a fast bowler from Hull called Dave Middlewood, who talked himself into Jackie Hampshire's four by claiming to have played 'quite a lot' of golf. Even as he hired his clubs from the pro it was patently obvious that he had never set foot on a golf course in his life but the other three tolerated him as cheerfully as possible by pretending he wasn't really with them. By the time they had reached the thirteenth, the others had virtually forgotten Dave, especially as he had put his tee-shot about two hundred yards out of bounds into the depths of a mowing field. As they reached the green they were hailed with a plaintive cry from far away to their left. It was Middlewood, playing his umpteenth shot outside the course and standing almost waist-high in potential hay, asking, 'Hey, Jake! Is a two-iron all right from here?'

I was introduced to golf while touring Australia in 1950-51 and developed a passion for the game equal to that of the most dedicated clubman. But I was advised by some of the senior players that it might affect my batting. So, always willing to work something out, I took up golf right-handed, so that it could not affect my left-handed batting. I continued with enthusiasm when I returned home, joined Bradford Golf Club (which looks down from the lower slopes of Ilkley Moor across the Aire Valley), and fairly quickly got down to a two handicap. Ultimately I had to settle on three, because it wasn't always easy to play enough golf to keep it there, with all the time I spent playing cricket. I was pleased with that handicap, though, apart from the nagging feeling in my mind that I could reach scratch if only I could play regularly enough. Well, I continued to play when I could and I kept my illustrious handicap for quite a few years. Then I went through about two years without managing to keep it at three, so one day while playing in the Gibson Cup (the Yorkshire players' and officials' championship which is usually staged in October) I was in the same four as Johnny Wardle, who golfed, as he batted, left-handed. While we were waiting to play our shots I idly borrowed one of his clubs and practised a few swings with it. It seemed natural enough. I couldn't resist it. I put down a ball and hit it as sweet as a nut; it went miles. I tried another; same thing. And another. I was hooked all over again.

I obtained a set of left-handed clubs, put some cards in at my club, and was given a handicap of nine. After my first competition I was pulled to five, but somehow after that I went through a period when I just did not seem able to find time for golf. In the meantime one-day cricket had started. It developed until Sundays disappeared from the cricketer's leisure calendar.

I didn't play regularly for several years and then, one day when I was sitting at home brooding despairingly on my sacking by Yorkshire, a friend called (my collaborator in this book as a matter of fact) and said, 'Come on, let's get out on the hills and try and forget about it for a bit.' We went up to the golf club and I suppose I was so miserable that I kept my head down and concentrated on the golf because he tells me I played to plus-two that day. That game became a regular weekly fixture, sometimes playing against cricketers – Peter Parfitt, Neil Hawke, Sonny Ramadhin, Johnny Sullivan, Tony Nicholson, Philip Sharpe – sometimes against business associates. I started to put in cards again at the Bradford Club to re-establish a handicap which had, of course, lapsed in my long lay-off. They gave me seven, but watch out now I have retired from cricket! There are times when I wish I had my time over again so that I could take up a career as a professional golfer. Well, who says it's too late at forty-seven?

Once I had cashed in on my ambidexterity, the usual crop of legends arose. I meet people today who believe I play shots right-handed or left-handed as the mood takes me or the lie of the ball dictates. Many of these tales arise from a round I once played with Ben Wright, the television commentator (who now spends most of his time in America), who at that time was a newspaperman in the north. He rang me up and challenged me over the championship course at Moortown, Leeds, off levels. Whereas Ben, a four-handicapper who had played since he was a child, knocked the ball round normally, he asked me to use my own, left-handed clubs, at odd holes and his right-handed sticks at the even holes – left-right, left-right, all the way round the course. I hadn't touched a right-handed club for quite some while before that game but I went round in gross 76 against Ben's 74 and I was proud of it. He made a good story out of the game for his magazine.

Nowadays in my left-handed set I carry a right-handed seven-iron, for insurance, if you like, but you'd be surprised how often it comes in useful. Playing at Scarcroft (another pleasant course on the out-skirts of Leeds) with Don Mosey against Ray Illingworth and Philip Sharpe, we were two up after two and Illy, who hates losing at any-thing just as much as I do, was beginning to moan already. But he cheered up a bit when he and his partner got away a couple of good tee-shots at the third, whilst mine seemed to be up against the base of a bush and Don was in the middle of a wood – out of bounds for good measure. Ray even managed a mock-sympathetic grin as we got to my ball and found it was indeed totally unplayable: to a left-hander. Then the grin faded as I took out the right-handed seven and put the ball on the green for a birdie putt. In best Illy fashion he complained bitterly that it was against the rules, counted the number of clubs in my bag and moaned solidly for the next fifteen holes.

At various stages of my life I have fancied the idea of being a pro-fessional golfer or a racing driver. I wish it were now not too late to take up one of these sports in a big way; from time to time, in these early days of retirement, I muse about the possibility that it may not, in fact, be too late. Certainly my golf is really on the top line but opportunities for getting on to the motor-racing circuit are fewer. I really got the taste for this in the seventies when I was invited to take part in a race at Oulton Park in a field of sportsmen from many different walks. I was as determined to win as Fred Trueman was determined to keep out of my way. (He and Don Mosey have told so many tales about my allegedly mad driving over the years that they now believe them!) I thought I *had* the race in the bag, too, when I got into a bit of a skid on a corner and I was literally pipped on the post by Stuart Hall, the television personality, who had quite a lot of experience at that game. Anyway, as soon as the chance of taking part in a similar race came up, I jumped at it – and won, at Brands Hatch.

25

CAPTAIN OF SOMERSET

After my Yorkshire sacking, it took me almost until the end of the year to think rationally again. I continued with the job I was doing outside cricket, and in quieter moments turned my thoughts over and over again, trying to see what the future had in store for me. I still loved the game and wanted to go on playing, if at all possible – but at the age of forty, how does one start again? Approaches from several counties for me to join them for the 1971 season helped to keep my spirits up. At least I was wanted somewhere and I wasn't a social outcast, which I must say was one of the thoughts which kept haunting my mind at that time. After all the events of my cricket career to date, I felt that other counties would have the 'wouldn't-touch-him-with-a-barge-pole', 'steer-clear-at-all-costs' attitude.

One morning near Christmas I woke up with a clear mind. If I was going to have to start my cricket life all over again, then I might as well make a complete break with everything, my job as well, and begin again from scratch. But this time the emphasis would be on a job outside cricket; no longer would I depend entirely on cricket. I'd had too many heartbreaks for that. I sent in my notice to quit my job that day, and for the first time in my life since leaving school, I was without work of any sort.

I mentioned my predicament to a few friends and it took only a few days before I was on my way to Newcastle to meet and be interviewed by the regional director of a national company. A few days later I was sent to Nottingham to the Bell Fruit (UK) Ltd's headquarters to meet the chairman, Dr W. Pilkington. After a very amicable interview I became their liaison executive in the north of

England. I mention this because something rather ironic happened at the end of the interview. I was offered a good contract with the company and immediately presumed that my first-class cricket career had ended and that the only cricket I would play from now on would be at weekends in my spare time. Then in the final moments of our meeting, Dr Pilkington asked me what I was going to do with my cricket now. I told him that I'd had several approaches but had not decided on anything until I'd sorted out the job I was going to take. I said it depended on what he thought. He told me that it would be good for the company if I continued to play first-class cricket alongside my work, whereupon he picked up the 'phone and rang Reg Simpson and mentioned that I had joined their staff – would Reg like me to play for Nottinghamshire? I was being offered to Notts on a plate and, under obligation to the company I had just joined, if there had been any sign of approval I would have gone. It didn't matter where or for whom I was going to play. Before that short meeting I'd thought my cricket career was finished and then, moments later, in the chairman's own words, 'I would like you to keep playing'. I would have agreed to play for anybody and it would still have been a thrill. However, for the next seven years Trent Bridge was not going to be my home ground, for Reg Simpson, after deliberating for a moment, replied that Nottinghamshire were not interested and that they were going to concentrate on bringing up their own youngsters. (Funny – just the job that I did for Somerset in the next few years!)

With all this behind me and my life and my family's future now secure, I spent the next few weeks settling into my new job, and looking for a county with renewed zest and vigour. Apart from the direct approaches from certain counties, Glamorgan also made a tentative inquiry and on the grapevine I heard that both Lancashire and Middlesex had toyed with the idea of asking me to join them. They were frightened off somewhat, I'm sure, by the thought of what my presence in the team might do to their current skippers – Tony Lewis, Jackie Bond and Mike Brearley. If only they'd known. All I wanted was to enjoy playing cricket again, to fit in and do my best for whoever I chose to play with – and who knows, with my experience, I might have taught them a thing or two. I might have

204

made them better players or better captains. In any case I lasted longer than two of them.

Somerset, through that great character, their ex-player Bill Andrews, had been the first county to approach me – by letter to start with and then by repeated telephone calls. I hadn't been ready to follow anything up then but now I was. I went down one weekend, stayed with Bill in Weston-super-Mare and met the Somerset people. I chatted with Jimmy James, then their secretary, with whom I found working a great pleasure over the next few years. I met the treasurer, John Evemy, and had a long chat with Colin Atkinson (whom I had known as a player, of course), now the chairman. They informed me of the financial state of the club, which wasn't good, but they impressed me with their all-round enthusiasm. They wanted to turn over a new leaf for the club, and to make progress. Between them, they had won me over. As I drove home back to the north to talk things over with my wife, the more I thought about joining the county, the more I liked the idea. Here was a place where I could do some good, as well as enjoy my last two or three years in first-class cricket, and perhaps show once again what I could do as a player without having the responsibilities I had had to shoulder one way or another in my previous twelve years. A few days later I rang Somerset and threw in my lot with them.

I was happy to play under the captaincy of Brian Langford, who had always been a nice lad and a very good bowler. His main trouble as captain stemmed from the fact that he wouldn't bowl himself enough. I hope that I helped him to overcome that. A young lad, Kerry O'Keeffe, had been signed from Australia and Tom Cartwright (one of the greatest bowlers ever in England) was established in the team after his move from Warwickshire. The future looked bright, interesting, and above all, challenging.

I suppose the players wondered how I would fit in as one of them. The Closey they knew as the Yorkshire captain was one thing – they knew exactly what to expect in that context – but Closey hanging up his gear with them in the same dressing-room and wearing the Somerset colours . . . well, that might be something else altogether. I found fielding close to the wicket to Brian, Tom and Kerry a real thrill – something was always liable to happen and it rekindled my attacking spirit – I felt like a 'two-year-old' again. We didn't have the best of wickets, but I topped the averages and hit five hundreds – one against Yorkshire which rather pleased me, and one against Surrey which should never have happened.

That game was one that started on the Saturday, at Taunton, and then we went off to Torquay for a Sunday League match in which I top-edged a ball straight into my mouth. Teeth splattered all over the place and there was a certain amount of hilarity at my expense when we stopped on our way back for a drink! The following morning Brian Langford picked me up and drove me to his dentist for emergency measures and then we went off to resume the match with Surrey. I had been not out on the Saturday evening, so I was opening on the Monday. I must admit that I felt extremely groggy and I can't see how I could have lasted very long if things had followed a normal course. But Robin Jackman bowled the first over at me – he could be a fiery so-and-so when he wanted – and let go a bouncer, first ball. It was the last thing I expected, I was still far from being all together, and how I avoided that ball I'll never know. It went off a top edge for six! That really shook me, and brought me to my senses; after that I was in an entirely different frame of mind. I got my head down and I made a hundred – all because of that bouncer. If Jackman had just bowled normally I can't see how, in that state, I would have lasted long against good bowling. Jackman should have known me better than to try intimidation.

At the end of the season Langie, due to his work outside cricket, wanted to give up the captaincy and I was asked to take over. I didn't want it, frankly. I had enjoyed helping Brian. From experience I knew the things a skipper wanted. Support, and one hundred per cent loyalty to his requests and orders; no grumbling behind his back when things looked bad. I offered a few choice remarks on occasions during the season to see that he got those requirements and we all had a happy and quite successful season.

I had also enjoyed the freedom to play my own game without the captain's responsibilities. They are formidable enough on the field, but they don't end there and the memories of my battles with the Yorkshire committee were still fresh in my mind. I hadn't been able to enjoy being just a player for a very long time before going to

Somerset, and now that I had tasted that freedom again I didn't want to lose it. However, I was persuaded that I could give a lot of help to the club and the younger players by taking over, so finally I agreed. There was not going to be the intensity of pressure which I had experienced in Yorkshire. Somerset players were not born and reared on success – winning was not the matter of life and death to them that it was to Yorkshire players. It was a good thing in some ways, but there were times when it was a disadvantage. Because they were not used to going all out for victory as a matter of course, the players were not geared to the intensity of concentration I regarded as the norm. It showed in fielding, it showed in batting and above all it showed in bowling. And that was where having Tom Cartwright in the side was so immensely valuable. He was a joy to watch as a bowler, a supreme artist, a master of accuracy, of variation, and total concentration, and he did a great deal to teach our bowlers a new set of values.

Kerry O'Keeffe had come back from winter in Australia a different bowler. The mauling he took from Sobers on a shirt-front wicket at Adelaide had completely changed his mental attitude. He no longer wanted to use the many variations of delivery he possessed for fear of punishment, and when batsmen had to look for fewer variations they had much more freedom in playing him. I travelled with him around the circuit in my car, spending hours talking to him, trying to coax him back to bowling as he had done for us in the previous year. He did not have much success in trying to become an orthodox leg-spinner and the lads, who were trying to alleviate his worries and make him less tense, used to pull his leg. Regretfully, he was very young and inexperienced and took this the wrong way. Unfortunately for us, he didn't return for the third year of his contract.

Setbacks like Kerry's are not unusual. Even experienced players suffer from them from time to time in their careers but mostly it is the young players who fall victim to bad runs of form as they try to think seriously about their game. Geoff Boycott, even during his illustrious career of run-making, fell into a couple of bad patches and needed help and guidance to get his thinking and his priorities right. It is all part of growing up in the game, and no player, no matter how gifted, claims exemption from that. I'm sure that if Kerry had come back for his third year, we would have seen a much wiser and better player and everyone would have benefited.

The first two seasons (1972 and 1973) I captained Somerset were quite a trying period. We had lost Brian Langford and Kerry O'Keeffe from our bowling strength. Roy Virgin, who had been one of Somerset's batting stalwarts for many years, decided to try his fortunes elsewhere and our cricketing staff at the club were sorely tried. At times we struggled to field eleven players, let alone a balanced side.

Nevertheless, I was still enjoying my cricket. I had to force myself to accept that, Cartwright apart, I couldn't achieve with the Somerset attack the sort of thing I had been able to do with Trueman, Illingworth, Wilson and their back-up team. We were not strong in bowling – we hadn't one top-class spinner in the side. But, with a man like Cartwright in the side, one could do quite a lot, and we put together some fine performances from time to time. Most of all, we played good cricket, and gradually caught the attention of the Somerset public.

In August 1972, at the end of the season, I had a most pleasant surprise. The official Test series against Australia had been completed with the sides sharing the honours, though England kept the Ashes, but Ray Illingworth, then captain of England, had been injured in the final Test. The Prudential series of one-day internationals were coming up soon afterwards and every likely candidate to lead England in these matches seemed to be either injured or indisposed in some way. I was approached to deputise for the injured. I was only too willing, in fact thrilled to bits, to be called on again and I enjoyed every moment of those three days, especially as we won the series 2–1.

In the winter of 1973–74 the Somerset cricket committee and I met to discuss the playing ability of the team for next season. Even the unenlightened could see that we were dismally under strength. A young man called Vivian Richards had joined us from Antigua the previous year but because of overseas registration difficulties he could not play straightaway. He would be available now. Experienced players wanting moves from other counties were contacted but with no success, so it was decided to throw everything into developing

Somerset's own youngsters from the talent available. Several were signed on contracts and we looked forward with optimism to the coming season.

A lot of hard work was put into pre-season April practices and training, and it paid off. We reached virtually the final stages of every competition. We finished fifth in the championship, were semi-finalists in both Gillette and Benson and Hedges Cups, and runners-up to that fine Leicestershire side in the John Player League. That was a momentous season by Somerset's standards and it was a delight to be part of it. Unfortunately, our one great bowler in the team, Tom Cartwright, badly injured his right shoulder attempting a diving catch in the Sunday League game against Kent at Yeovil on the 9 June. We were deprived of his services from then until the last couple of games of the season.

I'm sure if that hadn't happened, we would have had something to celebrate at the end of the season. However, the other lads all rose to the occasion when required. Vivian Richards often showed us glimpses of the talent and ability that in the next two years was to take him to the very top of international cricket. Ian Botham established himself as a fine all-rounder, Hallam Moseley (our other overseas player, another West Indian) had developed into a top-class medium-quick bowler. Mervyn Kitchen had worked hard over the previous couple of seasons on his batting technique against the quickies and the spinning ball, and he, too, was now a top-class player.

Another feature of that season was that after a short while out of the game, Brian Langford reappeared on occasions to play in the three-day first-class matches. His bowling experience helped us somewhat to get over Tom Cartwright's absence. As well as these players, Alan Jones showed moments of great hostility with his fast bowling and the general fielding standard of the team had become pretty good.

In our semi-final clash in the Gillette Cup at Canterbury (the 'lions' den' of cricket), we were just getting on top of the Kent batting in the dying overs of the game after tea. The ball was swinging around in the heavy atmosphere and Graham Burgess was bowling beautifully at one end, and was well supported at the other. Kent were struggling at 130 for 7, when rain came. It wasn't heavy enough to drive us off the field, but it dampened the ground, made the ball wet and stopped it moving and that was the end for us in that competition.

However, out of a pretty successful season, the nearest we came to winning a competition was in the John Player League. In the penultimate game we were playing Leicestershire at Leicester. At that time Leicestershire and ourselves were well clear of the field in the League, our opponents being two points in front of us. We had our full side available with Tom Cartwright back in harness – a bonus for us. The scene was set for a dramatic final round. As it was the end of the season and a lot of cricket had been played on the ground, the wicket wasn't of the highest standard. In the very first over of the game, I faced Ken Higgs. He went through the surface on a good length and I was lucky to get away with it – the ball fell in no-man's land out of reach of any fielder, much to the disgust of the bowler.

But we made a great start, scoring at a good rate without losing many wickets in the first 25 overs. Leicestershire, seeking to stem the assault, pulled back their fieldsmen and although they bowled several of their spinners, appeared in no hurry to get their overs in. During our innings, several of our leading players remarked that Leicestershire were not going to get the full 40 overs in before the tea interval at ten past four. So with wickets in hand and trying to get the maximum score possible, however many overs were bowled, our batsmen threw everything at the ball. Against a wily campaigner like Ray Illingworth and a good team like Leicester, things went against us and we lost several wickets almost immediately. The situation now took on an entirely different complexion for Leicestershire and there was a general rush and scamper around the field as they tried to get their full 40 overs completed in the time allotted and to bowl us out so that they would have a full 40 overs available in their innings to get the runs required. The whole ground was tense. It was after seven minutes past four when our ninth wicket fell with the fourth ball of the 39th over and Alan Jones, our tall fast bowler, got himself ready to go in. I issued hurried instructions to him to try to play the remaining two balls of that over and then have a bash at the last over for all he was worth.

He vanished out of the dressing-room but it was ages (it seemed like years!) before he appeared in front of the pavilion on the ground – there were cries from the crowd, angry grimaces from the Leicester players and I must admit to being embarrassed wondering what had happened to Jonesy. I'm sure the umpires were embarrassed, too, because sticking strictly to the law, if a batsman took more than two minutes to get to the wicket they should have ruled him out. Anyway, Alan Jones reached the wicket on the stroke of ten past four and was allowed to bat. Leicestershire's only chance of getting the full 40 overs in their innings was to get our last wicket with the two remaining balls of that over. They didn't. Jonesy held out and they all trooped off the field.

When Alan Jones arrived back I asked what had happened to him after he'd left the dressing-room; he replied that he'd tripped and fallen down the steep steps on his way out. Needless to say, Illy came in and accused me of sharp practice. I'd been blameless – I could only relate what Jones had told me. The press caught a whiff of the story and I suppose because it was Illy and me against each other they made quite a song and dance about the incident. Ray and I have amused ourselves over it many times since.

Anyway, we had made 162 for nine in 39 overs, and with the wicket playing as it was and our full bowling side available we were happy. If Leicestershire were going to win, they would have to play damn well. However, almost unnoticed, heavy thunderclouds had crept up and encircled the ground and suddenly, as we were contemplating the task in front of us, the skies opened and within minutes the ground was flooded and away went our chance to win the John Player League.

It was a sad disappointment, but the season had been good for us in general and the team had progressed immensely, played excellent all-round cricket and only an extreme pessimist would have had difficulty in seeing a rosy future for us. Over those few years we had built up tremendous enthusiasm and a large following amongst the Somerset public with the high competitive standard of cricket produced. It was great to feel that one had contributed something towards this success. I certainly couldn't count the number of drinks I had with the members, including some committee men, who told me they hadn't agreed with my coming to Somerset in the first place but were happy that I had. That gave me a wonderful feeling.

Unfortunately, the 1975 season proved a bit of a flop by comparison. We set off with great expectations, hoping to equal, and maybe improve on, our previous season's performances. We had reasons for optimism. Tom Cartwright was fit again and one could foresee improvement in many of the team, particularly the youngsters. We were without the services of Mervyn Kitchen, who had decided not to play that year. That was a pity, because he had become a really fine player; but the batting strength of our side was the least of our worries – we had an embarrassment of riches in that department. It was over our bowling that the biggest question-mark hung, but with Tom Cartwright around again, the hours we spent in the field would be interesting and enjoyable anyway. It is amazing what the presence of a great bowler can do for a side. He can shoulder responsibility and bowl day in, day out, on good or bad wickets. He helps the other bowlers along. He sets an example to the others who, having less responsibility on them and fewer overs to bowl, are able to concentrate more on each ball. As a result their confidence develops and they become better bowlers.

We started the season off well, qualifying for the Benson and Hedges knock-out rounds and winning three of our first four John Player League Sunday games. We would have won the other too but for a misguided moment at the end of the game against Leicestershire at Yeovil. With two balls to go they needed 10 runs to win (we had played exceptionally well in the field to be in that position). Alan Jones bowled the last two deliveries straight and on a perfect length and Norman McVicker despatched each for six. After the game I bought Alan a pint in the bar and joked 'don't drown in it'. He was more upset than any of us, for having let us down. Any two balls other than good length ones – even full tosses – would have won us the game.

Unfortunately, Tom Cartwright got into the wars again early in the season. He chipped a finger taking a catch in a championship match and then in May he had knee trouble and did not play again that season – a sad loss to us and the biggest single factor in producing our dismal record that season.

At one point we had hardly any fit bowlers. At the end of the 1974 season Hallam Moseley, who had improved and done so well, had to have an operation on his knee. Although he recovered, he lacked confidence and altered his action somewhat. This affected his ability to move the ball and he just wasn't the same bowler any more. Graham Burgess and Alan Jones had odd injuries that kept them out at times and we still didn't possess a top-class spin bowler. Denis Breakwell, our left-arm spinner, was settling in, but 37 wickets at an average of 33 was a poor return for a season's work and at least 10 of the wickets came in September.

On the other hand we put up some fine batting performances and at the end, we had six players who had scored over a thousand first-class runs. Amongst them were three youngsters: Brian Rose and Phil Slocombe, who were playing in their first full season, and Peter Denning, a gutsy little player who made his first thousand in a season.

It was in 1975 that I had my unhappiest couple of weeks ever playing cricket. After the good start we had to the season, by the middle of June our bowling attack looked decidedly ragged. We lost to Leicestershire and Warwickshire away from home, nearly lost to Yorkshire at Harrogate after making 423 for seven in our first innings, and then against Lancashire at Old Trafford we were put in on a wet flier and summarily despatched.

In the game that Sunday, because of the crop of injuries, I had to improvise and use Brian Rose and Viv Richards as bowlers. They didn't do badly at all – in fact they got us into a winning position – but the regular bowlers bowled the last few overs without thought or application and we lost. I had to give Ian Botham a rollicking for losing his temper and shouting at the others in the heat of the moment. After that I went home to Yorkshire for three days and when I returned to Taunton on the Friday night, I was met by Roy Kerslake, the cricket chairman, who accused me of being 'too hard on the young players'. I retorted, 'You must be joking'. When I realised he wasn't, I told him I had been a damn sight harder on them the season before when I was trying to convince them to take their cricket more seriously. 'If anything, I've been too lenient with them this season because some have found it difficult to progress from being promising youngsters to responsible first-class cricketers.' It was a ridiculous charge. God! If some of them had had to make their way into the Yorkshire side of the forties and fifties . . .

The following morning at the ground before our game with Northants, the club chairman, Mr Herbie Hoskins, brought up the same point. I repeated what I'd told Roy Kerslake and added for good measure: 'I don't know where all this has come from, but it's a stupid fallacy.' I told him, 'I shall be retiring from cricket in the near future. What do you want me to leave you with – a team that is capable of winning something, or a collection of players who will play well now and again when the mood takes them?'

The next few days of cricket were the saddest I have ever played. I went through the motions of my job as captain, putting the bowlers on at the right ends, changing them, placing fields etc, but refraining from pointing out mistakes there and then and from admonishing anyone for lack of attention or for carelessness. During the game one of our young players was bowling badly and started shouting at the fielders as if it was their fault. I would normally have dealt with that immediately, and told him to cut it out and concentrate on his own job. And since I hadn't anyone else in the team likely to use the conditions well and take a wicket, this continued. A few minutes later one of the lads asked me: 'Aren't you going to sort him out, skipper?' I replied, 'I would, but I've been told that I'm too hard on these young lads.' I did have a quiet word with the bowler in question later, off the field, but the lesson would have had much more impact on the spot. That fortnight I kept wondering whether it was worth the effort trying to improve things, trying to make promising players into good ones, trying to give the county some sort of future, when the committee didn't trust me enough to back me up and let me get on with it.

I was sorely tempted to pack it all in, and I very nearly did. What changed my mind was when two of the young lads asked me for a few minutes of my time and then told me I'd been 'got at' behind my back. I was relieved to know the youngsters weren't the cause of the trouble, as I had thought up until then, and they pleaded with me not to leave them high and dry. After that I did a little delving into the matter and found out that in my three days off after the Lancashire

Left: I shall not be second next time . . . (*John Holland*)
Below: On the starting grid at Oulton Park: (l-r) Reg Harris, myself, Meriel Tufnell, Ann Moore, Brian London, Tommy Mann, Robin Knox-Johnston, David Watkins, Freddie Trueman, Lord Lilford.

Above: Pro-am at Southport and Ainsdale with Neil Coles. (*E. A. Taylor*)
Left: Concentration in the nets. (*Kamragraphic*)

(*All pictures from here onwards by Patrick Eagar*)
Above: Playing for Yorkshire against Cambridge University at Fenner's, 1970.
Right: Second Test v West Indies at Lord's, 1976.
Following pages: First Test v West Indies at Trent Bridge, 1976 – England's second innings.

Left: A Benson and Hedges match – Somerset v Hampshire – at Taunton.
Above: Avoiding a bouncer from Holding in the Third Test at Old Trafford, 1976.
Right: I straight drive Holder in the Second Test at Lord's, 1976.

Above: I watch as Greenidge hooks Snow (Second Test) . . .
Right: . . . it went for six!

match, a committee member had run across a couple of senior players – whom I'd had cause to give a 'rocket' to for not setting the right example to the youngsters – and asked them what had been wrong with the team over the last few matches. Instead of replying truthfully that our bowling had not been up to scratch they probably felt that here was a chance to have a good old moan and get their own back by saying 'It's Closey – he's too hard on the young lads'. They probably never thought that it would go any further. But it did and caused a fair bit of anguish and discontent – although in the end I did get an apology.

Having got that sorted out, we all set about reviving our fortunes for the remainder of the season. We finished on a slightly better note, winning two and losing only one of our last seven matches. We put up some fine batting performances – but could we bowl the other side out . . . could we hell.

Sadly, things at Somerset changed that year. The committee had been remodelled and somehow the friendly, informal relationships which had so appealed to me when I first went there seemed to disappear. Jimmy James, with whom I had had a splendid captain-secretary relationship, had gone to Old Trafford. Through him and the meetings I had attended (even making special journeys from the north in the winter months) I had been closely involved with the cricket matters of the county. Although I only ever offered my opinion or advice on matters concerning our cricket and the players, somehow that year I was never invited to or even informed of any cricket committee meeting. It's funny, but I didn't even know who was on that committee except its chairman and my only contact with it was at informal meetings with the chairman of the club or the cricket chairman whenever we met, sometimes over a drink, sometimes watching the game or occasionally in the secretary's office where we usually picked the team. It was a little unsatisfactory to say the least. Perhaps if I'd been able to attend meetings, the unsavoury episode that season would have been sorted out with a few words and in no time at all, saving trouble all round.

But who was I to grumble at the way they wanted to run the club? Everyone has his own ideas, and my job was to play cricket and lead the Somerset team to the best of my ability and to success if at all possible. By the end of the 1975 season, I had made the chairman realise that we needed to strengthen our bowling, and this became even more of a priority when Alan Jones, our only fast bowler, wouldn't accept the one-year contract offered to him and left us. It was a decision I didn't agree with but I had little or no influence to change it. Alan joined Middlesex who next season, with his help, won the championship. I was sorry to see him go – he was quite a character and the Somerset crowds either loved or cursed him according to what he had done. They were never indifferent to his presence. He seemed a bit arrogant and this helped to make him, at his best, into a pretty good fast bowler. With my prompting and encouragement he had improved his fielding from incompetent to acceptable. I told him several times in the five years we played together that if he pulled his socks up and got more consistency into his game, he was good enough to play for England.

His leaving and the fact that we failed to attract any other bowler to the county that winter meant we were relying more than ever on Tom Cartwright being fit to play for us. His efforts in the nets and at training during April gave us hope, although I realised I would have to take care with him and nurse him a bit until his confidence was fully restored. Vivian Richards, who was now regarded as a world-class player after his exploits that winter (how the Somerset followers rejoiced in his performances for the West Indies in Australia – we didn't create his magnificent ability but we could be proud to have helped him develop in the two years he had spent with us and brought his talent to fruition), would be with the West Indies touring side visiting England so he couldn't be with us. But we still had a fine batting side available and the effect of Viv's absence would be lessened by Mervyn Kitchen's decision to come back into the game. He would add experience to what was now a very young side.

In the event, the 1976 season started disastrously for us. We didn't qualify for the knock-out stages of the Benson and Hedges Cup, winning only two out of our four zonal matches, and failing to bowl out the Worcestershire tail-enders when a win was on the cards. We should have beaten Hampshire in our first championship match – they were on the floor in their second innings when Bob Stephenson, their wicketkeeper, came in to score his maiden century. In the John

Player League we lost three of the first four games.

However, Tom Cartwright had made a nice start in his first few days' cricket, bowling some effective short spells – his old line and length were still with him. On 1 May we played Gloucestershire in the Benson and Hedges at Bristol and won well with Tom bowling superbly; every now and then as his confidence improved during the 11 overs he bowled, he would let one go with his old zest and zip. I was thrilled with the win, but even more thrilled to see him come through the match with flying colours and a Gold Award for his efforts.

That night I could visualise a good season in front of us: I could picture every other bowler doing better with Tom back in the team; I could see myself in the field being able to attack, being cheeky and imaginative again. That moment was short-lived. The following day, a Sunday, we played Sussex, and were put in to bat on a seamer's wicket. Tom was batting in the dying overs of the innings trying to scamper a few needed runs. The batsmen went for a sharp single on the leg side and John Spencer, the Sussex bowler (never the smoothest of movers!) dashed in to field. In his effort to throw the ball, he fell headlong in front of Tom who was trying to make his ground – the bat went flying, Tom almost completed a double somersault as he tripped over the prostrate bowler, came to earth with a bang and broke his shoulder-blade. It was a sad moment for Tom who never played again for Somerset. In all my years in sport I have never seen such a crestfallen team (myself included) as we were that night, as we reflected on how misfortune could strike us three years running like this. But we pulled ourselves together, won a championship match coming from behind with a good batting performance and managed to start a run of Sunday League wins.

An interesting game we had at that time was against Gloucestershire over the May Bank Holiday at Taunton. Having won the toss we made 333 for seven in our 100-overs first innings with Brian Rose, now developing into a very responsible batsman, contributing 104 (the first of his four hundreds that season). Helped by a little rain over the weekend, Ian Botham (6–25) and Bob Clapp (3–18) rolled Gloucestershire over for 79. Even with the limited bowling attack we had, as there was still some moisture in the wicket and we had a lead of over 250, I made them follow on. A heavy roller made the wicket somewhat easier and the Gloucestershire batsmen found it less troublesome the second time. It wasn't long before fatigue caught up with my three main bowlers who had bowled all through from the start of the day (my fourth bowler was off the field injured) and Zaheer was taking full toll of anything loose – as he did so often for Gloucestershire that season.

He and Mike Procter were establishing a partnership that was making life uncomfortable for us, so I thought I'd better lend a helping hand. Off came my sweater and in my second over (bowling spinners round the wicket), Mike drove hard, wide of my right hand along the ground towards mid-on. I leapt across, got my fingers round the ball and instantly realising that Zaheer would be backing up, I whipped it back-handed through my legs to the bowler's wicket. Everyone near at hand knew Zaheer was out of his ground but the umpire's attention was elsewhere. Zed was 70 then and he went on to murder us for 141, Gloucestershire totalling 372. However, I did break the stand, getting Mike Procter out a couple of overs later.

We now needed 119 to win – almost a formality with our batting strength. We were 108 for four when Procter, having failed to rout us with pace earlier, was put on by Tony Brown to bowl off-spin. He mesmerised the young lads so effectively that we were bowled out for 110, he finished with six wickets for 35 and Gloucestershire beat us by eight runs. You wonder why we never stop being fascinated by this wonderful game of ours?

By this time, we had realised that we weren't a strong enough all-round side to chase the championship, but that didn't stop us playing to win and, when things went our way, we came up with some good results, finishing in the end a good seventh in the table. We funnelled our main efforts into the John Player League games, where we still had a chance. However, in doing this, one of our most promising young batsmen, Phil Slocombe, suffered. He had played extremely well in 1975 to establish himself in the side and although in his second year he struggled a little as the opposition got to know a bit about him, he nevertheless played some good knocks in championship matches. But he simply could not adjust to the requirements of the limited-overs game, in which the batsman who can hit 20 to 30 quick runs is more important than one who can build an innings. Unfortunately Phil was left out of the side in order to give the players who were playing in the Sunday games, which had become vitally important for us, as much practice as possible.

Our winning run in the Sunday League continued with some brilliant batting performances, scoring 236 for eight to beat Middlesex, 244 for four to beat Derbyshire, and 207 for four to beat Yorkshire. We had a setback against Northants, losing by six runs, but a little luck with the weather the following week compensated us when we beat Warwickshire in a match reduced to 10 overs. We batted last, although our confidence was such that without the rain I'm sure we'd have got the 174 we would have needed to win.

For the past couple of seasons or more we had had a good batting side, but one thing had eluded us – a regular opening partnership. Brian Rose had emerged as a regular opener in 1975 and the following season the opportunity to open with him was given to Peter Denning. It worked wonderfully. Brian Rose was patient, steady and fairly orthodox, while Peter Denning was a 'cutter and carver', a gutsy, cavalier-type player. And they both ran well between the wickets. This pair gave us some wonderful foundations upon which we went on to build victories. No county had broken away from the rest in the John Player League and gradually, as the weeks went by, we made up the leeway we had lost at the beginning. The enthusiasm engendered by the team's cricket was spreading right through the club and our support was growing by the day – we had trouble at home matches trying to get everybody in to the grounds and even on marathon away-trips we had more than our share of loyal supporters.

We looked like losing at Trent Bridge but our eighth-wicket pair, Breakwell and Jennings, shared an unbeaten stand of 90-odd and pulled us out of the cart. We won the next three games and came to the final match against Glamorgan at Cardiff needing a win to clinch the League. As it turned out a tie would have been sufficient for us to be champions.

That weekend, the tension was at fever pitch as everyone in Somerset, it seemed, made their way to Cardiff. Glamorgan missed out on a bumper pay day when our thousands of supporters – fearful of not getting a seat or even entrance to the game – came early, and were well and truly entrenched in the ground before any officials came along to man the gates. It was a pity for Glamorgan, who had had a poor season all round. But our supporters weren't complaining about free admission to the grand finale of the season. There they were drinking cider, munching their sandwiches and waiting for what was to be a memorable game – a real classic.

I won the toss and put Glamorgan in to bat. Perhaps that was my first mistake, but batting was our strength and on many occasions that season we had succeeded when coming from behind. There was no earthly reason why we should change our tactics in the last match.

Glamorgan batted well in making the reasonable total of 191 for six, Alan Jones, the captain, making a good 70 and Malcolm Nash, their left-handed all-rounder, contributing a bright 43 in the closing stages. However, I remember vividly two mistakes in the field that I'm sure affected the result. One was mine. Alan Jones had made a steady start and was getting into double figures when he forced Hallam Moseley off his legs head high to me behind square leg. I caught the ball in front of my chin and Alan, seeing this, started walking towards the pavilion. A second or so later, as I was walking in to the wicket I brought my hands back to my waist and the ball slipped out of my fingers on to the ground. I was horrified – I could have dug my grave and gladly fallen into it – and before I could do anything about it, Alan Jones had turned around to give a second glance, seen what had happened and quickly retraced his steps to continue his innings.

The other mistake happened when Malcolm Nash came to the wicket for his innings. He was at the non-striker's end and hadn't received a ball when his partner pushed the ball back on the on-side and called for a run. Our fielder at straightish mid-wicket nipped in smartly and there was an almighty mix-up which left Nash high and dry in the middle of the wicket. All our fielder had to do was pick up the ball, take two steps and knock the wicket over, but he snatched at the ball twice, got into a tangle, and so Malcolm Nash survived to make a useful score. How many runs those two mistakes cost us no one can tell; if Nash and Jones had been out on those occasions, other batsmen might have scored the runs. Anyway, I shall remember that costly miss of mine long after I have forgotten the many good catches I took in the course of twenty-eight years.

It was never going to be easy to get this target, but the wicket was good and the form of our batsmen gave us the belief that a win was within our capabilities. We made a laborious start (by our standards) against some fine good-length bowling from Cordle and Nash. Denning was lbw, I went in and, for a couple of overs, struggled to get the ball away. After getting off the mark I went back and across to a short one from Nash and pulled it just behind square, little more than head high. It was a shot I'd have been proud of at any time, in any game, but as I followed the ball I groaned out loud – I had timed it so perfectly it carried all the way to the boundary straight to a fielder who caught it in front of his chest.

Ian Botham was soon out, and Rose and Kitchen were left to repair the innings. They did it well, if a little slowly, missing odd singles because of the pressure they were under. They pulled the innings round to respectability but our scoring rate required per over had almost doubled. It was now or never: a mad scramble for runs began. Kitchen went for 46, Rose for 39; but Burgess, going in at number six, speeded up the tempo and played a magnificent innings as we drew nearer the target.

Almost every Glamorgan fielder by this time was back on the boundary. We needed about seven an over and Derek Taylor was doing the trick but, after taking a two, he over-ran the wicket at the bowler's end by five yards. There was an overthrow at the other end and having run nearly ten yards more than he needed, Derek was run out a yard short of the third run. Keith Jennings was run out past the line with his bat in the air. Graham Burgess played at a wide one – he let go of the bat with one hand to reach it – and got a single (the umpire confirmed afterwards that if Graham had missed it it would have been a wide and we'd have got one run and another ball).

It came to the very last ball. We needed four to win and three to tie and Burgess had the strike. Young Colin Dredge had just gone in with instructions to keep on running till the death. 'Budgie' hit Nash to long-on and both batsmen set off. Dredge, the fresher of the two, was completing his second run when the ball, thrown to the bowler's end, went high over Nash's head. Colin turned for a third run while

Burgess, exhausted from his prodigious efforts, was still running the second. Glamorgan's wicketkeeper, Eifion Jones, collected the way-ward throw and dashed back to his wicket. I'm sure young Colin would have made his ground but he hesitated as Burgess set off on the third run and was run out by no more than a couple of feet.

History relates that Somerset lost the match by one run and thereby the championship of the John Player League. One run saved by us in the field or scored whilst batting would have given Somerset their very first title in their one hundred and first year. It would have been Somerset's finest hour and there would have been thousands to share it all with us. What a game!

In sport, there is often a very thin line between success and failure and we had finished on the wrong side of it, again. It was a sad team that went into the Glamorgan dressing-room moments later to congratulate them on their victory. I had always instilled into my team that there was no dishonour in defeat if they had put everything into their efforts to win. They could stand tall and say, 'you were better on the day, but just wait till next time' and heaven knows the Somerset team put every last drop of blood into that fight. Our followers could be proud of the team and if anyone had failed them it was me. I slipped away from the noise and hubbub to get quietly sloshed amongst Welsh friends. I was thankful in the end that I had young Colin Dredge to drive me back to Somerset.

To close that season on a different, if slightly more sober note, we played our last championship match against the powerful Leicester-shire side at Taunton. The team showed great character in shrugging off the disappointment of the previous weekend and finished with a fine victory to send the supporters off to their winter hives with plenty to talk about and keep them interested in Somerset cricket until the following spring.

I would like to pay tribute to two of my players in particular who gave a lot towards our successes of those years. First, my vice-captain, Derek Taylor. He had arrived from Surrey and was established as wicketkeeper before I came. He was the most responsible player in the side, quietly thinking about his game and turning out good performances behind the wicket day after day, season after season. He had as safe a pair of hands as anyone in the game at that time and some of his leg-side stumpings off the medium-pace bowler bordered on the miraculous. At first he did not have much chance to shine as a batsman and would score 20, 30 or 40-odd as a dependable number seven or eight. But in the 1974 season although we had plenty of batting talent we had no openers and when I offered him the opportunity he jumped at it. He applied himself sensibly and thoughtfully and did a most commendable job for two full seasons in all types of cricket, making his first thousand championship runs in a season in 1975. Keeping wicket and opening for a side are two very specialist jobs and to do one well is difficult enough. After he had done both for two seasons, I could sense the strain Derek was under, and at the beginning of 1976 he unselfishly offered to drop down the order to allow the developing young talent in the team their chance. That was a great gesture. His efforts and support were irreplaceable.

Ian Botham came into the team as a teenager at a time when we were struggling to field eleven players in 1974. He immediately made an impact in the Benson and Hedges quarter-final against Hampshire, showing that even Andy Roberts' reputation didn't mean a thing to him his fearless striking won us the day and he remained in the team from then on. A big, strong, powerful lad, gifted with natural talent in both batting and bowling and with an abundance of confidence, he is the ideal type for the present-day game, a natural all-rounder. At first his bowling was steady and he could bowl an out-swinger almost at will. As he learned more about the game, he added an in-swinger, and – surprisingly for his pace – found he could bowl an effective bouncer. With his youthful bubbling exuberance, he would try everything and anything in his search for wickets. This was not always the best policy, and he was often the victim of strong words from me as I tried to guide his talents into the best course for his team and himself. He bowled brilliantly at times for us and in both 1975 and 1976 was Somerset's chief wicket-taker. I look forward to seeing improvement in his batting. He is a fine striker and timer of the ball with a full, clean, flowing stroke of his bat, and – almost a 'must' in present-day cricket – he is not frightened to hit the ball. When he does, it fairly rockets to the boundary. In 1976, in view of his potential, I let him go in higher in the batting order and

223

he didn't let me down. His 167 not out at Trent Bridge was an innings almost out of the Vivian Richards mould – it won us the match against the clock and was worth going miles to see. His youthful impetuosity and confidence gets him out on occasions when he is well set, but experience and time will teach him to temper his aggression with a little patience: an exciting prospect for the future.

27

MY LAST SEASON

The new season came round so quickly it just wasn't true. The prospect of having Vivian Richards back in the Somerset side was quite pleasant, but with all the young talent around as well we were going to have a different problem – who to leave out. At first it was me, because an old shoulder injury had been bothering me (or was it just wear and tear?) since the end of the previous season. I had rested it until the year's end, but found it got worse as the muscles wasted with inactivity. I then had to go through weeks of intensive treatment to get it right. Dr David Challacombe, our acting MO from the local Taunton Hospital, did not give me the 'all clear' until well into May.

As a result I missed the first two Benson and Hedges matches, a championship match and a Sunday League match. We did not fare very well in these games so I was happy when the doctor eventually allowed me to play. My shoulder still wasn't one hundred per cent, but I would be able to bat. I snatched a few minutes batting practice with some young lads at the ground – all through April I had been allowed only to run and do special arm exercises for my shoulder, certainly not to take part in any cricket practices – and off I went to Bournemouth to play Hampshire in the Benson and Hedges. We won by four wickets in a low-scoring match in nasty weather and although I was one degree under with a virus cold, I felt justified in playing when I made 28 not out. Unfortunately the cold went to my chest; I was laid low for a week afterwards and missed two more matches.

In the end, a full half of the season was lost to me with illness and injury. A fall in the Roman Baths at a buffet-cocktail party given by the Bath Corporation to celebrate the visit of the Australian tourists put me out for another week, but not before I'd stayed around long enough to guide our lads to Somerset's first ever victory against an Australian team. Admittedly, the Australians were not a strong side in 1977, but nevertheless it was an occasion for everyone to rejoice.

I came back again, played in three championship matches and then caught gastric flu and missed another three weeks. It was a dreadful time for me – it was nearly July and I had hardly put bat to ball. I had missed most of Vivian Richards' magnificent batting onslaughts too – I could only read about them whilst recovering. I did witness his 241 not out against Gloucestershire at Bristol – it was absolutely fabulous – and his 118 against Warwickshire on a bad wicket, but he had been scoring almost every time he went to the wicket. Everyone marvelled at his excellence – even our opponents. The only thing they could do when he got going was to grin and bear it. However, even while this was going on our record in matches was abysmal.

At the end of June I was fit again, played in a second-team match to get the feel of the game and then joined the county at Hove. Ian Botham was having a great run with the ball and on a typically good Hove wicket proceeded to take 10 wickets in the match for 161. Bob Clapp, who hadn't played for two years for us, was drafted in at a late hour and took 4 for 37 in the match. Very tall and able to get bounce, he was difficult to 'slog' – when he played for us in the Sunday League in 1974, he broke the record for wickets taken in a season in that competition by taking 34. A nice, genuine lad with a slightly nervous nature, he looked a world beater in the nets, but out in the middle he grew tense and couldn't relax. As a result he had drifted back to club cricket and his teaching vocation. I had to be careful with him – I was, and he did his bit for us.

One of our openers, Peter Denning, had broken a thumb in the previous game so rather than upset anyone I threw myself in at the deep end and went in with Brian Rose to face Snowy and Co. – I made 30, but finding that the game was fun again, and enjoying myself, I got out with the first ball I failed to middle.

I returned a little annoyed to the pavilion, where I watched in comfort a most astounding innings of 204 by Viv Richards. At one time he had almost every Sussex fielder back on the boundary or near to it – fair enough, that might be the best policy in limited-overs cricket, but it cannot be right in the first-class game. I have often wondered in recent years who on earth teaches these players.

We won that game by an innings and went back to Taunton to take the pants off Hampshire by 152 runs. Life was all roses again except that I didn't consider my shoulder was fit enough for the Sunday League matches. These games, packed into 40 overs each innings, are played at a faster tempo and everyone has to be prepared to hurl himself around to stop runs and must be able to throw in the heat of the moment. With my injury I couldn't throw, and, knowing the way I tackle a game, I would probably get totally immersed, forget about my shoulder and do something that would knock me out for the rest of the season.

The fact that I couldn't get involved totally in all the different types of cricket contributed to the decision of my life, to retire from cricket. When I'd been off that season, I'd had time to contemplate and many thoughts ran through my mind. For seven years I had spent most of April to September in Somerset, away from my wife Vivienne and our two growing children. I wanted to spend more time with Lynn and Lance, to help them grow up, and to be a full-time husband to Vivienne for a change.

On top of this, in Somerset I had helped, considerably I think, to build a team of good young players, most of whom had already proved themselves. Now I was keeping one of them out of a place in the team and from further experience. I had given them what I could. No longer did they want 'Dad' (my nickname was 'The Godfather') around to look after them when things got tough. They would have to look after themselves from now on. But it was a tough decision to make after a lifetime in the game.

During the next game, against Sussex, I went out to dinner with Michael Hill, Somerset's cricket chairman. After a pleasant evening in which I explained my feelings and told him of my decision to retire at the end of the season, he remarked that it would make the selection committee's decision easier. I replied, 'Easier? What do you mean?' He told me that he and the others on the selection committee – my vice-captain and the secretary – had decided to leave me

227

out of the Gillette Cup side because, they said, I wasn't fit enough. I admit to feeling shocked. I was surprised to hear they had discussed the matter without consulting me and I argued that I'd just gone through four first-class games, three of which we had won, the other being drawn. And although I wasn't able to take part in the hectic Sunday League games, Gillette matches are 60 overs each innings, of which 50–55 overs are played in the normal championship way. I went on that I had set my heart on winning something for Somerset before I finished and the Gillette Cup was the one thing left in the season that we could win. I'm afraid I got a little indignant and went on the counter-offensive: 'Who's going to sort them out if things go wrong and players panic? Who's going to do this, who's going to do that? Just tell me how many matches we have won these last two seasons when I haven't been around? What's happened to the team whilst I've been away ill this season?' I'm afraid I gave Michael a hard time of it – he's a grand fellow who wishes no harm to anyone, but as chairman of cricket he had to tell me what had *almost* been decided.

In the end, it didn't happen: I led the side against Northumberland in the second round of the Gillette. In their first innings we didn't bowl very well or straight, and a weak batting side totalled 153 for eight in the 60 overs. It had taken all my skill at field placing to keep it to that. But if their batting had not been good, we had not bargained for the quality of their opening bowling attack. Callan (an Australian who very nearly made their 1977 touring side to England) and Johnson (ex Nottinghamshire) hit us with both barrels and had us reeling at 30 for four – another wicket then might have led to the surprise of the competition. So we were up to our knees in trouble when I joined Ian Botham at the wicket. I steadied him with a few strong words – he had fenced at quite a number of deliveries outside the off-stump without making contact – and we set about retrieving the position. Fortunately, Northumberland had no bowler of equal class to their openers, so after weathering the storm, we went on to win comfortably by five wickets, with Botham collecting the Gold Award for a splendid innings of 91 not out. In the merriment afterwards, over a drink with my cricket chairman, I will admit to a mild feeling of satisfaction.

Our wins in the championship had improved Somerset's position in the table considerably and we began to feel that we could attain a respectable position in that competition. Middlesex and Gloucestershire were steam-rollering every opponent into submission and were leading the field by quite a margin. We might not be able to overhaul them, but if we sustained our efforts of the previous few weeks we'd have a damn good try. We had been helped by the signing of West Indian fast bowler Joel Garner and the availability of a promising young fast bowler from Oxford University, David Gurr. Garner, because of weekend league commitments in Lancashire, was only able to play in mid-week matches. It was a pity, because, being six feet eight inches tall with a high action, he got tremendous bounce even on the most slow and docile wickets. He had been an instant success for us and, surprisingly for such a tall young man, he was a good fielder. It was a treat for his skipper when he was around. Somerset's relationship with Garner was rather unusual. We could not contact him by 'phone at his digs in Lancashire, so it was agreed that when able to play he would ring us. Joel only rang us three times for championship games (we won one, drew two) so we didn't get a great deal of help from him there, but he was able to play in the Gillette rounds.

Our next three championship games were at weekends and with poor results our position in the table slumped. We should have beaten Worcestershire at Taunton after making 351 for seven in our 100 overs, but just failed to bowl them out a second time after rain. We were thrashed by Lancashire on a fast lively Southport wicket but we had no Garner, no Botham (away playing in his first Test match), no Burgess (injured) and no Gurr (indisposed). Our attack that day looked decidedly sorry by comparison with Peter Lee and West Indian Colin Croft. They disposed of us in the second innings for 80 – our lowest score for three years. There, in our first innings, Vivian Richards treated everyone to an astonishing 189 – his striking of pace, bounce and spin were out of this world. When he was at the wicket and ticking like this, everyone (yes, even his partner at the other end) would sit back, watching every ball and wondering what he was going to do next. Watching an innings of Viv's, you just ran out of superlatives to describe his timing, his execution, his stroke

229

play. In all my years in the game I have never seen anything like it; so clean, so ferocious, so magnificent. In my last season he gave me a feast of wonderful memories to take with me into retirement. Many thanks, Viv.

It was the third of these games, against Northants at Weston, which was most disappointing. In batting first we totalled 383 in our 100 overs, with Richards this time taking a back seat to Brian Rose, who made his first double ton (205). On a wearing, rough-looking wicket we should have had the match over in two days but we lost by seven wickets in the end. Northants played and fought well to come out of it like that.

The remaining game of the Weston Festival was against Surrey. There was little need to have a selection meeting because we had only 12 players fit and available, but when I talked to the cricket chairman and secretary prior to the toss they said the cricket committee had given instructions that Phil Slocombe must play. I said, 'Okay – but who do we leave out?' The answer was Keith Jennings, a young lad who had bowled for us in an odd championship match. I disagreed. Our bowling was thin enough anyway and that would make it worse. A batsman would have to be left out. But they wouldn't be budged so I offered to drop out: 'Whoever captains the side will need all the bowlers available, otherwise we will be overrun again.' I got my way in the end and was justified when we ran out winners by 158 runs, with young Jennings bowling some good overs and taking two valuable wickets when we sorely needed them.

In this match too, Somerset nearly broke the record for the 100 over-limit first innings of a championship match when we scored 492 for eight. Needless to say Vivian Richards was involved, scoring another double century (204), but two youngsters from the universities also showed their mettle: Peter Roebuck scored his maiden Somerset ton (112) and Vic Marks made 69.

We had despatched an improving Derbyshire side led by the effervescent South African Eddie Barlow from the Gillette Cup in the quarter-final at Ilkeston and then found ourselves drawn against Middlesex at Lord's – a formidable hurdle to the final. We went to Lord's on 17 August with quiet confidence, feeling that we could surmount this obstacle and give our supporters a dream finish to the season. It was important to me to give them that – this was my last chance. Well, ten days later when, rainsoaked, bedraggled and beaten we returned to Taunton, my hopes of leading Somerset to a trophy had been ruined.

We hung around Lord's for three days whilst heavy rain turned the ground into a quagmire. On the Friday (19 August) the situation was desperate as there was no possible date open to settle the game before the final on 3 September. All kinds of solutions were discussed and rejected until it was agreed to take the unprecedented step of postponing a county championship game. We then went off to Canterbury, fielded all day on the Saturday and were rained off on the other three days. On the Tuesday evening we were back at Lord's hoping to settle the question the following day. But we still had to kick our heels for another couple of days waiting for fine weather and a fit ground until on the Thursday, both Middlesex and ourselves were told that something *had* to be done the next day, whatever the weather or state of the ground. By then our lads had been hanging around in hotels for ten days; they hadn't touched a bat in anger for that time and were somewhat frustrated. At least the Middlesex lads had homes to go to when we were rained off and they had also played some cricket whilst we had been in Canterbury.

Fortunately the weather was fine the next morning, but when we turned up at Lord's we heard that the ground was not fit. All of us, umpires, captains and officials, went out to inspect it to see what could be done, knowing that something had to be; we were about to agree to a 40- or 50-over game with a slightly delayed start to give the ground staff a chance to tidy up the square, when an official hurried out of the pavilion to inform us that the Met Office predicted heavy showers at lunchtime or in the early afternoon. At that I turned to Mike Smith, who was acting as captain for Middlesex and said, 'I'm prepared to leave it to the umpires to decide what to do, then there is no fear of favour.' He agreed and five minutes later we were informed that each side would have 15 overs. Obviously neither of us wanted it this way but with rain expected it was a certain way of sorting out the muddle.

Mike won the toss and put us in, leaving us to make the play. In such a short innings, we hurried, and only succeeded in making mistake after mistake. Four batsmen were out to full tosses, two dragged wide balls on to their wicket and two were run out. We were all out for 59 which, although we fought desperately in the field, was not enough to stretch Middlesex, who won by six wickets with one over to spare. It was unsatisfactory to lose in that way on such an important occasion, and whichever side had lost would have had cause for complaint.

We returned to a disappointed Somerset to play championship challengers Gloucestershire. This was to be my last first-class game in front of a Somerset crowd; and a cracker it turned out to be, full of rich batting performances. Gloucester – so ably led by Mike Procter throughout the season – escaped from a deficit of over a hundred on the first innings to total 384 for seven in the second; David Shepherd (142 not out) and Sadiq (88) being the main batsmen. Somerset were then set the hard task of getting 272 at over 90 an hour – obviously to take account of Vivian Richards. But Viv had had a knock on his finger in the field and it was found to be cracked, so he would bat only if necessary. That was a blow to our hopes of winning, but it didn't stop us having a go.

Peter Denning and Mervyn Kitchen didn't waste any time at the start and kept up with the clock. Later, I joined Denning, who was in great form, adding another century to the one he got in the first innings (122 and 107). After a hesitant start, I caught his enthusiasm and went on to my highest score of that ill-fated season. I had reached 87 when Brian Brain started a new over to me. As we needed only 18 to win, with wickets and time in hand, I could allow myself the luxury of thinking that it would be nice to go out with a century to my name in my last innings in Somerset. It had to be now or never. I struck the ball hard, but unfortunately not high enough. Zaheer, standing deep at mid-off, leapt up, stopped the ball with his outstretched fingers and caught it as it came down. I walked off the Taunton ground for the last time thinking to myself that nothing seems to turn out just right! But we won well and *that's* what it's all about.

*   *   *

232

I like to look back on my last season's cricket, not in terms of my personal performance: being interrupted so often, it was my poorest season (the only time with Somerset that I did not finish either first or second in the batting averages), but in terms of the team's performance. I played in fourteen championship matches of which we won six, lost two, and drew six; one Benson and Hedges match, which we won; two John Player matches, both of which we won; and three Gillette Cup games, two of which we won, and one of which we lost. I'm proud of that record – I think I offered something to those lads of ours.

In 1976 the Somerset committee most kindly granted me a testimonial. This presented certain difficulties: how would I organise it, when I was living 260 miles away and doing a full-time job as well? Out of the friends I had made in my time with Somerset I formed a small committee, chaired by Guy Payne, a Somerset committee member, a great character and a real Somerset enthusiast. Nothing was too much trouble for him where Somerset cricket was concerned, so we naturally spent a lot of time together. It was great fun. He seemed to know everyone in Somerset as we visited towns and villages around the county. The efforts which Guy, Pat Mitchard, John Bail, George Wheeler and many others put in on my behalf were simply terrific. The Somerset public supported me tremendously and gave me a marvellous year.

If I didn't know Somerset and its people before my testimonial year, I certainly did at the end of it. It is a lovely picturesque county with wonderful, warm-hearted people who had flocked in their thousands to support their team when it started to improve its standing. I spent many happy days amongst those green hills of Somerset and made a host of real and important friendships.

I very badly wanted to win something for Somerset, to repay a little to the county which had given me such a warm and sincere welcome when my cricket career seemed shattered. Unfortunately, I failed in the end but we had fun – and a few near misses. I hope their memories of me are as warm as mine of Somerset and its cricket.

233

26

REFLECTIONS

In my twenty-eight years in cricket I have seen a lot of changes. When I was capped for Yorkshire at the age of 18 in my first season, my pay was about £1,000 a year, out of which I had to pay certain expenses such as travel and meals. Even so this was more than three times the average wage of a working man at that time, and the same as Len Hutton, then the greatest batsman in the world, was paid. It was daft, but not as daft as it is now with the top handful of players reaping rich rewards and the ordinary first-class cricketer – who keeps the game going, day in, day out struggling to eke out a decent living. In 1977, as captain of Somerset, my basic pay was £2,268 (less than most of the players under my leadership), but captain's expenses and other allowances brought my total pay up to £3,218 – all of it taxable and a fair part of what was left swallowed up in expenses such as hotel bills, travelling expenses and all the bits and pieces involved in doing the captain's job properly. Many things changed considerably in my twenty-eight years, but cricketers' pay wasn't one of them.

It took Kerry Packer and his circus to do that and even then the benefit went principally to the Test player rather than the bread and butter cricketers who keep the game going season after season. My recommendation would be to look after the ordinary players and the stars, who have all the perks of Test matches, advertising and sponsorships, will look after themselves. But even as I say this I must emphasise that in my time in the game, pay (until the last twelve months) was never the first consideration of a county cricketer – I hope everyone will understand that. Most of us would play for nothing if we could afford to because you do not become involved in cricket and the way of life of a county cricketer unless you have a genuine love of the game.

Most cricketers may despise the shabby way they have been treated over the years but are still far more concerned with what they can put into the game than what they get out of it. There are exceptions of course – as we saw in 1977 – but, by and large, cricketers have looked on their game as a way of life they love. They are closely involved with their public and have given up a lot of their modest free time to spend it with them.

I disagree with Packer's approach to cricket, but in all fairness I cannot blame any of the players who have cashed in on it. In an indirect way, Mr Packer has proved to be a 'good thing' for those Test cricketers who ignored his overtures, and even for those who were not invited to join him. That is fine. But let no one kid himself, or try to kid others, that Mr Packer's 'Super Tests' can ever be Tests at all in the sense understood by cricket lovers, or that they were ever designed in themselves to improve the position of the average county cricketer. That would be hypocritical and cynical. Kerry Packer's enterprises were purely and simply intended as a profit-making venture. (With, it seems, the corollary of 'doing' the Australian Board of Control and the Australian Broadcasting Commission.) It is probably true to say that cricket's administration has failed the players in this country for too long. We saw in 1977 that there *was* money available to sponsor the game and to boost the pay of players, at least at Test level; and it took Packer to make that evident. Post-war cricket was run for a long time by administrators who stuck rigidly to pre-war mental attitudes. Professionals were treated almost as serfs, and were expected to regard themselves as fortunate, even privileged, to be in the game at all. I do feel that in recent times there have been improvements that bode well for the future of cricket.

When I began my career, the captains were amateur players. Life was such that quite a number of men who were good players could devote themselves to the game without thought of financial reward. They were good for cricket – they loved it and made sure that the highest principles were upheld both on and off the field. In addition, they encouraged individual flair. They could speak to committees on the players' behalf, and because they were amateurs with no personal axe to grind, people took notice of what they said, and acted on it. Players on the whole were well looked after. Then in the fifties, the genuine amateur started to drift away from the game. In his place came the skipper who was still of amateur status, but was not a true amateur in the strict interpretation of the term. We had young men – good players, too – coming from the universities, and because of the old traditions of the game they were often appointed captains over seasoned professionals before they had had time to learn very much. The administration seemed to think that the professional had neither the dignity nor the intelligence to lead. So we had captains who were more interested in their own performances – and setting the stage for those performances – than in the performance, and the well-being, of their players. This did not do the standard of the game much good. A lack of imagination and adventure became evident – too much medium-pace bowling, defensively-set fields, and less and less spin bowling, characterised play. Rules were altered almost year by year to try to accommodate the changes, until eventually limited-overs cricket was introduced. Coincidentally, from the sixties we had an influx of overseas players. Rather than spend time and money on the development of home talent, the administration seemed to prefer to pay large amounts of money to ready-made overseas stars. Opportunities for English players were therefore limited, which had a catastrophic effect on the emergence of young English talent – particularly middle-order batsmen and spin bowlers.

Limited-overs cricket is negative cricket. It is negative because whilst it certainly encourages run-making from batsmen, it forces bowlers to try to curtail run-scoring rather than get batsmen out. It is negative because it encourages run-saving fields rather than fields which help a bowler to exhibit and develop his arts. True cricket is a contest between batsman and bowler, with each trying his damndest – by applying all his skill and ability, and using the conditions – to get on top. Limited-overs cricket gives the bowler another weapon but puts the batsman under a different kind of tension and pressure – even the best stroke-players find more is demanded of them than they can give. It is impossible for them to play naturally. In first-class cricket, it can be said the players dictate the way the game shall be played; in limited-overs cricket, the game dictates to the player. Spin bowlers dare not tease or lure a batsman to self-destruction, swing bowlers cannot indulge in the luxury of moving the ball away with no slips giving the batsman more room to hit the ball, even with the edge of the bat.

In short, first-class cricket is a highly complex game demanding deep thought from its practitioners, and consequently deep thought from those who want to derive pleasure from watching it. Sadly, there are not enough spectators with enough time available to keep the game alive in economic terms. Instant cricket, although cutting across the grain of most positive thinking cricketers, has become a necessary evil to keep the game financed through sponsorship. Spectators see a competitive match between teams of first-class cricketers in one day, and regardless of the quality, most seem to enjoy it.

As a result, players have had to come to terms with limited-overs cricket too. It is no accident that certain sides have dominated these competitions. On the opening day of the 1968 season, I took part in a broadcast, along with several other famous cricket names, to discuss the new John Player League (just starting that season). I said then that it would affect the first-class game badly, and in particular the youngsters. So it has proved. Asked to prophesy who would win the League – various counties were mentioned, the strong ones at the time being Surrey and Kent – I threw a spanner in the works by suggesting that Lancashire would be a strong force. (Lancashire had been drifting downwards in the championship since the early sixties.) Brian Johnston, the MC for the programme, looked at me as if I was out of my mind, and asked why. I replied, 'Well, they play well the defensive cricket in the field that is demanded for this type of cricket, and with Clive Lloyd and Farokh Engineer, two hard-hitting batsmen, to strengthen their line-up, I feel they are admirably equipped to win.'

In actual fact, Lancashire won the John Player League in its first two seasons. These successes gave the county confidence, and they went on to a run of Gillette Cup wins. They thus became one of the top sides of the early seventies; but although on paper they were a powerful team, they could never find the imagination or adventure in the field to prosper in the championship.

Lancashire and Kent have been the two counties who have most nearly achieved perfection, for present-day requirements, in the last few years. Both have powerful squads (with players to spare) and containing quite a number of good all-rounders with plenty of experience. Analysing the two sides, the main feature is batting strength. Most of those batsmen are able to hit the ball hard, while the others are good runners between the wickets. In addition, each county has its fair share of bowlers who can bat, giving more depth. It is essential these days to have depth in batting, as the tempo required for run-scoring in limited-overs cricket is somewhat risky. It can lead to mistakes, and minor crises. A strong tail can save a side on occasions and perhaps mean the difference between winning and losing three or four matches a season – the difference between success and failure.

In the field, each of these sides have plenty of bowling with a predominance of experienced medium to quickish seamers. In the spin department, Kent have Derek Underwood, a master of length and line, and adept at hurrying the ball along to give opposing batsmen less time in which to judge his strike. Leicestershire are in the enviable position of having four experienced spinners, each of whom could get into the side on his batting merits. Also, each of these sides has a top-class wicket-keeper batsman, and enough athletically-built players with 'good arms' to patrol the outfield and save the runs in the key fielding positions. Add an experienced knowledgeable captain, a little luck with the toss, the weather and the run of the ball, and you have the ingredients for success.

It is an economic fact that the one-day game has come to stay, whatever any purist would like to think. The days of the public and press thirsting for blood if success is not achieved are over. There are more trophies for the competing teams, so if a county fails in one, there are others to try for and supporters can be kept happy till much later in the season. And, of course, the much needed pounds and pence are brought into the game.

In defence of limited-overs cricket, one can say that it has improved the general standard of fielding, and the running between the wickets, by bringing greater urgency into the game. This type of cricket appeals to a much wider audience around the country, which must be good for the game provided that we can find ways of keeping the class of the 'real' game at its highest. If we can, then perhaps that wider audience might take the trouble to find enjoyment in first-class cricket once again, as leisure time increases.

You don't need me to tell you that in the last eight or nine years we have seen a gradual lessening of class amongst England's players. This is not altogether their fault – rather the fault of the present structure of the game. Take the talented player who is representing his country. In the course of the season, he plays in the four domestic competitions, and for his country in Test cricket. Each type of competition has different rules and regulations, different tempos, and the player has to change his game completely, sometimes literally from day to day. Much more important, he is constantly having to change his mental approach and attitudes. The experienced class player finds this adjustment terribly difficult, if he is to be consistently successful. But he does know that he is good, and that he won't be dropped from the team for a few low scores or inconsistent performances. What about the effect on the youngster trying to make his way in the game with only enthusiasm and talent to guide him?

Compare these demands on a cricketer, with the demands of another sport: for instance horse racing. A brilliant horse, put over a mile and a half flat race one day, a two-mile hurdle a few days later, followed by a five furlong sprint and finally a three-mile steeplechase, would eventually become a mediocre product and give mediocre performances, if these demands continued over a period of time.

Some years ago, I first spoke up about the effect of the limited-overs game, especially on the development of youngsters in the game. I could see that some of them were floundering, in spite of their obvious talent, and not making any progress at all in either type of game. I felt for them, and I felt for the game, so I spoke. Needless to say, the press never let me forget it, and to this day I cannot escape reference to my remarks. A few seasons later, other people, including the chairman of selectors, made the same sort of comments. But limited-overs cricket is here to stay, and we must make the best of it.

Whilst I was captain of Yorkshire, we won the Gillette Cup twice (1965 and 1969) – years when for one reason or another we had no chance in the championship. The second of those two years, 1969, came after our great sixties side had partially broken up and we were reforming. We adapted ourselves to the Gillette game. I remember one game where we kept a batsman at the crease for 30 overs or more on a good wicket, fearing what might happen if we allowed their stroke-players too many overs. In fact we even played hell (in an amusing way, of course!) with the bowler who did eventually get him out. We won the game easily as a result – but our main aim in Yorkshire in those days was the championship. We didn't fare too badly in that, winning it seven times in ten seasons. The Gillette Cup was good – it was knock-out, unlike league cricket, and although it meant changing one's ideas on the game to a certain extent, to win it only meant four or five games at the most.

It wasn't until 1968 that limited-overs cricket became a force in the game, with the advent of the John Player League. It took me two seasons to come to terms with it. If I'd just been a player, it would probably have been less because I would have had only myself to think about. But I was skipper – captain of Yorkshire – and at that time we were trying to reshape another championship side after losing Freddie Trueman, Ray Illingworth and Ken Taylor in 1968 and Jimmy Binks in 1969. For several years I'd been the buffer between a none-too-considerate and autocratic committee, and a strong, powerful and professional team; whilst trying to keep the team together and guide them to success. I was tired of being kicked from pillar to post, and of taking the blame for things when most of the time I was fighting other people's battles. I had lost the ability to enjoy the game through my own performance, as my energies were swallowed up doing the captain's job – schooling and coaxing the up-and-coming replacements, and the team in general, teaching them to think and play positively in the true Yorkshire mould. That left me little to put into my own game. In fact, my good performances at that time came only when the others had failed, and I was trying to rescue the team. At that time, I admit to taking a dislike to the one-day game. I hated having to encourage my team, in particular my bowlers, to think and act positively for six days of the week, and then on the Sunday to have to blast them for doing the very things that I'd been coaxing them to do. It really went against the grain.

241

By the third year, my last year with Yorkshire, I had accepted that sort of cricket and set about playing whatever type of cricket was demanded in each competition, regardless of what I had to say to the players to make them play well as a team. Unfortunately, in the very first Sunday League match I played in I suffered a severe injury to my shoulder, and missed half the season. I came back less than fit, because the team was doing so badly, and I did guide them to five consecutive wins (our first that season). I proved later that I wasn't the worst player at one-day cricket either. A couple of years later I broke the record for six hits (19) in the Sunday League, and held it until 1977, when that marvel Viv Richards did better.

The present structure of the game puts a tremendous strain on the captain. The four different types of competition mean so many more things to think about, both on and off the field, and quite naturally the quality of play has suffered. It is hardly surprising that something suffers: either the captain's own performance, or more usually his team duties. I suppose cricket will eventually follow other sports and appoint team managers to take some of the strain. That will not lessen the captain's responsibility with regard to the cricket, but it will certainly leave him with more energy and time to devote to the actual play. I'm sure that the well-to-do counties will certainly use such a plan before too long.

My one regret is that I wasn't more successful personally in the highest sphere of the game. In my infrequent and short stays in Test cricket, it always seemed that my luck ran out. More often than not the first ball that I missed or edged I lost my wicket and off I would go into the wilderness again. Even when I did manage to stay in for a whole series, as in the West Indies tour of England in 1963, and when I was captain of England in 1966-67, someone found a way to remove me soon afterwards. Now that it is all over, it strikes me as rather funny that many players in the game have said to me that I play at and miss the ball less frequently than any other batsman they have seen. If that is so, I put it down to my upbringing in the game – watching and learning from that master of all time, Len Hutton – to good positioning behind the ball, having good hands with the top hand strongest, and a fair knowledge of what the bowler is trying to do, or may do, with the ball. This doesn't mean, of course, that I didn't miss the ball or that I was never beaten; but over the years I have marvelled at players, particularly in recent years, who make hundreds, and yet regularly, over after over, play at and miss the ball . . . but keep their wickets intact.

Despite the glamour attached to the honours of the three one-day competitions, the county championship remains to this day the one which cricketers feel is most worthwhile – the one they would all most like to win. That, at least, has not changed since I took up cricket as my way of life. I wish that I could say the same of the great cricketers which this country produced for so long. Boycott is a great run-gatherer with a marvellous technique, but he has not the grace of a Hutton, the charm of a Graveney, or the gift for improvisation which was Compton's great attraction. Willis is currently outstanding in a thin crop of fast bowlers but he has nothing on Trueman or Statham or Tyson. With the exception of Barry Richards and Procter, the great players of today tend to come from the West Indies.

The greatest of these is Isaac Vivian Alexander Richards. He is the sort of player who makes you gasp rather than grope for extravagant adjectives. Never have I seen a man who times the ball better, and few who hit it as hard. To be at the other end when he is batting is to marvel at the extent of his ability. And what a super bloke he was to have in my side at Somerset. I never had one minute's trouble from him, never the slightest suggestion of temperament. He was one of a team – a delightful and immensely popular one but always a team man. Yet he only joined us by accident.

In the close season, 1972-73, the Mendip Acorns went on a tour of some of the West Indian islands. Accompanying them was a Somerset committeeman who later became chairman, Len Creed, and on their way over he said, 'Let's see if we can bring a cricketer back for Somerset.' This was known when the Acorns played in Antigua, and quite a lot of the locals wanted to do well enough to have a chance of playing in English cricket. One of these was Vivvy Richards, who was out for about 20; another was either his brother or cousin – I'm not sure which – who made more than 50. Len wanted to sign him. However, Danny Livingston – remember him

243

as a Hampshire player in the fifties and sixties? – who is the sports director in Antigua, offered the view that Viv was the better player. Len didn't know what to do. Late one night he was in the Blue Waters Hotel still debating the problem with another of the tourists, Richard Cooper, and finally decided: 'There's nothing else for it. We'll toss a coin.' It came down 'Heads – Vivvy Richards' and Somerset consequently took on one of the greatest batsmen I have ever seen. Even then it was not exactly plain sailing, because when the party arrived back at London Airport the immigration officers were determined not to let Viv into the country. He had no work permit; they couldn't accept the word of a party of tourists that he was going to make it as a professional cricketer. It looked as though Len's new acquisition was going to have to take the next plane back to Antigua. In desperation the party asked to see the chief immigration officer, and at last their luck changed. He came from Chard and was a Somerset supporter! He said, 'All right, I'll issue a twenty-one day permit but before that expires I want to hear from the Bath Labour Exchange that this man has found a job.' Viv did – working for Len and playing for the Lansdowne Club for a season, because at that time we hadn't a spare registration for another overseas player. But in 1974 he was in action and someone with great perception wrote in the *John Player Cricket Yearbook*: 'Here is a batsman with a wide range of attacking strokes who has the ability to transform the whole course of a match. He has not yet fully adapted himself to English conditions but once he has, he is palpably going to score heavily for Somerset in the years that lie ahead; additionally, he should also have a distinguished Test career. There is no substitute for class and it shows from the start.'

I took an immediate liking to Vivian. He was straight, honest and sincere. He wanted to learn, and learn quickly, and it gives me the most immense pleasure to think that I was involved in his development. If I had done nothing else in twenty-eight years of first-class cricket, I would be happy to feel I had played some part in giving Vivian Richards to the game.

Looking back over my career as a whole, I have had loads of fun and excitement, and the thrill of sharing team success with many great colleagues. I have played with and competed against the greatest – I take with me so many wonderful memories. I have been lucky to have travelled the world and made a host of sincere friends who share my feelings and emotions. I was more than surprised, and particularly thrilled, to be presented to the Queen at Buckingham Palace and awarded the CBE for doing something that I love and feel so privileged to have had the opportunity to do.

I have been fortunate in that I had a wonderful sporting father from whom I inherited the ability to play games, and that he encouraged me in every way – I run into the old fellows sometimes and they still say 'tha'll niver be as good as thi' dad'. I married a wonderful girl and now have a young family growing up: at least I shall be able to spend more time with them now.

I can remember so vividly my own childhood days, when my dear mother, who sacrificed so much for me to develop my sport as a youngster at school, used to recite poems to me night after night. A verse that I always remember, taken from *Play the Game* (*Vita Lampada*) goes like this:

> There's a breathless hush in the close tonight
> Ten to make and a match to win
> A bumping pitch and a blinding light
> An hour to play and the last man in.
> And it's not for the sake of a ribboned coat
> Or the selfish hope of a season's fame
> The captain's hand on his shoulder smote
> Play up! Play up and play the game.

I hope that I have.

245

APPENDIX: CAREER RECORD 1949-77

Compiled by Roy D. Wilkinson

BRIAN CLOSE IN FIRST-CLASS CRICKET 1949-77

Debut for Yorkshire: *v* Cambridge University at Cambridge – 11 May, 1949
Captain: 1963–1970
Debut for Somerset: *v* Leicestershire at Leicester – 1 May, 1971
Captain: 1972–1977

Season	M	Inns	NO	Runs	HS	Avge	100s	50s	Overs	Mdns	Runs	Wkts	Avge	C/st
1949	31	50	10	1098	88*	27.45	0	4	1245	334	3150	113	27.87	19
1950	4	7	1	202	92*	33.66	0	2	153.1	46	386	20	19.30	5
1950-51 (Aus.)	9	13	3	231	108*	23.10	1	0	†98	9	475	13	36.53	9
1951	6	12	1	384	135*	34.90	1	2	101.4	37	246	4	61.50	5
1952	33	45	9	1192	87*	33.11	0	8	1106.4	330	2746	114	24.08	27
1953	2	2	1	14	10	14.00	0	0	45	19	105	3	35.00	1
1954	31	43	7	1320	164	36.66	2	7	534	138	1474	66	22.33	25
1955	32	53	5	1330	143	27.70	2	5	871.4	257	2274	97	23.44	38
1955–56 (Pak.)	12	20	1	684	92	36.00	0	5	145	58	313	11	28.45	12
1956	27	37	5	802	88	25.06	0	3	266.5	75	674	24	28.08	23
1957	34	56	4	1666	120	32.03	4	6	290	93	787	32	24.59	37
1958	34	53	5	1497	120	31.18	2	7	342.1	85	921	34	27.08	33
1959	33	56	3	1879	154	35.45	5	8	757	210	2162	88	24.56	37
1959–60 (SA)	3	5	1	111	78	27.75	0	1	125	28	442	10	44.20	1
1960	36	51	3	1699	198	35.39	3	8	611.3	207	1493	64	23.32	44
1961	37	64	8	1985	132	35.44	5	9	615	220	1716	67	25.61	47
1962	29	46	6	1447	142*	36.17	3	7	413.5	164	929	32	29.03	30
1963	31	50	3	1529	161	32.53	1	10	425.2	134	1176	43	27.34	27
1964	36	55	7	1455	100*	30.31	1	8	563.5	199	1360	52	26.15	48/1
1964–65 (I.)	1	2	0	52	52	26.00	0	1	30.1	4	170	4	42.50	2
1965	30	46	7	1127	117*	28.89	3	2	527.2	202	1217	58	20.98	31
1966	34	56	11	1331	115*	29.57	3	6	563.3	201	1362	60	22.70	46
1967	23	32	4	884	98	31.57	0	8	372.1	143	870	29	30.00	29
1968	27	34	8	660	77*	25.38	0	3	340	139	772	32	24.12	34
1969	20	27	4	812	146	35.30	1	4	115	47	282	7	40.28	10
1970	20	28	2	949	128	36.50	1	6	34	10	95	2	47.50	20
1971	26	42	10	1389	116*	43.40	5	6	39	11	160	5	32.00	34
1972	20	33	4	1396	135	51.70	3	7	35	10	128	3	42.66	17
1972–73 (SA)	2	4	0	59	27	14.75	0	0	40	6	218	6	36.33	6
1973	21	32	5	1096	153	40.59	3	3	159.5	29	560	10	56.00	21
1973–74 (SA)	7	11	3	200	50	25.00	0	1	47	9	184	2	92.00	8
1974	24	40	9	1153	114*	37.19	1	5	104	30	287	14	20.50	25
1974–75 (SA)	7	13	4	332	102	36.88	1	0	27.5	1	129	4	32.25	7
1975	22	38	6	1284	138*	40.12	1	8	294.1	87	931	29	32.10	14
1976	20	34	5	1137	88	39.20	0	8	163.1	36	605	15	40.33	17
1977	16	25	2	438	87	19.04	0	2	0.2			0	—	19
Totals	780	1215	169	34824	198	33.29	52	170	11505.1 †98	3598	30807	1167	26.39	808/1

† 8 ball overs

CENTURIES

For Yorkshire

v Derbyshire	108 at Bradford, 1957	v Surrey	198 at The Oval, 1960
	120 at Chesterfield, 1957		132 at The Oval, 1961
v Essex	142* at Sheffield, 1962		100* at Bradford, 1964
v Glamorgan	120 at Swansea, 1958		101* at Bradford, 1965
	103 at Leeds, 1961	v Sussex	103 at Hove, 1957
v Gloucestershire	105 at Bristol, 1966	v Warwickshire	140* at Sheffield, 1962
v Hampshire	102 at Portsmouth, 1960	v Cambridge	114 at Cambridge, 1955
v Lancashire	128 at Sheffield, 1959	University	100 at Cambridge, 1961
	111 at Manchester, 1961		103 at Cambridge, 1966
v Northamptonshire	161 at Northampton, 1963	v Combined Services	164 at Harrogate, 1954
	128 at Northampton, 1970	v New Zealanders	115 at Bradford, 1965
v Nottinghamshire	154 at Nottingham, 1959		146 at Bradford, 1969
	184 at Scarborough, 1960	v Oxford University	144 at Oxford, 1959
	115* at Worksop, 1966	v Pakistanis	123* at Sheffield, 1954
v Somerset	143 at Taunton, 1955	v South Africans	117* at Sheffield, 1965
	128 at Bath, 1959		
	103 at Hull, 1961		
	121* at Taunton, 1962		

For Somerset

v Essex	114* at Taunton, 1973	**For Players**	
v Glamorgan	108 at Swansea, 1972	v Gentlemen	112 at Lords, 1959
	108 at Neath, 1973	**For International Wanderers**	
v Gloucestershire	135 at Taunton, 1972	v Rhodesia	102 at Salisbury, 1974-75
	138* at Bristol, 1975	**For Combined Services**	
v Leicestershire	104* at Leicester, 1971	v South Africans	135* at Portsmouth, 1951
	114* at Weston-super-Mare, 1974	**For MCC**	
v Middlesex	153 at Lord's, 1973	v Western Australia	108* at Perth, 1950-51
v Northamptonshire	116* at Northampton, 1971	v West Indies	108* at Lord's, 1957
v Surrey	114 at Taunton, 1971	**For an England XI**	
v Warwickshire	108 at Weston-super-Mare, 1972	v A Commonwealth XI	102 at Torquay, 1958
v Yorkshire	102 at Taunton, 1971		
v Indians	103* at Taunton, 1971		

TEN WICKETS IN A MATCH

For Yorkshire

v	Kent at Gillingham 1965	11 for 116 (5 for 67 and 6 for 49)
v	Glamorgan at Sheffield 1963	10 for 74 (6 for 55 and 4 for 19)

For Combined Services

v	Essex at Chelmsford 1950	10 for 94 (6 for 61 and 4 for 33)

EIGHT WICKETS IN AN INNINGS

For Yorkshire

8 for 41 v Kent at Leeds 1959
8 for 43 v Essex at Leeds 1960

CENTURY PARTNERSHIPS

Brian has shared in 93 Century Partnerships – 4 for the first wicket, 11 for the second, 32 for the third, 16 for the fourth, 20 for the fifth, 7 for the sixth and 3 for the seventh. Doug Padgett has been his partner in 17 of these stands, Ray Illingworth in 9, Vic Wilson in 7, Phil Sharpe in 5 and Mervyn Kitchen in 4. Eleven of the stands have exceeded 200 runs.

OVERSEAS TOURS

1950–51	MCC to Australia.
1955–56	MCC to Pakistan.
1959–60	Commonwealth XI to South Africa.
1964–65	Commonwealth XI to India.
1972–73	International Wanderers to Rhodesia.
1973–74	D. H. Robins' XI to South Africa.
1974–75	International Wanderers to Rhodesia and South Africa.
1974–75	D. H. Robins' XI to South Africa.

FOR YORKSHIRE
COUNTY CHAMPIONSHIP

	M	Inns	NO	Runs	HS	Avge	100s	50s	Overs	M	Runs	W	Avge	5 in Inns	C/st
Derbyshire	28	44	5	1317	120	33.76	2	7	503.1	155	1221	52	23.48	2	32
Essex	25	41	8	1187	142*	35.97	1	6	416.4	141	977	46	21.23	3	36
Glamorgan	22	34	3	797	120	25.71	2	4	418.5	143	971	47	20.65	2	22
Gloucestershire	31	50	5	1158	105	25.73	1	6	526.3	168	1355	52	26.05	3	42
Hampshire	23	39	2	837	102	22.62	1	4	381	126	1016	45	22.57	2	18
Kent	26	37	6	894	77	28.83	0	5	504.1	191	1205	66	18.25	6	30
Lancashire	34	47	9	1120	128	29.47	2	7	512.4	164	1189	55	21.61	2	36
Leicestershire	22	29	3	953	78	36.65	0	8	387	128	850	41	20.73	1	27
Middlesex	31	47	2	1034	90	22.97	0	6	529.5	159	1366	44	31.04	1	30
Northants	22	39	4	1249	161	35.68	2	7	402.2	123	996	36	27.66	2	27
Nottinghamshire	33	45	8	1566	184	42.32	3	8	672.5	214	1640	69	23.76	2	37
Somerset	33	49	6	1493	143	34.72	4	5	511.4	171	1292	53	24.38	2	23
Surrey	30	55	8	1585	198	33.72	4	5	480.4	132	1426	49	29.10	3	28
Sussex	27	38	5	880	103	26.66	1	2	555.5	191	1367	48	28.47	2	26
Warwickshire	33	47	5	1294	140*	30.81	1	9	503.5	175	1161	52	22.32	1	45
Worcestershire	28	42	4	1057	93	27.81	0	6	624.4	229	1469	62	23.69	1	33
Totals	448	683	83	18421	198	30.70	24	95	7931.4	2610	19501	817	23.86	35	492

OTHER MATCHES

	M	Inns	NO	Runs	HS	Avge	100s	50s	Overs	M	Runs	W	Avge	5 in Inns	C/st
Australians	5	8	1	230	49	32.85	0	0	92	22	285	5	57.00	0	3
Cambridge Univ.	12	16	1	712	114	47.46	3	2	307.1	99	675	32	21.09	1	11
Canadians	1	2	—	66	45	33.00	0	0	25.4	8	68	5	13.60	0	2
Comb. Services	1	1	—	164	164	164.00	1	0	18.1	3	55	2	27.50	0	3
Hampshire	1	1	—	23	23	23.00	0	0	25	6	114	1	114.00	0	0
Indians	2	2	1	93	71*	93.00	0	1	18	6	50	1	50.00	0	1
Lancashire	2	3	—	99	71	33.00	0	1	18	5	52	2	26.00	0	3
MCC	34	55	9	1343	88*	29.19	0	6	387	82	1240	43	28.83	1	25
New Zealanders	4	5	—	324	146	64.80	2	1	100	41	196	9	21.77	1	3
Oxford Univ.	12	14	4	447	144	44.70	1	1	247.3	85	531	25	21.24	1	9
Pakistanis	2	1	1	123	123*	—	1	0	89	40	185	6	30.83	0	1
Rest of England	2	3	—	199	86	66.33	0	2	27.4	2	139	6	23.16	1	2
Scotland	2	3	—	49	20	16.33	0	0	55	24	91	2	45.50	0	2
South Africans	3	5	1	156	117*	39.00	1	0	97	35	189	5	37.80	0	3
West Indians	5	9	1	201	51	25.12	0	1	38	13	118	6	19.66	0	4
Other Matches for Yorkshire	88	128	19	4229	164	38.79	9	15	1545.1	471	3988	150	26.58	5	72
All Matches for Yorkshire	536	811	102	22650	198	31.94	33	110	9476.5	3081	23489	967	24.89	40	564

FOR SOMERSET
COUNTY CHAMPIONSHIP

	M	Inns	NO	Runs	HS	Avge	100s	50s	O	M	Runs	W	Avge	5 in Inns	C/st
Derbyshire	5	8	2	216	77	36.00	0	2	37.1	6	121	3	40.33	0	4
Essex	10	18	4	665	114*	47.50	1	4	105.3	36	307	12	25.58	0	8
Glamorgan	12	18	1	711	108	41.82	2	3	62	21	195	7	27.85	0	14
Gloucestershire	14	23	5	601	138*	33.38	2	1	113.2	32	400	8	50.00	0	17
Hampshire	9	17	3	587	86*	41.92	0	5	80.2	20	241	6	40.16	0	10
Kent	6	9	1	349	58*	43.62	0	3	36	8	159	1	159.00	0	3
Lancashire	8	13	3	395	65	39.50	0	3	35	3	145	6	24.16	1	2
Leicestershire	6	11	4	578	114*	82.57	2	3	31	6	137	1	137.00	0	3
Middlesex	8	11	—	298	153	27.09	1	1	34	11	92	3	30.66	0	9
Northants	11	16	1	424	116*	28.26	1	0	18	8	36	4	9.00	0	10
Nottinghamshire	6	8	1	230	46	32.85	0	0	25.1	2	121	5	24.20	0	4
Surrey	8	13	1	271	114	22.58	1	0	24	6	73	3	24.33	0	12
Sussex	9	15	4	501	78	45.54	0	4	55	20	130	2	65.00	0	8
Warwickshire	8	15	2	471	108	36.23	1	1	57	10	187	3	62.33	0	17
Worcestershire	7	12	2	272	64	27.20	0	2	19	4	61	4	15.25	0	8
Yorkshire	5	9	2	386	102	55.14	1	2	13	2	53	1	53.00	0	4
Totals	132	216	36	6955	153	38.63	12	34	745.3	195	2458	69	35.62	1	133

FOR SOMERSET (cont.)
OTHER MATCHES

	M	Inns	NO	Runs	HS	Avge	100s	50s	O	M	Runs	W	Avge	5 in Inns	C/st
Australians	3	5	—	169	59	33.80	0	2	5	0	30	0	—	0	2
Cambridge Univ.	1	1	1	28	28*	—	0	0	11	2	39	2	19.50	0	1
Indians	2	3	2	184	103*	184.00	1	0	2	0	6	0	—	0	2
New Zealanders	1	1	—	26	26	26.00	0	0							0
Oxford Univ.	1	1	—	29	29	29.00	0	0							1
Pakistanis	1	2	—	48	46	24.00	0	0							1
West Indians	1	2	—	128	88	64.00	0	1	14	3	53	3	17.66	0	0
Other Matches for Somerset	10	15	3	612	103*	51.00	1	3	32	5	128	5	25.60	0	7
All Matches for Somerset	142	231	39	7567	153	39.41	13	37	777.3	200	2586	74	34.94	1	140

TEST CRICKET

	M	Inns	NO	Runs	HS	Avge	100s	50s	O	M	Runs	W	Avge	5 in Inns	C/st
England v Australia	2	4	—	42	33	10.50	0	0	†7 8	2	61	1	61.00	0	3
India	4	5	1	129	47	33.25	0	0	76.4	21	197	13	15.15	0	6
New Zealand	1	1	—	0	0	0.00	0	0	42	14	85	1	85.00	0	0
Pakistan	3	5	—	95	41	19.00	0	0	27	10	65	2	32.50	0	6
South Africa	1	2	—	47	32	23.50	0	0							0
West Indies	11	20	1	574	70	30.21	0	4	39	9	124	1	124.00	0	9
Totals	22	37	2	887	70	25.34	0	4	†7 192.4	56	532	18	29.55	0	24

SUMMARY

	M	Inns	NO	Runs	HS	Avge	100s	50s	O	M	Runs	W	Avge	5 in Inns	C/st
For England	22	37	2	887	70	25.34	0	4	†7 192.4	56	532	18	29.55	0	24
For Yorkshire	536	811	102	22650	198	31.94	33	110	9476.5	3081	23489	967	24.89	40	564
For Somerset	142	231	39	7567	153	39.41	13	37	777.3	200	2586	74	34.94	1	140
For Other Teams	80	136	26	3720	135*	33.81	6	19	†91 1058.1	261	4200	108	38.88	2	80/1
Totals	780	1215	169	34824	198	33.29	52	170	†98 11505.1	3598	30807	1167	26.39	43	808/1

† 8-ball overs

GROUNDS IN YORKSHIRE

	M	Inns	NO	Runs	HS	Avge	100s	50s	O	M	Runs	W	Avge	5 in Inns	C/st
Bradford	59	82	7	2346	146	31.28	5	12	920.5	331	2217	119	18.63	7	60
Harrogate	16	21	1	611	164	30.55	1	3	279.3	83	810	26	31.15	0	27
Huddersfield	4	5	1	38	17*	9.50	0	0	100	28	270	11	24.54	1	4
Hull	20	32	3	998	103	34.41	1	8	348	120	822	34	24.17	2	23
Leeds	48	69	7	1769	103	28.53	1	10	890.3	303	2151	92	23.38	6	42
Middlesbrough	19	27	3	693	98	28.87	0	6	129	39	345	19	18.15	1	30
Scarborough	59	98	16	2684	184	32.73	1	13	946.2	270	2804	96	29.20	2	48/1
Sheffield	62	99	17	2999	142*	36.57	5	14	1197.3	404	2678	107	25.02	3	67
Totals	287	433	55	12138	184	32.11	14	66	4811.4	1578	12097	504	24.00	22	301/1

GROUNDS IN SOMERSET

	M	Inns	NO	Runs	HS	Avge	100s	50s	O	M	Runs	W	Avge	5 in Inns	C/st
Bath	17	29	5	876	128	36.50	1	4	127.2	42	298	13	22.92	1	19
Bristol (I.C.G.)	1	1	0	26	26	26.00	0	0							1
Glastonbury	2	1	0	34	34	34.00	0	0							6
Taunton	52	83	15	3155	143	46.39	7	16	489.1	143	1536	46	33.39	1	50
Wells	1	2	0	5	5	2.50	0	0	38	7	105	5	21.00	0	0
Weston-S-Mare	17	25	4	955	114*	45.47	2	5	101.5	23	344	13	26.46	0	16
Totals	90	141	24	5051	143	43.17	10	25	756.2	215	2283	77	29.64	2	92

OTHER GROUNDS IN UK

	M	Inns	NO	Runs	HS	Avge	100s	50s	O	M	Runs	W	Avge	5 in Inns	C/st
Birmingham	23	37	5	911	82	28.46	0	5	359.1	120	900	30	30.00	0	22
Blackpool	1	2	0	15	15	7.50	0	0	27.4	2	234	4	58.50	0	1
Bournemouth	10	20	3	509	78	29.94	0	3	141.1	37	396	18	22.00	1	8
Bristol	20	34	5	827	138*	28.51	2	2	256	72	712	21	33.90	1	22
Cambridge	13	17	2	742	114	49.46	3	2	318.1	101	714	34	21.00	1	12
Canterbury	3	2	0	3	2	1.50	0	0	34	10	85	4	21.25	0	2
Cardiff (Arms Pk)	3	6	0	73	36	12.16	0	0	39	9	139	0	—	0	3
Cardiff (Sophia Gdns)	4	7	0	171	81	24.42	0	2	38	17	76	1	76.00	0	6
Chelmsford	3	4	0	44	23	11.00	0	0	40.5	8	114	10	11.40	1	6
Cheltenham	1	2	0	17	10	8.50	0	0	9	2	22	1	22.00	0	1
Chesterfield	14	23	3	662	120	33.10	1	3	302.1	95	677	32	21.15	1	19
Clacton	1	1	0	38	38	38.00	0	0	5	1	12	0	—	0	0
Colchester	4	7	1	165	88	27.50	0	1	18	6	60	0	—	0	7
Coventry	1	1	0	57	57	57.00	0	1	12	6	17	2	8.50	0	1
Derby	2	2	0	1	1	0.50	0	0	2	1	1	0	—	0	1
Dover	5	7	2	129	36	25.80	0	0	109	37	286	12	23.83	1	7
Eastbourne	2	4	2	117	41	58.50	0	0	7	1	32	1	32.00	0	2
Folkestone	1	2	0	59	48	29.50	0	0	17	4	73	0	—	0	0
Gillingham	2	4	2	153	47	76.50	0	0	69	28	177	13	13.61	2	4
Glasgow	1	2	0	40	20	20.00	0	0	46	23	67	2	33.50	0	2
Gloucester	2	3	1	119	78	59.50	0	1	51	24	102	3	34.00	0	2
Gravesend	2	3	0	109	44	36.33	0	0	57	24	122	5	24.40	0	3
Guildford	1	2	0	22	20	11.00	0	0							0
Hastings	1	2	0	36	19	18.00	0	0	28	5	111	3	37.00	0	1
Hove	15	23	4	623	103	32.79	1	1	286	89	742	20	37.10	0	12
Kidderminster	2	3	1	62	41	31.00	0	0	45.5	20	110	5	22.00	0	4
Leicester	15	23	4	759	104*	39.94	1	5	267.3	89	643	26	24.73	1	20
Leyton	4	8	3	178	62*	35.60	0	2	75.5	30	173	11	15.73	0	9
Liverpool	1	2	0	28	25	14.00	0	0	11	2	35	0	—	0	1
Lord's	52	77	6	2050	153	28.87	3	9	643	160	1849	60	30.81	2	38
Lydney	1	1	0	0	0	0.00	0	0							1
Maidstone	3	6	1	246	62	49.20	0	3	11	1	64	1	64.00	0	3
Manchester	26	39	6	985	111	29.84	1	8	267.2	84	681	20	34.05	0	29
Neath	1	2	0	119	108	59.50	1	0							1
Newport	1	2	0	19	19	9.50	0	0	9	1	38	1	38.00	0	0
Northampton	14	25	4	953	161	45.38	3	3	202.1	64	535	18	29.72	1	12
Nottingham	20	28	4	825	154	34.37	1	4	392.2	124	978	40	24.45	2	20
Oxford	13	15	4	476	144	43.27	1	1	247.3	85	531	25	21.24	1	10
Pontypridd	1	2	0	28	20	14.00	0	0	11	2	30	1	30.00	0	2
Portsmouth	4	6	1	331	135*	66.20	2	1	77	20	220	4	55.00	0	6
Romford	2	2	0	61	31	30.50	0	0	37	7	126	5	25.20	0	1
Southampton	2	4	1	139	86*	43.33	0	1							1
Southend	2	4	1	65	46*	21.66	0	0	12	4	27	2	13.50	0	3
Southport	1	2	0	33	31	16.50	0	0							1
Swansea	10	16	1	481	120	32.06	2	2	162.1	53	332	24	13.83	1	14
The Oval	25	44	3	1157	198	28.22	2	3	299.1	71	1000	31	32.25	2	22
Tunbridge Wells	1	1	0	8	8	8.00	0	0	6	3	27	0	—	0	0
Torquay	2	4	1	162	102	54.00	1	0	18	3	65	2	32.50	0	3
Wellingborough	2	3	0	58	36	19.33	0	0	52	17	108	3	36.00	0	2
Westcliff	2	4	1	38	18	12.66	0	0	5	1	12	0	—	0	2
Worcester	17	29	5	775	92*	32.29	0	5	362.1	116	956	37	25.83	1	14
Worksop	2	2	1	211	115*	211.00	1	1	10	2	28	0	—	0	7
Worthing	1	2	0	77	77	38.50	0	1	26	9	57	4	14.25	0	0
Totals	362	573	78	15966	198	32.25	26	71	5522.1	1690	14496	536	27.04	19	370

GROUNDS—SUMMARY

	M	Inns	NO	Runs	HS	Avge	100s	50s	O	M	Runs	W	Avge	5 in Inns	C/st
In Yorkshire	287	433	55	12138	184	32.11	14	66	4811.4	1578	12097	504	24.00	22	301/1
In Somerset	90	141	24	5051	143	43.17	10	25	756.2	215	2283	77	29.64	2	92
Others in U.K.	362	573	78	15966	198	32.25	26	71	5522.1	1690	14496	536	27.04	19	370
Totals—U.K.	739	1147	157	33155	198	33.48	50	162	11090.1	3483	28876	1117	25.85	43	763/1
In Australia	9	13	3	231	108*	23.10	1	0	†98	9	475	13	36.53	0	9
In India	1	2	0	52	52	26.00	0	1	30.1	4	170	4	42.50	0	2
In Pakistan	12	20	1	684	92	36.00	0	5	145	58	313	11	28.45	0	12
In South Africa	19	33	8	702	102	28.08	1	2	239.5	44	973	22	44.22	0	22
Totals—Overseas	41	68	12	1669	108*	29.80	2	8	†98 415	115	1931	50	38.62	0	45
Totals	780	1215	169	34824	198	33.29	52	170	†98 11505.1	3598	30807	1167	26.39	43	808/1

† 8-ball overs

HOW HE WAS OUT

Caught	608	(58.1%)
Bowled	282	(27.0%)
Lbw	81	(7.8%)
Stumped	38	(3.6%)
Run out	36	(3.4%)
Hit wicket	1	(0.1%)
Total	1046	(100.0%)

HOW HE TOOK HIS WICKETS

Caught	742	(63.6%)
Bowled	275	(23.6%)
Lbw	108	(9.2%)
Stumped	39	(3.3%)
Hit wicket	3	(0.3%)
Total	1167	(100.0%)

BRIAN CLOSE AS CAPTAIN

	Matches Captained	Won	Tied	Lost	Drawn
FOR ENGLAND	7	6	0	0	1
FOR YORKSHIRE	200	75	0	28	97
FOR SOMERSET	118	36	0	27	55
FOR OTHER TEAMS	27	7	1	7	12
TOTALS	352	124 (35.2%)	1 (0.3%)	62 (17.6%)	165 (46.9%)

As will be seen from the above table, Brian led England to victory in 6 of the 7 Test matches in which he was captain, the other was drawn. He also led England to victory over Australia in the Prudential Trophy in 1972 – a three-match series of one-day matches won by England by 2 matches to 1.

Brian led Yorkshire to win the County Championship four times during his 8 seasons as captain. Yorkshire also won the Gillette Cup twice under his leadership.

His best season as captain of Somerset was 1974, when the county came fifth in the championship, were semi-finalists in both Gillette and Benson and Hedges Cups, and second in the John Player League. He was captain when Somerset beat the Australians for the first time in their history in May 1977.

CENTURIES FOR AND AGAINST YORKSHIRE

Brian was only the fourth player to score first-class centuries both for and against Yorkshire. P. J. Sharpe became the fifth in 1976, the others were Norman Kilner, Paul Gibb and Brian Bolus. It is typical of Brian Close that he should have scored his century against Yorkshire in his very first innings against them – 102 for Somerset at Taunton in 1971. He has scored two centuries in one-day cricket (both of them for Somerset in the John Player League) and one of these was against Yorkshire – 131 at Bath in 1974.

BRIAN CLOSE IN ONE-DAY CRICKET

	M	Inns	NO	Runs	HS	Avge	100s	50s	O	M	Runs	W	Avge	C
ONE-DAY INTERNATIONALS 1972	3	3	0	49	43	16.33	0	0	3	0	21	0	—	1
GILLETTE CUP														
For Yorkshire	15	15	2	399	96	30.69	0	2	131	29	357	22	16.22	6
For Somerset	12	11	0	160	69	14.54	0	1	16	3	64	2	32.00	5
Total Gillette Cup	27	26	2	559	96	23.29	0	3	147	32	421	24	17.54	11
JOHN PLAYER LEAGUE														
For Yorkshire	17	16	0	224	50	14.00	0	1	21	2	118	1	118.00	8
For Somerset	91	88	7	2054	131	25.35	2	6	146.3	14	636	33	19.27	28
Total John Player League	108	104	7	2278	131	23.48	2	7	167.3	16	754	34	22.17	36
BENSON AND HEDGES CUP														
For Somerset	23	20	1	444	88	23.36	0	1	58.5	6	240	6	40.00	4
TOTALS— ONE-DAY MATCHES	161	153	10	3330	131	23.28	2	10	376.2	54	1436	64	22.43	51